**CHEAT SHEET**

## Accessing the CD-ROM Files

*Note:* If you don't already have Netscape Communicator, see Unit 1 to find out how to get it.

Follow the instructions in CD-5, located on the CD, and Appendix B of this book to install and access the files on the CD-ROM.

## Browsing the World Wide Web

| To See... | Click... |
| --- | --- |
| The preceding page | The Back button |
| Your starting page | The Home button |
| A link's Web page | The link (underlined text) |
| A page at a Web address (URL) | The Location box; then type the URL and press Enter |
| A list of pages you've visited | Go on the menu bar |
| A list of bookmarks | The Bookmarks button or menu |
| The *Dummies 101: Netscape Communicator 4* home page | The Location box; then type `net.dummies.net/ncomm101` and press Enter |
| A page that lets you search the Web | The Location box; then type `net.dummies.net/internet101/search.htm` and press Enter |

Refer to Units 1, 2, 3, and 4 to learn how to use the Netscape browser.

## Reading Usenet Newsgroups

| To Do This... | Click... |
| --- | --- |
| Open the Message Center window | The Discussions icon (third icon in the lower-right corner of any Netscape window) |
| List a server's newsgroups | The server name and then the Subscribe button |
| Subscribe to a newsgroup | The newsgroup name and then the Subscribe button |
| List the articles in a newsgroup | The newsgroup name twice (that is, double-click) from the Message Center |
| Read the contents of an article | The article header |
| Reply to an article by e-mailing its author | The Reply button and then the Reply to Sender option |
| Reply to an article by posting a response to the newsgroup | The Reply button and then the Reply to Group option |

Refer to Unit 7 to learn how to use Netscape Collabra to read Usenet newsgroups.

CHEAT SHEET

# Setting Up Netscape to Send and Receive Your E-Mail

See Lesson 5-1 to learn how to get this information. ISP is short for Internet Service Provider.

Your ISP's POP Server (for storing your incoming mail):

_____

Your ISP's SMTP Server (for sending your outgoing mail over the Internet):

_____

Your ISP's NNTP Server (for getting Usenet newsgroup articles): _____

Your e-mail user name _____

Your e-mail password (write on a separate piece of paper and store in a safe place)

Your Netscape Communicator folder (from Lesson 1-1; for example, C:\Program Files\Netscape or C:\Netscape):

_____

# Managing Your E-Mail

| To Do This... | Click... |
| --- | --- |
| Open the Messenger window | The Mailbox icon (second icon in the lower-right corner of any Netscape window) |
| Get your new messages | The Mailbox icon or the Get Msg button |
| Read a message | The message heading |
| Reply to a message | The message and then the Reply button |
| Create a new message | The New Msg button |
| Attach a file to a message | The Attach button |
| Send a message | The message and then the Send button |
| Print a message | The message and then the Print button |
| Delete a message | The message and then the Delete button |
| Close the Messenger window | File⇨Close |
| Open the Address Book window | Communicator⇨Address Book |
| Add an Address Book entry | The New Card button |
| Change an Address Book entry | The entry and then the Properties button |
| Delete an Address Book entry | The entry and then the Delete button |

Refer to Units 5 and 6 to learn how to use the Netscape Messenger window.

IDG
BOOKS
WORLDWIDE

# DUMMIES 101: NETSCAPE COMMUNICATOR™ 4

**by Hy Bender and Margaret Levine Young**

**IDG BOOKS WORLDWIDE**

IDG Books Worldwide, Inc.
An International Data Group Company

Foster City, CA ✦ Chicago, IL ✦ Indianapolis, IN ✦ Southlake, TX

**Dummies 101**® **: Netscape Communicator**™ **4**

Published by
**IDG Books Worldwide, Inc.**
An International Data Group Company
919 E. Hillsdale Blvd.
Suite 400
Foster City, CA 94404
www.idgbooks.com (IDG Books Worldwide Web site)
www.dummies.com (Dummies Press Web site)

Library of Congress Catalog Card No.: 97-70732

ISBN: 0-7645-0162-3

Printed in the United States of America

10 9 8 7 6 5 4 3 2 1

1M/TQ/QX/ZX/IN

Distributed in the United States by IDG Books Worldwide, Inc.

Distributed by Macmillan Canada for Canada; by Transworld Publishers Limited in the United Kingdom; by IDG Norge Books for Norway; by IDG Sweden Books for Sweden; by Woodslane Pty. Ltd. for Australia; by Woodslane Enterprises Ltd. for New Zealand; by Longman Singapore Publishers Ltd. for Singapore, Malaysia, Thailand, and Indonesia; by Simron Pty. Ltd. for South Africa; by Toppan Company Ltd. for Japan; by Distribuidora Cuspide for Argentina; by Livraria Cultura for Brazil; by Ediciencia S.A. for Ecuador; by Addison-Wesley Publishing Company for Korea; by Ediciones ZETA S.C.R. Ltda. for Peru; by WS Computer Publishing Corporation, Inc., for the Philippines; by Unalis Corporation for Taiwan; by Contemporanea de Ediciones for Venezuela; by Computer Book & Magazine Store for Puerto Rico; by Express Computer Distributors for the Caribbean and West Indies. Authorized Sales Agent: Anthony Rudkin Associates for the Middle East and North Africa.

For general information on IDG Books Worldwide's books in the U.S., please call our Consumer Customer Service department at 800-762-2974. For reseller information, including discounts and premium sales, please call our Reseller Customer Service department at 800-434-3422.

For information on where to purchase IDG Books Worldwide's books outside the U.S., please contact our International Sales department at 415-655-3200 or fax 415-655-3295.

For information on foreign language translations, please contact our Foreign & Subsidiary Rights department at 415-655-3021 or fax 415-655-3281.

For sales inquiries and special prices for bulk quantities, please contact our Sales department at 415-655-3200 or write to the address above.

For information on using IDG Books Worldwide's books in the classroom or for ordering examination copies, please contact our Educational Sales department at 800-434-2086 or fax 817-251-8174.

For press review copies, author interviews, or other publicity information, please contact our Public Relations department at 415-655-3000 or fax 415-655-3299.

For authorization to photocopy items for corporate, personal, or educational use, please contact Copyright Clearance Center, 222 Rosewood Drive, Danvers, MA 01923, or fax 508-750-4470.

# About the Authors

## Hy Bender

Hy Bender is the author or coauthor of nine computer books to date. Among his solo titles are *PC Tools: The Complete Reference* (Osborne/McGraw-Hill, 1990/1992), which was selected as one of the dozen "Best Books of the Year" by *Computer Currents* magazine, and *Essential Software for Writers* (Writer's Digest Books, 1994), which was designated "Byte's Book of the Month" by Jerry Pournelle at *Byte Magazine*, praised as "exhaustive" and "lots of fun" by L. R. Shannon at *The New York Times*, and proclaimed "the best of its kind" by mega-selling author Peter McWilliams in his syndicated Personal Computers column.

Hy is also coauthor — with his writing partner Margy Levine Young — of *Dummies 101: Netscape Navigator* (IDG Books Worldwide, 1996), *Dummies 101: The Internet for Windows 95* (IDG Books Worldwide, 1996), and the book that you hold in your hands. In addition, Hy teamed up with Margy, John Levine, and Carol Baroudi to write *The Internet for Dummies, Starter Kit Edition* (IDG Books Worldwide, 1997).

When he's not busy with computers, Hy writes humor articles for such publications as *Mad Magazine*, *Spy*, *American Film*, and *Advertising Age*. Hy also runs a fiction reading group for New York writers, and he's currently pursuing several nontechnical projects (stay tuned!).

## Margaret Levine Young

Unlike her peers in that 30-something bracket, Margaret Levine Young was exposed to computers at an early age. In high school, she got into a computer club known as the R.E.S.I.S.T.O.R.S., a group of kids who spent Saturdays in a barn fooling around with three antiquated computers. She stayed in the field through college against her better judgment and despite her brother's presence as a graduate student in the Computer Science department. Margy graduated from Yale and went on to become one of the first microcomputer managers in the early 1980s at Columbia Pictures, where she rode the elevator with Paul Newman, Bill Murray, and Jeff Goldblum.

Since then, Margy has coauthored more than two dozen computer books on such topics as the Internet, UNIX, WordPerfect, Microsoft Access, and (stab from the past) PC-File and Javelin, including *Dummies 101: Netscape Navigator*; *Dummies 101: The Internet for Windows 95*; *The Internet For Dummies, Starter Kit Edition*; *The Internet For Dummies, Fourth Edition*; *More Internet for Dummies, Third Edition*; *Internet FAQs: Answers to Frequently Asked Questions*; and *UNIX For Dummies, Third Edition* (all from IDG Books Worldwide).

Margy met her husband Jordan in the R.E.S.I.S.T.O.R.S., and her other passion is her children, Meg and Zac. She loves gardening, chickens, reading, and anything to do with eating. Margy lives near Middlebury, Vermont.

# ABOUT IDG BOOKS WORLDWIDE

Welcome to the world of IDG Books Worldwide.

IDG Books Worldwide, Inc., is a subsidiary of International Data Group, the world's largest publisher of computer-related information and the leading global provider of information services on information technology. IDG was founded more than 25 years ago and now employs more than 8,500 people worldwide. IDG publishes more than 275 computer publications in over 75 countries (see listing below). More than 60 million people read one or more IDG publications each month.

Launched in 1990, IDG Books Worldwide is today the #1 publisher of best-selling computer books in the United States. We are proud to have received eight awards from the Computer Press Association in recognition of editorial excellence and three from *Computer Currents'* First Annual Readers' Choice Awards. Our best-selling *...For Dummies*® series has more than 30 million copies in print with translations in 30 languages. IDG Books Worldwide, through a joint venture with IDG's Hi-Tech Beijing, became the first U.S. publisher to publish a computer book in the People's Republic of China. In record time, IDG Books Worldwide has become the first choice for millions of readers around the world who want to learn how to better manage their businesses.

Our mission is simple: Every one of our books is designed to bring extra value and skill-building instructions to the reader. Our books are written by experts who understand and care about our readers. The knowledge base of our editorial staff comes from years of experience in publishing, education, and journalism — experience we use to produce books for the '90s. In short, we care about books, so we attract the best people. We devote special attention to details such as audience, interior design, use of icons, and illustrations. And because we use an efficient process of authoring, editing, and desktop publishing our books electronically, we can spend more time ensuring superior content and spend less time on the technicalities of making books.

You can count on our commitment to deliver high-quality books at competitive prices on topics you want to read about. At IDG Books Worldwide, we continue in the IDG tradition of delivering quality for more than 25 years. You'll find no better book on a subject than one from IDG Books Worldwide.

John Kilcullen
CEO
IDG Books Worldwide, Inc.

Steven Berkowitz
President and Publisher
IDG Books Worldwide, Inc.

*Eighth Annual Computer Press Awards ≥ 1992*

*Ninth Annual Computer Press Awards ≥ 1993*

*Tenth Annual Computer Press Awards ≥ 1994*

*Eleventh Annual Computer Press Awards ≥ 1995*

IDG Books Worldwide, Inc., is a subsidiary of International Data Group, the world's largest publisher of computer-related information and the leading global provider of information services on information technology. International Data Group publishes over 275 computer publications in over 75 countries. Sixty million people read one or more International Data Group publications each month. International Data Group's publications include: **ARGENTINA:** Buyer's Guide, Computerworld Argentina, PC World Argentina; **AUSTRALIA:** Australian Macworld, Australian PC World, Australian Reseller News, Computerworld, IT Casebook, Network World, Publish, Webmaster; **AUSTRIA:** Computerwelt Osterreich, Networks Austria, PC Tip Austria; **BANGLADESH:** PC World Bangladesh; **BELARUS:** PC World Belarus; **BELGIUM:** Data News; **BRAZIL:** Annuário de Informática, Computerworld, Connections, Macworld, PC Player, PC World, Publish, Reseller News, Supergamepower; **BULGARIA:** Computerworld Bulgaria, Network World Bulgaria, PC & MacWorld Bulgaria; **CANADA:** CIO Canada, Client/Server World, ComputerWorld Canada, InfoWorld Canada, NetworkWorld Canada, WebWorld; **CHILE:** Computerworld Chile, PC World Chile; **COLOMBIA:** Computerworld Colombia, PC World Colombia; **COSTA RICA:** PC World Centro America; **THE CZECH AND SLOVAK REPUBLICS:** Computerworld Czechoslovakia, Macworld Czech Republic, PC World Czechoslovakia; **DENMARK:** Communications World Danmark, Computerworld Danmark, Macworld Danmark, PC World Danmark, Techworld Denmark; **DOMINICAN REPUBLIC:** PC World Republica Dominicana; **ECUADOR:** PC World Ecuador; **EGYPT:** Computerworld Middle East, PC World Middle East; **EL SALVADOR:** PC World Centro America; **FINLAND:** MikroPC, Tietoverkko, Tietoviikko; **FRANCE:** Distributique, Hebdo, Info PC, Le Monde Informatique, Macworld, Reseaux & Telecoms, WebMaster France; **GERMANY:** Computer Partner, Computerwoche, Computerwoche Extra, Computerwoche FOCUS, Global Online, Macwelt, PC Welt; **GREECE:** Amiga Computing, GamePro Greece, Multimedia World; **GUATEMALA:** PC World Centro America; **HONDURAS:** PC World Centro America; **HONG KONG:** Computerworld Hong Kong, PC World Hong Kong, Publish in Asia; **HUNGARY:** ABCD CD-ROM, Computerworld Szamitastechnika, Internetto online Magazine, PC World Hungary, PC-X Magazin Hungary; **ICELAND:** Tolvuheimur PC World Island; **INDIA:** Information Communications World, Information Systems Computerworld, PC World India, Publish in Asia; **INDONESIA:** InfoKomputer PC World, Komputek Computerworld, Publish in Asia; **IRELAND:** ComputerScope, PC Live!; **ISRAEL:** Macworld Israel, People & Computers/Computerworld; **ITALY:** Computerworld Italia, Macworld Italia, Networking Italia, PC World Italia; **JAPAN:** DTP World, Macworld Japan, Nikkei Personal Computing, OS/2 World Japan, SunWorld Japan, Windows NT World, Windows World Japan; **KENYA:** PC World East African; **KOREA:** Hi-Tech Information, Macworld Korea, PC World Korea; **MACEDONIA:** PC World Macedonia; **MALAYSIA:** Computerworld Malaysia, PC World Malaysia, Publish in Asia; **MALTA:** PC World Malta; **MEXICO:** Computerworld Mexico, PC World Mexico; **MYANMAR:** PC World Myanmar; **NETHERLANDS:** Computer! Totaal, LAN Internetworking Magazine, LAN World Buyers Guide, Macworld Netherlands, Net, WebWereld; **NEW ZEALAND:** Absolute Beginners Guide and Plain & Simple Series, Computer Buyer, Computer Industry Directory, Computerworld New Zealand, MTB, Network World, PC World New Zealand; **NICARAGUA:** PC World Centro America; **NORWAY:** Computerworld Norge, CW Rapport, Datamagasinet, Financial Rapport, Kursguide Norge, Macworld Norge, Multimediaworld Norge, PC World Ekspress Norge, PC World Nettverk, PC World Norge, PC World ProduktGuide Norge; **PAKISTAN:** Computerworld Pakistan; **PANAMA:** PC World Panama; **PEOPLE'S REPUBLIC OF CHINA:** China Computer Users, China Computerworld, China InfoWorld, China Telecom World Weekly, Computer & Communication, Electronic Design China, Electronics Today, Electronics Weekly, Game Software, PC World China, Popular Computer Week, Software Weekly, Software World, Telecom World; **PERU:** Computerworld Peru, PC World Profesional Peru, PC World SoHo Peru; **PHILIPPINES:** Click!, Computerworld Philippines, PC World Philippines, Publish in Asia; **POLAND:** Computerworld Poland, Computerworld Special Report Poland, Cyber, Macworld Poland, Network Poland, PC World Komputer; **PORTUGAL:** Cerebro/PC World, Computerworld/Correio Informático, Dealer World Portugal, Mac*In/PC*In Portugal, Multimedia World; **PUERTO RICO:** PC World Puerto Rico; **ROMANIA:** Computerworld Romania, PC World Romania, Telecom Romania; **RUSSIA:** Computerworld Russia, Mir PK, Publish, Seti; **SINGAPORE:** Computerworld Singapore, PC World Singapore, Publish in Asia; **SLOVENIA:** Monitor; **SOUTH AFRICA:** Computing SA, Network World SA, Software World SA; **SPAIN:** Communicaciones World España, Computerworld España, Dealer World España, Macworld España, PC World España; **SRI LANKA:** Infolink PC World; **SWEDEN:** CAP&Design, Computer Sweden, Corporate Computing Sweden, Internetworld Sweden, it.branschen, Macworld Sweden, MaxiData Sweden, MikroDatorn, Natverk & Kommunikation, PC World Sweden, PCaktiv, Windows World Sweden; **SWITZERLAND:** Computerworld Schweiz, Macworld Schweiz, PCtip; **TAIWAN:** Computerworld Taiwan, Macworld Taiwan, NEW ViSiON/Publish, PC World Taiwan, Windows World Taiwan; **THAILAND:** Publish in Asia, Thai Computerworld; **TURKEY:** Computerworld Turkiye, Macworld Turkiye, Network World Turkiye, PC World Turkiye; **UKRAINE:** Computerworld Kiev, Multimedia World Ukraine, PC World Ukraine; **UNITED KINGDOM:** Acorn User UK, Amiga Action UK, Amiga Computing UK, Apple Talk UK, Computing, Macworld, Parents and Computers UK, PC Advisor, PC Home, PSX Pro, The WEB; **UNITED STATES:** Cable in the Classroom, CIO Magazine, Computerworld, DOS World, Federal Computer Week, GamePro Magazine, InfoWorld, I-Way, Macworld, Network World, PC Games, PC World, Publish, Video Event, THE WEB Magazine, and WebMaster; online webzines: JavaWorld, NetscapeWorld, and SunWorld Online; **URUGUAY:** InfoWorld Uruguay; **VENEZUELA:** Computerworld Venezuela, PC World Venezuela; and **VIETNAM:** PC World Vietnam.

3/24/97

# Dedication

Hy dedicates this book, with love, to Tracey Michele Siesser.

Margy dedicates this book to the memory of her cousin Esther Gilman.

# Authors' Acknowledgments

First, we give our heartfelt thanks to Kelly Ewing for the special care she provided as she expertly shepherded this book through the editing and production process. We also thank all the folks mentioned in the Publisher's Acknowledgments section that appears on the back of this page.

Hy thanks his beloved pal and fellow writer Tracey Siesser for 21 years of cherished friendship. Hy also thanks all his old classmates for their cooperation and help in making the 25th anniversary S.A.R. Academy reunion a success.

Margy thanks all the people who have made her family feel welcome in Vermont, her new home.

# Publisher's Acknowledgments

We're proud of this book; please send us your comments about it by using the IDG Books Worldwide Registration Card at the back of the book or by e-mailing us at feedback/dummies@idgbooks.com. Some of the people who helped bring this book to market include the following:

*Acquisitions, Development, and Editorial*

**Project Editor:** Kelly Ewing

**Acquisitions Editor:** Michael Kelly

**Media Development Manager:** Joyce Pepple

**Associate Permissions Editor:** Heather H. Dismore

**Copy Editor:** Susan Christopherson

**Technical Editor:** Mike Lerch

**Editorial Manager:** Seta K. Frantz

**Editorial Assistant:** Donna Love

*Production*

**Project Coordinator:** Regina Snyder

**Layout and Graphics:** Lou Boudreau, Linda M. Boyer, J. Tyler Conner, Maridee V. Ennis, Jane E. Martin, Drew R. Moore, Kate Snell

**Proofreaders:** Christine Berman, Joel K. Draper, Robert Springer

**Indexer:** Rebecca R. Plunkett

*Special Help*

Joell Smith, Associate Technical Editor; Colleen Rainsberger, Senior Project Editor; Stephanie Koutek, Proof Editor

*General and Administrative*

**IDG Books Worldwide, Inc.:** John Kilcullen, CEO; Steven Berkowitz, President and Publisher

**IDG Books Technology Publishing:** Brenda McLaughlin, Senior Vice President and Group Publisher

**Dummies Technology Press and Dummies Editorial:** Diane Graves Steele, Vice President and Associate Publisher; Judith A. Taylor, Product Marketing Manager; Kristin A. Cocks, Editorial Director; Mary Bednarek, Acquisitions and Product Development Director

**Dummies Trade Press:** Kathleen A. Welton, Vice President and Publisher

**IDG Books Production for Dummies Press:** Beth Jenkins, Production Director; Cindy L. Phipps, Manager of Project Coordination, Production Proofreading, and Indexing; Kathie S. Schutte, Supervisor of Page Layout; Shelley Lea, Supervisor of Graphics and Design; Debbie J. Gates, Production Systems Specialist; Tony Augsburger, Supervisor of Reprints and Bluelines; Leslie Popplewell, Media Archive Coordinator

**Dummies Packaging and Book Design:** Patti Sandez, Packaging Specialist; Lance Kayser, Packaging Assistant; Kavish + Kavish, Cover Design

◆

The publisher would like to give special thanks to Patrick J. McGovern, without whom this book would not have been possible.

◆

# Files at a Glance

ABC 123

Here's a list of all the programs, plug-ins, exercise files, and document files that are stored on this book's CD-ROM, and where in the book you can find more information about them. For instructions on how to install this software, see Appendix B.

## Part I

## Part II

# Contents at a Glance

# Table of Contents

# Introduction

Welcome to *Dummies 101: Netscape Communicator 4,* part of the new hands-on tutorial series from IDG Books Worldwide. Like our *...For Dummies* books, this book gives you lots of information in a form you can understand, without taking computers and software too seriously.

Netscape Communicator is the most popular program in the history of the Internet. You can use Netscape to browse the World Wide Web, the Internet's zoomiest and friendliest face. You've probably grown awfully curious about those Web addresses at the bottom of every advertisement, article, and business card you come across these days. Using Netscape, you can take a look at those Web pages and find out what all the fuss is about. You can even use Netscape's Composer window to create and publish your own Web pages!

Netscape gives you more than just access to the World Wide Web, however. Netscape's Messenger component is a powerful program that you can use to send and receive e-mail messages over the Internet. And Netscape Collabra lets you join any of 30,000 ongoing discussions covering every topic under the sun that take place via a section of the Internet called Usenet newsgroups.

One of the coolest things about Netscape is the way it can accept *plug-ins*, which are programs that add special capabilities to Netscape. The CD-ROM in the back of this book has a bunch of plug-ins that you can install and use for free. You'll also learn how to find other plug-ins on the Internet itself.

If you are new to Netscape, the best way to learn about it is to take a course, with step-by-step instructions that build up your expertise as you go along. That's just what this book does. As opposed to a stuffy reference book with vague guidelines, this book provides a series of specific, detailed lessons that take you through getting and installing the latest version of Netscape, browsing the World Wide Web, sending and receiving e-mail, joining newsgroups, and more. The tutorials in this book take the place of a class, with lessons, exercises, quizzes, and tests.

This is the book for you if:

- ▶ You want to use Netscape but are daunted by all the incomprehensible technical terms and all the different choices that you need to make to get started.

- ▶ You have an older version of Netscape and want to upgrade to the latest version and learn about all the new stuff it can do.

- ▶ You want to take a class so that you can learn how to use Netscape's Web browser, e-mail, and newsgroups facilities but you just don't have time or the inclination to spend weeks going out to sit-down classes.

- ▶ You want to learn all the basic tasks of using Netscape so that you don't have to run for help every time you need to get some work done.

Notes:

Unlike most of the other books in the *Dummies 101* series, this book does *not* assume that you already have the programs we describe. In case you don't have Netscape, we tell you where to get it. And in case you don't have an Internet account, the CD-ROM in the back of this book includes AT&T WorldNet sign-up software, which you can use to sign up for a new account. You learn about all the programs on the CD-ROM over the course of the book and in Appendix B.

# You, the Reader

This book is designed for the beginning or intermediate computer user who wants more than just technical geekspeak about the Internet. We have to make some assumptions about you in order to make the course work for you. We assume that:

- You have Windows 95 or Windows 3.1 installed on your PC, or you use a Macintosh-compatible computer.

- You have a modem that communicates at 14,400 bps or faster (for example, 33,600 bps or 56,000 bps) and that your modem is connected to your computer.

- You have a phone line connected to your modem.

- You have at least some understanding of how to use Windows 95, Windows 3.1, or the Macintosh. (If you don't, consider checking out *Dummies 101: Windows 95* or *Dummies 101: Windows 3.1,* which are both by Andy Rathbone, or *Macs for Dummies* by David Pogue. All three are published by IDG Books Worldwide, Inc.)

If you already have Netscape Communicator installed on your computer, so much the better!

# How the Book Works

This book contains a course in using Netscape Communicator, including how to upgrade to the latest version (in case you have, for example, Netscape Navigator 3.0) and how to sign up for an AT&T WorldNet account (in case you don't have an Internet account yet). The step-by-step approach leads you through each Netscape feature by telling you exactly what to do and what your computer will do in response. Each unit has hands-on procedures to follow as you learn the basics. At the end of each unit are fun quizzes and an additional exercise that helps you review what you've learned.

After you've covered the basics, you can skip to the units that discuss what you need to learn right away. Each unit indicates what you have to know before beginning the unit, in case you're skipping around, as well as what you'll learn in the unit. You can even find a progress check at the end of each lesson so that you can gauge how you're doing.

Best of all, we don't take Netscape, the Internet, or computers very seriously. After all, there's more to life than cruising the Net (or so we hear)!

Here's how to follow the lessons in this book:

♦ The course contains eight *units,* each starting with an introduction to the topic to be covered. Then you get to the *lessons* that delve into the topic with step-by-step instructions on what to do.

♦ Topics that are more complicated or less widely used are covered in *Extra Credit* sidebars. These topics aren't critical for your learning, but they may contain just the information you need to make your Internet use more productive or more fun.

♦ When we tell you something important to remember, we summarize the information in a note in the margin (like the one in this margin).

♦ A *Recess* section indicates a good place to stop and take a breather (perhaps a walk around the block — or the block of cubicles — would clear your head). When you reach a Recess section, we tell you how to stop what you're doing and how to get started again when you come back.

♦ At the end of each unit, a quiz provides a way for you to review what you've learned and it also adds some comic relief. If a question stumps you, flip back through the unit to find the point that you missed. You'll also find an exercise that lets you practice what you've learned. At the end of each part of the book is a review of all the units in that part, along with a grueling test. (Well, maybe it's not so grueling, considering that the answers are in the back of the book.)

In the text, stuff that you need to type appears in **boldface**.

When you have to press more than one key at a time on a PC, we show the names of the keys connected with a plus sign, like this: Ctrl+C. Hold down the first key (Ctrl, in this example), press the second key (C), and then release them both.

When you have to press more than one key at a time on a Macintosh, if the first key is the Command (⌘) key, which is typical, we show the second key directly following it, like this: ⌘C. Hold down the first key (⌘), press the second key (C), and then release them both.

Every time we tell you about a keystroke, we list the keystroke for both the PC and the Macintosh. For example, if we tell you to "press Ctrl+C or ⌘C," you should press Ctrl+C on your PC or press ⌘C on your Mac.

*a note in the margin summarizes an important point*

*Notes:*

When we tell you to choose a command from the menu bar, a little arrow appears between the parts of the command, like this: File⇨Open. Click the first part of the command (File, in this example) on the menu bar and then click the second part of the command (Open) on the menu that appears. If you're using a PC, the underlines under the letter F in File and O in Open indicate that you can press Alt+F, then O to choose the command if you don't feel like using your mouse.

A note about the Internet and moving targets: The Internet is in a perpetual state of flux. The ever-changing face of the Internet makes it an interesting place but also makes writing a book about it a little problematic. If you find that an electronic address in this book doesn't work, don't panic: the address may simply have changed. Luckily, we provide online updates to the book. See the section "Send Us E-Mail" at the end of this introduction to learn how to get updated information.

# How the Book is Organized

This book is divided into two parts.

## Part I: Browsing the World Wide Web

The first part of this book gets you up and running with Netscape Communicator. If you don't have Version 4 or later, you'll also find out how to get the latest version of Netscape. Then we describe the World Wide Web, the newest, zoomiest part of the Internet. You'll use Netscape's Navigator program, or *browser,* to browse through colorful Web pages; cruise links from one Web page to another; search the Web for just about any kind of information; and copy all kinds of nifty program, graphics, and sound files from the Web.

## Part II: Communicating via E-Mail, Newsgroups, and Web Pages

In Part II, you'll learn to use Netscape's Messenger program to read and send e-mail. You'll also learn how to organize e-mail messages, maintain an address book of the e-mail addresses of your friends and coworkers, and send all kinds of data files by e-mail. Next, you find out how to use Netscape's Collabra program to participate in any of the tens of thousands of online discussions called Usenet newsgroups. Finally, you'll learn how to use Netscape's Composer program to create and publish your own Web pages, giving you the opportunity to put your words and pictures in front of tens of millions of Web users.

## Appendixes

The back of this book offers two appendixes. Appendix A gives you the answers to the test questions that appear at the ends of Parts I and II. Appendix B tells you how to install and use the dozens of fabulous programs that are stored on this book's *Dummies 101* CD-ROM.

# Icons Used in This Book

We put one of the following four icons in the margin when we want to point out important information:

**on the CD**

This icon tells you when you need to use a file that comes on the *Dummies 101* CD-ROM.

**on the test**

Here's an item that you need to know when you get to the quiz at the end of the unit. If it's on the test, it must be important!

**extra credit**

Descriptions of advanced topics appear in sidebars highlighted with this icon.

**heads up**

Heads up! Here's a piece of information that can make your life easier or may avert disaster.

# About the *Dummies 101* CD-ROM

**on the CD**

The *Dummies 101* CD-ROM at the back of this book contains all the programs and files that you'll need to do the exercises in this book. In case you don't have an Internet account, the CD-ROM also includes three AT&T WorldNet software sign-up kits (for Windows 95, Windows 3.1, and the Macintosh) that you can use to sign up for an Internet account (see Unit 1). In addition, the CD-ROM houses a bunch of Netscape plug-ins, which are programs that increase the abilities of Netscape in a variety of spectacular ways (see Unit CD-5, which is a bonus unit that's also stored on the CD-ROM). Finally, the CD-ROM provides more than a dozen powerful Internet programs that you can run independently of Netscape, including Eudora Light for managing e-mail; Free Agent and InterNews for participating in Usenet newsgroups; mIRC and Ircle for chatting live with others on the Net; WinZip and Stuffit Expander for making compressed files usable again; Paint Shop Pro and Graphic Converter for viewing and revising picture files; and ThunderBYTE Anti-Virus and

Disinfectant for detecting computer viruses (see Appendix B).

The CD-ROM comes with a handy Windows Installer program that copies to your hard disk the programs you decide to use. See Appendix B for specific instructions, as well as a list of the programs and files that the CD-ROM contains.

If you have trouble with the CD-ROM (for example, if your computer can't read it or it arrives in three pieces), call IDG Books Customer Support at 800-762-2974.

# Send Us E-Mail

We love to hear from our readers. If you have questions or comments about the book, send us e-mail at ncomm101@dummies.net. We can't answer all your questions about the Internet — after all, we are authors, not consultants — but we'd love to hear how the course worked for you.

If you want to know about other ...*For Dummies* books, call 800-762-2974, write to info@idgbooks.com, or look at this page on the World Wide Web:

http://www.dummies.com

For more information about the Internet and updates to this book, look at this Web page:

http://net.dummies.net/ncomm101

If you can't send e-mail, you can always send plain old paper mail by using the registration card in the back of this book. You'll receive a catalog of IDG Books in return. Don't worry — we authors will see your comments, too.

# Browsing the World Wide Web

## Part I

## In this part . . .

**N**etscape Communicator can do a lot of cool things, but it's most famous for its capability to let you cruise the amazing World Wide Web. This part of the book first tells you how to sign up for an Internet account and get a current copy of Netscape. It then steps you through using Netscape to take in the many colorful and fascinating sights on the Web; locate information on virtually any topic on the Web; and copy any of thousands of programs, electronic pictures, sound and video clips, and other fun files from the Web.

# Getting Started with Netscape Communicator

**Objectives for This Unit**

✓ Preparing to go online

✓ Jumping onto the World Wide Web using Netscape Communicator

✓ Moving around a Web page and identifying its links

✓ Using links to move to Web pages

✓ Switching between Web pages

**Prerequisites**

▶ A PC running Windows 95 or Windows 3.1, or a Macintosh

▶ A CD-ROM drive connected to your computer

▶ A 14,400 bps or faster modem connected to your computer

The Internet has been popping up everywhere lately. Hundreds of articles about it appear regularly in newspapers and magazines, dozens of TV specials and videotapes are devoted to it, major motion pictures such as *The Net* are based on it — coffee shops are even springing up that let you cruise the Internet while you sip an espresso!

Does the Internet deserve all this hoopla? In a word, *yes*. The Internet's most famous component, the visually striking World Wide Web, lets you find information about any subject with a few keystrokes or mouse clicks. The Internet also enables you to send electronic mail (or *e-mail*) messages to friends and colleagues around the globe in seconds; participate in ongoing discussions about virtually any topic via Internet talk groups (called *newsgroups*); chat with people live through your keyboard by using Internet Relay Chat (or *IRC*); and freely copy thousands of programs, picture files, and other goodies that are just waiting for you to come and get them.

To take advantage of such Internet features, you need software that lets you access and interact with the Net. The best program for doing so is Netscape Communicator, which is published by Netscape Communications Corporation. Most people refer to Netscape Communicator as just *Netscape,* and that's what we'll do from now on, too.

Netscape is the Internet program of choice by an overwhelming margin — it's used by more than 70 percent of folks on the Net, or about 40 million people! In fact, Netscape isn't simply the best-liked Internet program around — it's one of the three most popular programs of *any* kind in the history of computers. Netscape is packed with features that let you cruise the World Wide Web, send and receive e-mail, participate in newsgroup discussions, and much more.

> *Netscape lets you cruise the Web, send and receive e-mail, and join newsgroups*

This book and the CD-ROM that comes with it are designed to teach you how to run Netscape and use it to take advantage of all the wonderful things on the Internet. By the time you finish this book, you'll have turned from a *newbie* (Internet newcomer) to a *Nethead* (Internet expert)!

The version of Netscape Communicator that we'll be covering is 4, which is the most current version at the time of this writing. Because Netscape tends to keep its key features operating the same way across versions, however, much of the material in this book also applies to Netscape Navigator 2.0 and 3.0 (and is likely to apply to future versions of Netscape as well).

This first unit tells you what you need to know to get started. It then guides you through an initial look at the World Wide Web using Netscape.

## Lesson 1-1

# Preparing to Go Online with Netscape Communicator

Before you can cruise the Internet with Netscape, you have to prepare yourself for the journey. Specifically, you need to own the right equipment, set up an Internet account, have a recent copy of Netscape, and know a few basic terms.

## Understanding what equipment you need

You need several pieces of equipment to make full use of this book.

First, you need a PC that runs Windows 95 (or its advanced sibling, Windows NT); or a PC that runs some version of Windows 3.1 (such as Windows 3.11 or Windows 3.11 for Workgroups). For you Macintosh folks, you need an Apple Macintosh computer (such as the PowerMac or PowerBook) or a Macintosh-compatible unit (such as Power Computing's PowerTower Pro).

You also need a CD-ROM drive so that you can transfer the terrific software on this book's CD-ROM to your hard disk.

In addition, you need a phone line that's available for use with your computer.

Finally, you need a device called a *modem*. This special piece of equipment requires some explanation.

**on the test**

To *go online* means to get your computer to communicate with other computers over a phone line. (In fact, while on the Internet, you can access *millions* of other computers.) Talking over the phone isn't a capability built into your machine, however, so it needs help from your modem. The modem converts your computer's digital language into audio that can travel over phone wires and converts the audio signals from other computers back into digital data.

Not all modems are created equal. For example, if you have an internal modem, it's tucked away in a slot inside your computer, and you don't have to think much about it because it's always on and available. If you have an external modem, it resides outside your computer, has an on/off switch, and is connected to a socket in the back of your machine by a special cable. (If you ever encounter a problem getting online with an external modem, always start off by making sure that the modem's power switch is turned on and that its cable is still tightly attached to your computer.)

Modems also have different speed capabilities, which are measured in bits per second, or *bps*. As we write this book, the current standard speed is 33,600 bps, which can transmit and receive data very quickly — for example, transferring the contents of a 1.44MB floppy disk at 33,600 bps takes about six minutes. An up-and-coming standard is 56,000 bps, which is about twice as fast as 33,600 bps — transferring 1.44MB at this speed takes about three minutes. The bare minimum speed you need to use the Internet effectively is 14,400 bps, which is less than half as fast at 33,600 bps (and which may cause you to tap your foot impatiently while waiting for data to appear on your screen).

To sum up, if you have a computer running Windows or Macintosh software, a CD-ROM drive, a modem, and a phone line that you can plug into your modem, you're set as far as equipment goes. Your next step is to decide how to connect to the Internet.

## Getting an Internet account

One of the wonderful things about the Internet is that no one owns it — it's a resource that millions of people and organizations around the world share. Before you can go online, however, you need to sign up with a company that has the proper hardware and software to provide you with access to the Internet. Such a company is called, appropriately enough, an *Internet Service Provider* or *ISP,* and it typically charges a monthly fee for its service. Thousands of such providers exist, so you have lots of choices.

For example, if you're running Windows 95, you can sign up for the Microsoft Network service by doing little more than *double-clicking* (that is, clicking twice in rapid succession) the MSN icon on your desktop and then answering some questions (with credit card in hand).

*Notes:*

online = connected
to other computers
via phone line

*Notes:*

AT&T WorldNet
sign-up software is
on your *Dummies*
*101* CD-ROM

Three other popular services are MindSpring, Concentric, and Netcom, each of which provides hundreds of telephone numbers across the U.S. that let you dial into the Internet for the price of a local call.

Another excellent ISP is AT&T WorldNet Service, which offers technical support 24 hours a day, seven days a week via an 800 number. We feel that AT&T WorldNet Service is an ideal choice for beginners, so we've included the Windows 95, Windows 3.1, and Macintosh versions of its software kits — each of which consists of a sign-up program and a customized edition of Netscape Navigator — on the CD-ROM that comes with this book. (For more information, see Appendix B.)

You can also access the Internet through an online service such as America Online or CompuServe. The advantage of an online service is that it provides a number of features in addition to Internet access, such as easy-to-use discussion sections and special databases that furnish information not available on the Net. An online service may be more expensive than a vanilla ISP, however, or it may be more prone to problems such as excessive busy signals or slow Net access.

Of course, if you use online resources as serious business tools, you can always sign up with more than one provider. (For example, we belong to both America Online and CompuServe so that we can access their extra features, but we do all our Internet work through a dedicated ISP.) If you'd like to contact any of the companies we just mentioned, see Table 1-1.

| Table 1-1 | Some Popular Internet Service Providers | |
|---|---|---|
| *Company* | *Telephone Number* | *Comments* |
| America Online | 800-827-6364 or 703-448-8700 | Online service that includes Internet access among its many features |
| AT&T WorldNet Service | 800-967-5363 or 201-967-5363 | International ISP; we provide its sign-up software on this book's CD-ROM |
| CompuServe | 800-848-8199 or 614-457-8600 | Online service that includes Internet access among its many features |
| Concentric | 800-939-4262 or 408-342-2800 | U.S. ISP |
| IBM Global Network | 800-455-5056 or 404-238-1234 | International ISP |
| The Microsoft Network | 800-386-5550 or 206-882-8080 | Online service that includes Internet access among its features; you can join it by double-clicking the MSN icon on your Windows 95 desktop |
| MindSpring | 800-719-4332 or 404-815-0082 | U.S. ISP |
| Netcom | 800-353-6600 or 408-881-1815 | U.S. ISP |

Then again, you might consider hooking up with a small local service. Although such companies aren't able to provide local telephone numbers for connecting to the Net outside your area, you don't need such numbers unless you travel frequently. In addition, local companies can sometimes provide a more personal touch (for example, offering beginner classes or organizing subscriber get-togethers) than their national competitors. You can locate ISPs in your area by checking the Internet and/or Computer Services sections in your phone book's Yellow Pages, leafing through ads in your newspaper's Science or Technology section, or asking your friends and colleagues which providers they recommend. Alternatively, if you have a friend who already knows how to use the Net and is willing to spare a few minutes, ask your friend to go to the World Wide Web location `thelist.iworld.com`. This location is the home of a search program named The List that contains information on over 5,000 ISPs and lists them based on the criteria you specify (such as your country, state, or area code).

> you can search for ISPs at World Wide Web site thelist.iworld.com

Whether you select a large national ISP, a small local ISP, or an online service, the important thing is that you have an account with a company that can serve as your connection to the Internet. After you're signed up, you need just one more thing: a copy of Netscape itself.

# Getting and installing Netscape Communicator

Before you can tackle the various exercises that teach you how to use Netscape Communicator, you need to *have* Netscape Communicator.

The program actually comes in two different editions: Standard and Professional. The only difference between them is that the Professional edition contains three extra corporate features: group scheduling over a Local Area Network, access to your office's expensive IBM 3270 computers, and software to help set up and manage multiple copies of Netscape. In a nutshell, if you aren't working in a large office with a Local Area Network, choose the Standard edition.

You can get Netscape in a variety of ways. One approach is simply to buy the program directly from Netscape Communications Corporation by calling 415-937-3777 or 415-937-2555 with a credit card in hand. If you're upgrading from an older version of Netscape that you or your company paid for, be sure to say so when speaking to your salesperson, because that fact may entitle you to buy the current version at a lower price. After the Netscape installation software — which is typically stored on a CD-ROM — arrives in your mailbox, you can follow the instructions included in the package to copy the new version of Netscape to your hard disk.

Alternatively, you can purchase Netscape from a local computer store, or from a mail-order vendor that advertises in computer magazines and software catalogs such as *PC Connection/Mac Connection* (800-800-5555), *MicroWarehouse* (800-367-7080), or *MacWarehouse* (800-255-6227). Such retailers typically charge less for a program than the actual publisher of the program, so buying Netscape from a third-party vendor is likely to save you money. Again, after you receive the software package, you can follow the instructions that are included to install Netscape on your hard disk.

Another option is to get Netscape directly from the Internet. When you signed up for an Internet account, your provider probably included a Web browser as part of your start-up kit. (For example, if you used the software on this book's CD-ROM to subscribe to AT&T WorldNet Service, you now have a copy of Netscape Navigator 3.0 for Windows or Netscape Navigator 2.02 for the Macintosh.) The browser that you have may not be the latest version of Netscape, but you can use it to connect to the Net and then copy, or *download*, the latest version of Netscape from any of hundreds of areas on the Web. (For example, we recommend the superb Tucows Internet software library at the Web location www.tucows.com.) You can skip to Lesson 3-2 for instructions on downloading software from the Web; or you can simply ask a friend who already knows her way around the Net to download Netscape for you.

After you download Netscape, you have a single installation file that contains dozens of program and data files in compressed form. To make Netscape useable, follow these steps:

**1  Save any documents that you have open and then exit all programs that are currently running.**

It's best to close all programs before installing a new one to ensure that no conflict between programs occurs during the installation process.

**2  Move to the folder containing the file that you just downloaded.**

For example, if you're using Windows 95, use a My Computer or Windows Explorer window; if you're using Windows 3.1, use File Manager; and if you're using a Mac, use the Finder.

**3  Position your mouse pointer over the file and double-click — that is, click your left mouse button twice in rapid succession.**

If nothing happens, you may have paused too long between your two clicks, so just try again. When you've double-clicked successfully, a message asking you to confirm that you want to install Netscape appears.

**4  Click the <u>Y</u>es button to run the installation program and then follow the instructions that appear on-screen.**

You may soon see a license agreement. (If you're asked to pick a folder first, skip to Step 6.) This is the only time the agreement will appear, so take a few minutes to examine it. You can move down and up in the window by pressing the PgDn and PgUp keys.

Notice that the agreement states that your downloaded copy of Netscape is an evaluation copy. If you decide that you like Netscape and want to keep using it, you're supposed to register the program by paying for it. Doing so entitles you to certain extra privileges, such as telephone technical support from Netscape Communications.

copy, or download,
the latest version
of Netscape
from World Wide
Web site
www.tucows.com

**5 If you accept the terms of the license agreement, click the <u>Y</u>es button.**

If you don't click <u>Y</u>es, Netscape won't run. After you click the <u>Y</u>es button, you're asked to pick the folder that will store Netscape's program and data files.

**6 Select a folder for storing the Netscape program or accept the folder name suggested.**

For example, you might choose `C:\Program Files\Netscape` for Windows 95, `C:\Netscape` for Windows 3.1, or `Netscape Communicator Folder` for Macintosh. After you select the folder, write down its full name on the Cheat Sheet in the front of this book so that you can refer to the folder in later exercises.

**7 Click the <u>N</u>ext button and then answer any additional questions to proceed with the installation.**

After you're done with its initial questions, the installation program expands and copies all its files to the Netscape folder that you selected. You may then be asked whether you want to go online to the Netscape Communications area on the World Wide Web to complete the installation. If this occurs, go ahead and click <u>Y</u>es and follow the instructions online.

**8 Answer any additional questions to complete the installation.**

When the installation program has finished, you may be asked whether you want to restart, or *reboot,* your computer. If this happens, click <u>Y</u>es and let your machine shut down and restart.

You should now see a folder (or, under Windows 3.1, a Program Group) on your desktop that contains an icon for Netscape Communicator. If you're using Windows 95, you should also see a Netscape Communicator icon on your desktop. Double-clicking either icon runs the Netscape program.

**9 Double-click the Netscape Communicator icon.**

A Profile Setup Wizard dialog box may pop up to help you customize your version of Netscape. If this happens, follow its instructions.

In addition, if you didn't see a license agreement previously, you see one now. If the agreement appears, examine it and then press the <u>Y</u>es button to accept it. (See Steps 4 and 5 of this exercise for more information.)

Finally, Netscape opens and is ready for use. You may also see an Internet dialer program (such as the Windows 95 Connect To dialog box) that allows you to connect to the Internet. You'll be running both the dialer and the Netscape programs in the next lesson. For now, though, simply exit.

**10 Choose <u>F</u>ile⇨E<u>x</u>it or <u>F</u>ile⇨Quit — that is, click the <u>F</u>ile heading on the Netscape menu bar and then click the E<u>x</u>it option (if you're using Windows) or the Quit option (if you're using a Mac).**

Alternatively, press Ctrl+Q or ⌘Q. The Netscape program and the dialer program disappear.

Fantastic! You're now set to use Netscape as your window on the Internet!

*Notes:*

*press Yes button to accept license agreement*

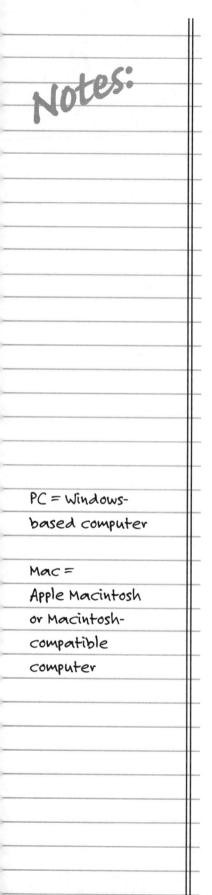

**Notes:**

**heads up**

## Getting an Internet dialer program

In addition to Netscape, you need an Internet dialer program that can dial one of your ISP's phone numbers and connect you to the Net. Windows 95 has a dialer program built-in, and many new Macintoshes come with a dialer program included. In addition, an ISP will typically provide a dialer to you as part of its service. If you don't have a dialer program, though, or if you'd simply like to try using a different dialer, you can get one from the CD-ROM that comes with this book. If you use Windows, you can install the excellent Trumpet WinSock program from your *Dummies 101* CD-ROM; and if you use the Macintosh, you can install the acclaimed FreePPP program from the CD-ROM. For more information, see Appendix B.

You have just one more thing to do before you start running Netscape, and that's to become familiar with some key words and phrases related to using your computer and the Internet.

## Understanding a few basic terms

We try to avoid jargon as much as possible, but writing a computer book requires throwing in some technical words. We introduce most new terms as they're needed over the course of the book (and, we hope, always clearly define them when they pop up!). You should know a few words and phrases right away, though, so here's a quick list:

PC = Windows-based computer

Mac =
Apple Macintosh
or Macintosh-
compatible
computer

▶ **PC:** Short for personal computer. In the context of this book, PC refers to a computer that's designed to run Microsoft Windows (as opposed to a Macintosh).

▶ **Mac:** Short for Apple Macintosh or Macintosh-compatible computer.

▶ **Click:** Press your left mouse button.

▶ **Click the OK button:** Position your mouse pointer over the OK button and then press your left mouse button.

▶ **Double-click:** Press your left mouse button twice in rapid succession.

▶ **Right-click:** Press your right mouse button.

▶ **Click and drag:** Click an object that you want to move and, while keeping your mouse button held down, move your mouse to another location; the object will be dragged along by your mouse.

▶ **Dialog box:** A box that displays a message and/or various options.

▶ **Run, launch, or fire up a program:** Get a program going.

- **Dial in or log in:** Use your modem and phone line to call up an ISP and get connected to the Internet.

- **Go online:** Take steps to connect with other computers by using your modem and a phone line.

- **Go offline:** Disconnect from your online session.

- **The Net:** Short for the Internet.

- **Default option:** The option that's selected before you make any adjustments (sort of like the factory setting).

- **Character:** A single letter, number, punctuation mark, or other symbol that you can type on your keyboard. (For example, the word *cat* has three characters, as does the date *5/9*.)

- **Extension:** The one to three characters following the final period in a filename. (For example, the filename *Letter.txt* has the extension *txt*, the filename *Program.exe* has the extension *exe*, and the Web page file *My Home Page.htm* has the extension *htm*.)

- **Filename:** The name of an electronic file. Under Windows 95, a filename can be up to 255 characters, and can include spaces and punctuation. On a Mac, a filename can be up to 31 characters long, including spaces and punctuation. Under Windows 3.1, a filename can consist of up to 8 characters and a 3-character extension, with no spaces or punctuation. If you're using Windows 3.1 and see a long filename in this book (or on the Net), keep in mind that you need to use relatively short names for files.

- **Folder:** An area on your hard disk that's used to store files. Folders help keep your files organized in logical groups, just as physical folders help organize your papers in a filing cabinet.

- **Directory:** The term typically used for *folder* in Windows 3.1. *Directory* and *folder* mean the same thing, however, and this book simply uses the term *folder*.

- **Program Group:** Another area used to store files under Windows 3.1. Folders are used for this purpose under Windows 95 and the Macintosh.

on the test

- **Maximize a window:** Under Windows 95, click the middle button of the three buttons residing in the upper-right corner of every window. Under Windows 3.1 or the Mac, click the button that's in the upper-right corner of every window. Maximizing expands a window so that it fills the screen. (If the window already fills the screen, clicking this button shrinks the window back to its former size.)

  On a Macintosh, you click a button that's actually called a *Zoom box*, and doing so may only partially expand a window. If you're instructed to maximize a window and clicking the Zoom box doesn't fully do the job, click and drag the Size box in the every window's lower-right corner to manually expand the window to fill the screen.

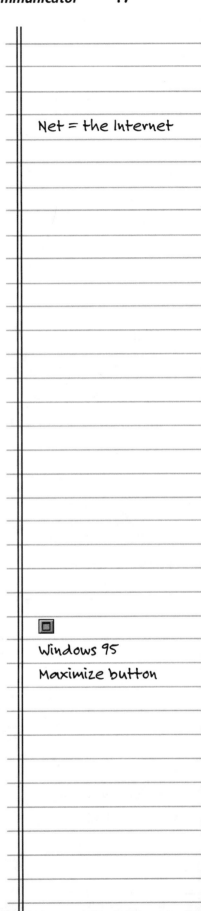

Net = the Internet

Windows 95
Maximize button

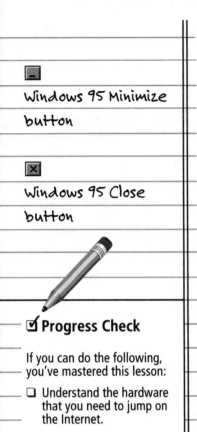

Windows 95 Minimize button

Windows 95 Close button

☑ **Progress Check**

If you can do the following, you've mastered this lesson:

❏ Understand the hardware that you need to jump on the Internet.

❏ Understand how to sign up with an Internet Service Provider (ISP).

❏ Understand how to get the current version of Netscape Communicator.

❏ Understand fundamental computer terms.

▸ **Minimize a window:** Under Windows, click the leftmost button of the buttons residing in the upper-right corner of every window. Clicking Minimize makes a window disappear from your screen but keeps it active (as indicated by the window being represented as a button on the Windows 95 Taskbar or as a small icon at the bottom of the Windows 3.1 desktop). You can restore a minimized window to your screen at any time by clicking its button on the Taskbar (under Windows 95) or double-clicking its icon (under Windows 3.1). There's no equivalent to the Minimize button on a Mac.

▸ **Click the window's Close button:** Under Windows 95, click the button directly to the right of the Maximize button. Under Windows 3.1, double-click the Control-menu box that's in the upper-left corner of every window. On a Macintosh, click the Close box that's in the upper-left corner of every window. Closing a window makes it disappear from your screen, deactivate, and free up space in your computer's memory for new windows.

▸ **Press Ctrl+D:** On a PC, hold down the Ctrl key and, while keeping it pressed, tap the D key.

▸ **Press ⌘D:** On a Macintosh, hold down the Command key and, while keeping it pressed, tap the D key.

▸ **Choose File⇨Save:** Click the File heading near the top of your window to display a menu of options and then click the Save option that appears on the menu. Alternatively (if you're using a PC), hold down the Alt key and press F followed by S.

*Note:* If you're using a Mac, you won't see underlines under menus or options because the Mac edition of Netscape doesn't support keystroke equivalents the way the PC version does. As a result, ignore such underlines when they appear in this book and just use your mouse to click the commands.

If you don't memorize all these terms on the spot, don't worry; we'll go over their definitions again as needed. If most of these terms are entirely new to you, however, doing some additional reading about Windows may be helpful. Three (of many) fine books are *Dummies 101: Windows 95* and *Dummies 101: Windows 3.1,* which are both written by Andy Rathbone, and *Macs For Dummies* by David Pogue (all published by IDG Books Worldwide, Inc.).

## Lesson 1-2    Jumping onto the Web

Web = shorthand for World Wide Web section of Internet

It's time that all the preparation work you did in Lesson 1-1 pays off. You're about to crawl onto the World Wide Web!

*World Wide Web* may sound like the title of a 1950s conspiracy movie involving radioactive Communist spiders. However, the WWW, or *Web* (as savvy Net users refer to it) is much cooler than that. Though it didn't even exist until 1990, the Web is rapidly becoming the most popular feature of the Internet.

The Web consists of electronic pages that display text and pictures, similar to the pages of a paper book or magazine (though some jazzier Web pages also can play sound and video clips). Well-designed Web pages are a visual treat, and they cover virtually every topic that you can think of — from the stock market to stock car racing, from bass to baseball, and from Picasso to Prozac. The neatest thing about the Web, however, is that each page typically contains *links* to other pages, allowing you to jump from one page to another with a single mouse click.

For example, you might be reading a Web page about the life of William Shakespeare and notice that various phrases and pictures in the biography are underlined, are a different color, or are marked in some other special way. This special marking usually means that clicking the phrase or picture (called a *link*) with your mouse takes you to another page covering that topic in more depth. At the William Shakespeare page, clicking the phrase *Romeo and Juliet* might take you to a page with the full text of that play, and clicking an image of the Globe Theatre could take you to a page with a series of detailed drawings of that famous Elizabethan playhouse.

Your voyage wouldn't have to end there, either. For example, the Globe Theatre page might contain a link to *modern theatre.* Clicking the phrase could offer you additional links to such disparate topics as Arthur Miller, movie adaptations, and Andrew Lloyd Webber's *Cats.* Clicking the latter might furnish — in addition to information about other Lloyd Webber hits, such as *Evita* and *The Phantom of the Opera* — links to Web pages about *real* cats. And any feline Web page worth its fur inevitably offers a link to pictures of Socks, the First Cat of the Clinton White House.

This hypothetical journey from Shakespeare to Socks shows you what jumping around the Web, also known as *cruising* or *surfing,* is all about. Because these electronic pages — which are created independently by thousands of individuals and organizations around the planet — are all linked together in various intricate ways, they truly form a World Wide Web of information.

In this unit, you get on the Web by using the Netscape *browser* window, which lets you browse through electronic pages. (It's also called the *Navigator* window because it helps you navigate your way along the Web.) You first learn how to examine a Web page and use its links to move to other pages. You then learn how to use Netscape buttons to switch among a few pages, and how to use Netscape's Go menu and History window to switch among many pages.

## Opening Netscape and connecting to the Net

In Lesson 1-1, you signed up with an ISP and installed Netscape on your hard disk. Now follow these steps to actually run Netscape and use it to browse the Web:

**1** Make sure that your modem is turned on, that you have a phone line connected to your modem, and that you don't have another telecommunications program running.

*Notes:*

browser = program
that lets you
cruise the Web

**Figure 1-1:** When you run Netscape, a Netscape browser window and your Internet dialer program appear.

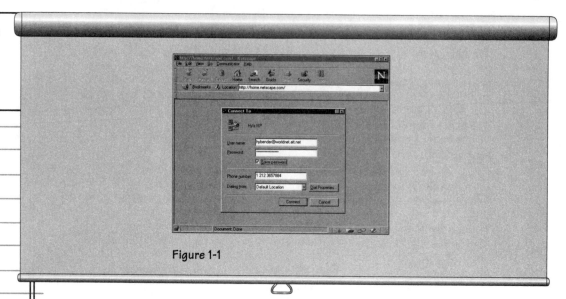

Figure 1-1

Netscape Communicator icon

**2. Start Netscape Communicator.**

- If you're using Windows 95, double-click the Netscape Communicator icon on your desktop. (Alternatively, click the Windows 95 Start button, click Programs, click the Netscape Communicator option from the second menu that appears, and then click the Netscape Navigator icon from the third menu that appears.)

- If you're using Windows 3.1, double-click the Netscape Communicator icon from the Netscape Program Group.

- If you're using a Macintosh, double-click the Netscape Communicator icon from the Netscape folder.

The Netscape browser window opens, and whatever Internet dialer program you're using appears. For example, if you're using the Windows 95 Dialer, a Connect To dialog box appears in front of the Netscape window, as shown in Figure 1-1.

**Note:** Some dialer programs don't pop up automatically when you run Netscape. If that's true of your dialer, simply run it manually by double-clicking its icon.

**3. Click the appropriate button on your dialer program to connect to the Internet.**

For example, if you're using the Windows 95 Dialer, click the Connect button. After a few moments, your dialer program dials into the local phone number that you're using to access your ISP, gets your modem talking to your provider's modem, and transmits the user name and password that identify you to your provider. If all goes well, you're connected to the Internet. If you're using Windows, your dialer program then becomes minimized — that is, it disappears from your screen but stays active, and is represented as a button on the Windows 95 Taskbar or an icon on the Windows 3.1 desktop. (If you're using a Mac, the dialer simply remains displayed on your desktop.)

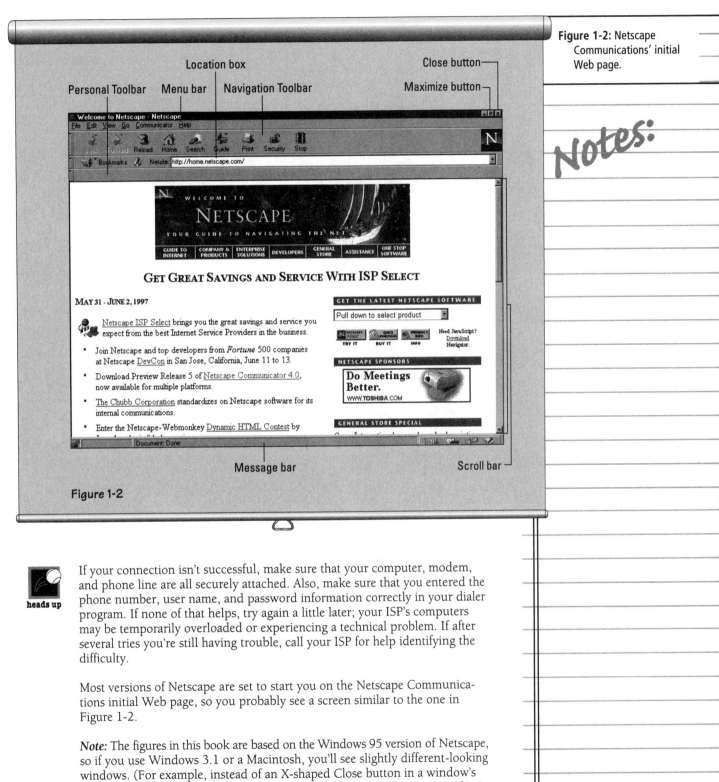

**Figure 1-2:** Netscape Communications' initial Web page.

Personal Toolbar    Menu bar    Location box    Navigation Toolbar    Close button    Maximize button

**GET GREAT SAVINGS AND SERVICE WITH ISP SELECT**

MAY 31 - JUNE 2, 1997

Netscape ISP Select brings you the great savings and service you expect from the best Internet Service Providers in the business.

- Join Netscape and top developers from *Fortune* 500 companies at Netscape DevCon in San Jose, California, June 11 to 13.
- Download Preview Release 5 of Netscape Communicator 4.0, now available for multiple platforms.
- The Chubb Corporation standardizes on Netscape software for its internal communications.
- Enter the Netscape-Webmonkey Dynamic HTML Contest by

Message bar    Scroll bar

Figure 1-2

*Notes:*

**heads up**

If your connection isn't successful, make sure that your computer, modem, and phone line are all securely attached. Also, make sure that you entered the phone number, user name, and password information correctly in your dialer program. If none of that helps, try again a little later; your ISP's computers may be temporarily overloaded or experiencing a technical problem. If after several tries you're still having trouble, call your ISP for help identifying the difficulty.

Most versions of Netscape are set to start you on the Netscape Communications initial Web page, so you probably see a screen similar to the one in Figure 1-2.

*Note:* The figures in this book are based on the Windows 95 version of Netscape, so if you use Windows 3.1 or a Macintosh, you'll see slightly different-looking windows. (For example, instead of an X-shaped Close button in a window's upper-right corner, you have a Control-menu box or Close box in a window's upper-left corner.) The visual differences are small, however, and this book's explanations and exercises apply to all three types of computers, so you'll be able to follow along regardless of what machine you're using.

Notes:

If your window doesn't fill the screen, click the Maximize button (represented by a box symbol in Windows 95 and an upward-pointing triangle in Windows 3.1) in the window's upper-right corner. If you use a Mac, manually resize the window until it fills the screen.

Congratulations! You've successfully landed on the World Wide Web. (Now we're getting somewhere!)

The initial Netscape Communications Web page that you're on is called a *home page* because it's the place from which you set off on your Web journey. Every Web area, or *site,* has its own home page that contains links to other pages on the site (and elsewhere).

The text and pictures that you see on your screen will look different from the screen shots that appear in this book, because Web page content is constantly being updated and improved. However, the basic skills on how to use the Web that we cover still apply.

## Moving up and down a Web page

If you take a close look at the page displayed in your Netscape window, you see that only part of the page is visible. Web pages are almost always longer than a browser's window, so you typically must view them a section at a time. One way to view different sections of a page is to use the vertical scroll bar — that is, the gray stripe along the right edge of your Netscape window.

The vertical scroll bar has three main elements: the down and up scroll arrows on its ends and the scroll box between them, which indicates by its position in the bar just how far down you are on the page (see Figure 1-3). Clicking the down or up arrow moves the page about a line at a time, and clicking and dragging the scroll box, as described in the next exercise, moves you around the page more rapidly.

**1 Click the down arrow of your window's vertical scroll bar.**

The page scrolls down a bit in your window, allowing you to see more of the page's content.

**2 Click the down arrow repeatedly until the scroll box is at the bottom of the bar.**

The page continues to scroll down until the end of its content appears in the window.

**3 Click the up arrow of the vertical scroll bar.**

The page scrolls up a bit in the window.

**4 Click the scroll box in the vertical scroll bar and, while keeping your mouse button pressed, drag the box to the top of the bar.**

This procedure is called *clicking and dragging.* After you move the scroll box, the page jumps back up in the window to its top section.

clicking and
dragging = clicking
object and, while
keeping your mouse
button held down,
moving mouse

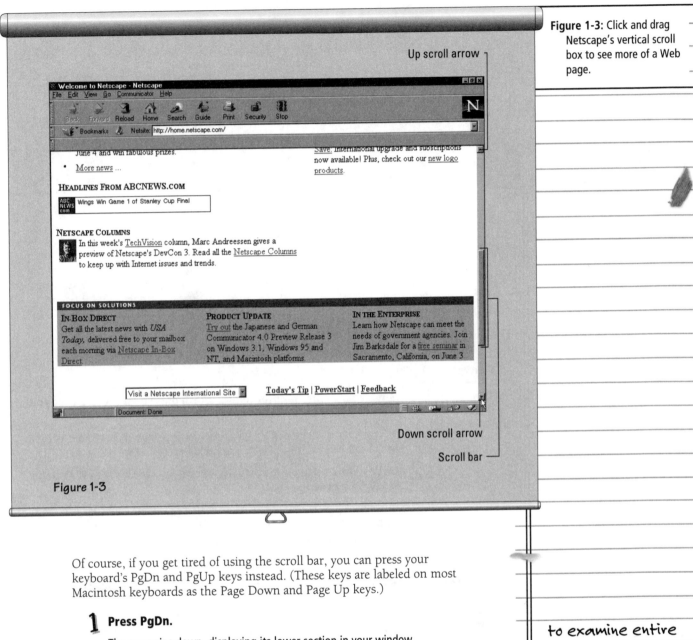

**Figure 1-3:** Click and drag Netscape's vertical scroll box to see more of a Web page.

Up scroll arrow

Down scroll arrow

Scroll bar

Figure 1-3

Of course, if you get tired of using the scroll bar, you can press your keyboard's PgDn and PgUp keys instead. (These keys are labeled on most Macintosh keyboards as the Page Down and Page Up keys.)

**1 Press PgDn.**

The page zips down, displaying its lower section in your window.

**2 Press PgUp.**

The page swooshes up to its top section again.

That's all there is to moving up and down in a Web page!

To sum up: Your browser window is almost always shorter than the Web page you're looking at. To see the whole page, simply use the vertical scroll bar or the PgDn and PgUp keys.

*to examine entire Web page, click vertical scroll bar arrows or press PgDn and PgUp keys*

**Figure 1-4:** When you point to regular text on a Web page, your mouse pointer retains its arrowhead shape.

**Figure 1-5:** When you point to a Web page link, your mouse pointer changes to the shape of a pointing hand.

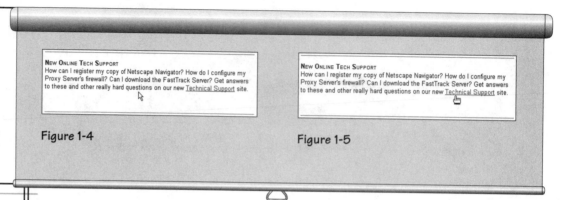

Figure 1-4                                    Figure 1-5

*Notes:*

URL = electronic address of Web page or other information area on Net

# Finding links on a Web page

Notice that certain phrases and images on the Web page that you're viewing are distinguished from the other text and pictures by underlines, different colors, or other effects. Such markings indicate that these areas are links that you can use to jump to other Web pages.

**on the test**

Finding out whether a highlighted phrase or image is really a link is easy. All you have to do is move your mouse.

**1** **Move your mouse pointer over a word, phrase, or picture that you suspect is a link.**

If the area that you choose is a link, your mouse pointer changes from its usual arrowhead shape to a hand with a pointing finger (see Figures 1-4 and 1-5).

**2** **Move your mouse pointer slowly over every area of the Web page in your window.**

Your mouse pointer turns into a hand when it's over areas that are links, and the pointer reverts to its usual arrowhead shape when it's over areas that contain only normal text and pictures.

# Identifying a link's electronic address

**on the test**

Another way to prove that you found a link is to keep an eye on the gray message bar at the bottom of your window (see Figure 1-6). When your mouse is pointing to a link, the message bar displays the Internet location, or electronic *address*, of the page to which the link takes you. This location is called a *URL*. (Actually, the official techie term is *Uniform Resource Locator* but, understandably, almost everybody just calls 'em URLs.) For example, the URL of the page that you're currently viewing is `http://home.netscape.com/`. That's why the address `http://home.netscape.com/` appears in the Location box in the upper portion of your window.

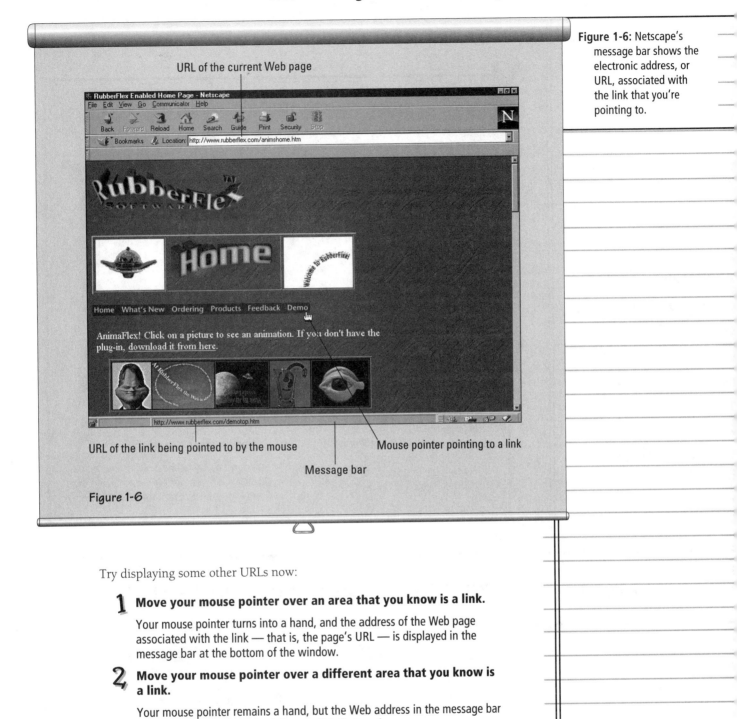

URL of the current Web page

**Figure 1-6:** Netscape's message bar shows the electronic address, or URL, associated with the link that you're pointing to.

URL of the link being pointed to by the mouse

Mouse pointer pointing to a link

Message bar

Figure 1-6

Try displaying some other URLs now:

**1 Move your mouse pointer over an area that you know is a link.**

Your mouse pointer turns into a hand, and the address of the Web page associated with the link — that is, the page's URL — is displayed in the message bar at the bottom of the window.

**2 Move your mouse pointer over a different area that you know is a link.**

Your mouse pointer remains a hand, but the Web address in the message bar changes to reflect the URL of the new link that you're on.

**3 Move your mouse pointer over an area that you know is *not* a link.**

Your mouse pointer reverts to its arrowhead shape, and the message bar either goes blank or displays a previous message (such as `Document: Done`) because you're no longer pointing to an area associated with a URL.

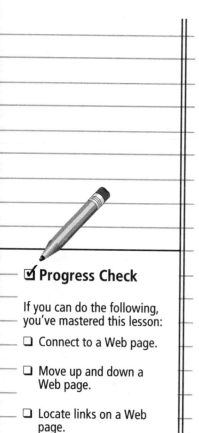

extra credit

## The wacky world of URLs

Some fun facts about Web page URLs:

▶ Web URLs usually have the format `http://www.name.com`.

▶ Web URLs usually begin with *http://*, which stands for *HyperText Transfer Protocol. HyperText* refers to the art of linking disparate sections of text together; *transfer* refers to the transmission of data; and *protocol* refers to the rules and standards that allow computers to communicate with each other.

▶ Following the double slash *(//),* Web URLs usually sport a www — which stands for World Wide Web, 'natch — and a period (also referred to as a *dot*).

▶ Following www., URLs usually contain a name representing the organization affiliated with the Web site, plus another period; for example, *att.* for AT&T or *microsoft.* for — well, you know.

▶ U.S. Web sites have URLs that usually end with a three-letter code, such as *com* for a commercial organization, *gov* for a government department, *mil* for a military site, *edu* for an educational institution, *net* for groups running a network (that is, a bunch of connected computers), and *org* for miscellaneous others (such as nonprofit organizations).

▶ Non-U.S. Web sites have URLs that usually end in a two-letter country code, such as *au* for Australia, *ca* for Canada, *fr* for France, *jp* for Japan, and *se* for Sweden.

▶ URLs can also refer to other areas of the Internet. Non-Web codes include *ftp://* for FTP file transfers (see Appendix B) and *news://* for newsgroups (see Unit 7).

You don't really need to remember any of this stuff. Then again, the info may prove handy for impressing people at parties.

### ✓ Progress Check

If you can do the following, you've mastered this lesson:

❑ Connect to a Web page.

❑ Move up and down a Web page.

❑ Locate links on a Web page.

❑ Identify the URL associated with a link.

---

## Lesson 1-3    Cruising the Web by Using Links

to use a link, click it

Now that you know how to move around a Web page and identify its links, you're ready for the big step — jumping to another Web page.

To perform this incredible technical feat, you need to do two things: point to a link, and click. It's that simple!

After you click, Netscape uses the Web address associated with the link to connect you to the page to which you want to jump. If the page is available (for example, if it isn't tied up by too many other people trying to access it simultaneously), Netscape connects to the page and copies its text, pictures, and other data to your browser window. When that process is complete, you're all set to explore the new page.

*Notes:*

Sound good? Then go for it!

**1** **If you aren't still online, repeat the steps at the beginning of Lesson 1-2 to run Netscape and connect to the Internet.**

Your Netscape browser window should be maximized and displaying a Web page.

**2** **Point to a link that interests you on the current Web page.**

Your mouse pointer turns into a hand, and the URL of the link — that is, the address of the Web page that the link is associated with — appears in the message bar.

**3** **Click (that is, press your left mouse button).**

In the Netscape logo in your window's upper-right section (which consists of a large N hovering over a planet), you see comets begin to shoot past the planet. This eye-catching activity is a cool way of letting you know that Netscape is operating to fulfill your request for new data.

At the same time, several notices appear in the message bar, though some may flash by too quickly for you to read. First, you see `Contacting host`, which indicates that Netscape is trying to connect to the URL you selected. Next — if you connect to the page successfully — you see a `Transferring data` message, which means that Netscape is transmitting the text and graphics of the new Web page to your computer. As bits of the new page appear, Netscape continuously flashes what percentage of the data has been transferred and — if it's an especially long transfer — how many more seconds it will take to complete the process. Finally, you see the message `Document: Done`, which means that Netscape successfully copied all the new Web page's data to your computer. Also, comets stop flying over the planet in the Netscape logo to show that the attempt to make a new connection is complete. (If the connection was *not* successful for some reason, simply try again by clicking a different link.)

**4** **Read the new page.**

Skim through the page. When you're done, pick out a link on this page that interests you.

**5** **Point to a link on the page that you want to explore and then click your left mouse button.**

Once again, the message bar displays `Contacting host` and `Transferring data` notices. A short time after that, the page you selected appears on your screen.

**6** **Read the new page.**

Notice that this page contains links leading to additional Web pages.

**7** **Point to a link on the page that you want to explore and then click your left mouse button.**

Again, the message bar displays `Contacting host` and `Transferring data` notices. A short time after that, the page you selected appears on your screen.

Clearly, you could go on and on like this, jumping from Web page to Web page. (Indeed, we've lost more people that way. . . .) However, for now you should push on to the next exercise.

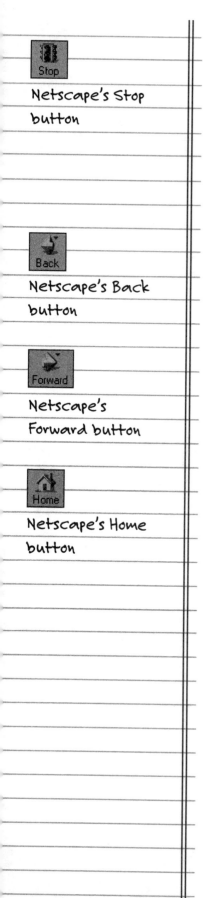

Netscape's Stop button

Netscape's Back button

Netscape's Forward button

Netscape's Home button

Typically, you receive all of a Web page's data within a minute or two. Occasionally, however, a page requires more time. In such a case, the page may have lots of pictures (which take much longer to transmit than text), or numerous other people may be trying to access the page simultaneously, or the Web site may be experiencing technical problems. If you become impatient, you can abort a transfer by clicking the Stop button, which is the rightmost button on the Navigation Toolbar near the top of the browser window. You can then read whatever information and use whatever links on the page were transmitted before you clicked Stop.

Another way to avoid long waits is to prevent Netscape from automatically transferring pictures at all. For more information about this option, see Lesson 4-1.

## Moving back and forth on the Web

Constantly leaping to new Web pages is all well and good, but what if you want to go back to a previous page? No problem! All you've gotta do is click Netscape's cleverly named Back button, which is the leftmost button on the Navigation Toolbar (see Figure 1-7).

Similarly, if you want to move forward again, you can click — you guessed it! — Netscape's Forward button. (Who says that computers are complicated?)

Finally, if you want to jump directly to your starting point, you can click Netscape's Home button. This button instantly returns you to the place where you began your session (in this case, the Netscape Communications home page).

But don't take our word for it; check it out for yourself. (You should still be connected to the Internet from the preceding exercise.)

**1  Click the Back button in the upper-left section of the Netscape window.**

The current Web page is quickly replaced in your window by the preceding page you viewed.

**2  Click the Back button again.**

Again, the current page is replaced by the preceding page.

**3  This time, don't click right away, but simply hold your mouse pointer over the Back button for a few seconds.**

After a short pause, the name of the Web page that you'll go to if you click the Back button is displayed! You can use this nifty look-ahead feature to avoid revisiting Web pages that don't interest you. In this case, however, keep going.

**4  Click the Back button again.**

The current page is replaced by the preceding page. Also, notice that the title bar at the top of the window displays the same Web page name that you saw moments ago by pointing to the Back button.

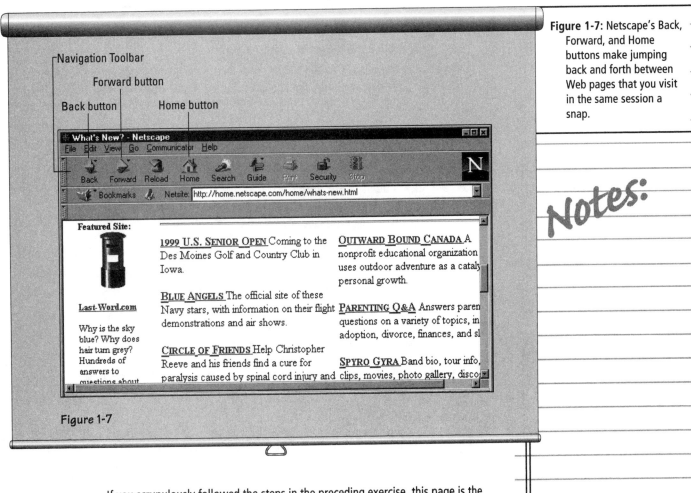

**Figure 1-7:** Netscape's Back, Forward, and Home buttons make jumping back and forth between Web pages that you visit in the same session a snap.

Figure 1-7

If you scrupulously followed the steps in the preceding exercise, this page is the page that you started on. (And if you didn't, simply click the Back button a few more times until you return to the page where you started.) The Back button is now dim, or *grayed out,* indicating that you can't move back any farther.

**5** **Click the Back button again.**

Nothing happens because you returned to your starting point.

**6** **Click the Forward button, which is directly to the right of the Back button.**

Your initial Web page is quickly replaced by the second page that you visited during this session.

**7** **Click the Forward button again.**

Your current page is replaced by the third page that you moved to during this session.

**8** **This time, don't click right away, but simply hold your mouse pointer over the Forward button for a few seconds.**

After a short pause, the name of the Web page you'll go to if you click the Forward button is displayed. That's because Netscape's look-ahead feature works with both the Back and Forward buttons.

*Notes:*

**9  Click the Forward button again.**

Again, your current page is replaced by the next page that you visited during this session. Also, the title bar at the top of the window displays the same Web page name that you saw moments ago by pointing to the Forward button.

If you scrupulously followed the steps in the preceding exercise, this page is the last page that you visited. (And if you didn't, simply click the button a few more times until you arrive at your last page.) The Forward button dims to indicate that you can't move forward any farther.

**10  Click the Forward button again.**

Nothing happens because you reached the end of the sequence of Web page links that you selected.

**11  Click the Home button (the fourth button on the Toolbar).**

You immediately jump back to your starting point, the Netscape Communications home page.

We're tempted to note the last step of this exercise proves that, through the wonders of technology, you *can* go home again. However, we're worried that you'd want to hit us if we did, so we won't.

**on the test**

Remember, click Netscape's Back button to move to the preceding Web page, click the Forward button to move to the next Web page, and click Home to return immediately to your initial Web page.

**heads up**

Netscape's Back, Forward, and Home buttons keep track of only the Web pages that you select during your *current* Internet session. When you disconnect by closing Netscape, these buttons "forget" the Web pages that you just visited; and when you reopen Netscape for a new session, the buttons start from a clean slate, paying attention only to the Web pages that you visit during your new session.

## Using the Go menu and History window

The Back and Forward buttons are all you need for moving among a few Web pages. If you're using ten or more Web pages during a session, however, you may find it a nuisance to click through lots of intermediate pages to reach the one you want. In such cases, you can use Netscape's Go menu, which lists the URL of each page that you've visited and lets you move you directly to whichever URL you select. For a demonstration, follow these steps:

*to return directly to a Web page, use the Go menu*

**1  Choose Go (that is, click the Go heading on the menu bar).**

A menu pops down that lists the URL of each Web page you've visited during this session. Also, a check mark appears next to the URL of the page you're currently on.

**2  Click a URL without a check mark next to it.**

You move to the Web page located at the URL that you selected.

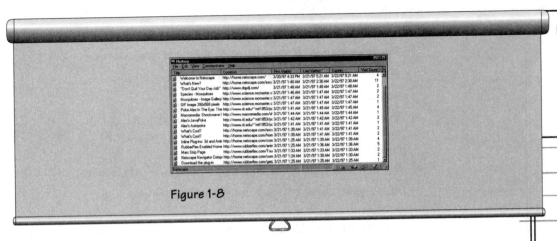

Figure 1-8

**Figure 1-8:** The History window shows you all the Web pages that you've recently visited. You can move to any listed page by double-clicking it.

**3** **Choose <u>G</u>o again.**

The menu pops down, and the check mark now appears next to the URL that you selected.

**4** **Click a URL without a check mark next to it.**

You move to the Web page located at the new URL that you selected, and so on.

That's all there is to using the Go menu!

**extra credit**

You can also display a mini-Go menu by clicking the Back or Forward button and keeping your mouse button pressed. After a few seconds, a list pops down with the names of the pages that you can go back to (from the Back button) or forward to (from the Forward button). To move to any listed page, simply click the page's name.

**heads up**

Like the Netscape Back, Forward, and Home buttons, the Go menu keeps track of only the Web pages that you select during your current Internet session. Every time you restart Netscape for a new session, the Go menu begins with a clean slate, paying attention only to the Web pages that you visit during your new session.

The only other thing to know is that if you visit too many pages during a session to be listed on the Go menu, you may have to choose Communicator⇨History (or press the keystroke shortcut Ctrl+H on a PC or ⌘H on a Mac) to get at the URL that you want. Doing so opens a History window that can display a virtually unlimited number of URLs. Try it!

**1** **Choose <u>C</u>ommunicator⇨<u>H</u>istory.**

A window like the one in Figure 1-8 appears that lists the name and URL of each Web page you've visited. If you're using Windows the History window also lists the date on which you first visited the page, the date you last visited the page, the number of times you've visited the page, and the date on which the page entry is set to expire and be automatically deleted from the History window. The History window normally stores a page's URL for one day, but you can optionally extend that storage period. (For more information, see the last exercise in Lesson 4-2.)

*to switch between lots of Web pages, choose Communicator→ History or press Ctrl+H or ⌘H*

**2** **Double-click a Web page listed in the History window.**

After a pause, the Web page appears in the browser window.

**3** **Select the History window again.**

If you're using Windows, press Alt+Tab to switch to it. If you're using a Mac, click its window or select it from the Applications menu. The History window returns to the front of your screen.

**4** **Double-click a different Web page listed in the History window.**

After a pause, the Web page appears in the browser window, and so on.

Because the History window can store many Web page names, you may sometimes have trouble finding the page you're looking for. In such cases, you can click the headings near the top of the window to reorder the list by name, date, or number of times visited. (***Note:*** This feature is available only under Windows. If you're using a Mac, skip to Step 7.)

**5** **Select the History window again, but this time click the Visit Count heading near the top of the window. (If you don't see this heading, repeatedly click the left-pointing arrow in the upper-right section of the window until you do.)**

The list is reorganized based on the number of times that you've visited each page, in ascending order (lowest to highest).

**6** **Click the Visit Count heading again.**

The list is reorganized again, but this time in descending order (highest to lowest).

**7** **Click the Title heading.**

The list is reorganized based on the names of the Web pages, and so on.

**8** **Finally, close the History window by clicking its Close button (or choosing File⇨Close, or pressing Ctrl+W or ⌘W).**

The History window disappears.

Unlike the Go menu, the History window doesn't close until you tell it to. Therefore, when you need to switch among many Web pages frequently, you may find it convenient to leave the History window open and then quickly move to each page you want by double-clicking it from the window.

## Recess

Well, all right. There's much more to learn about cruising the Web, but you just mastered the basics. (And performed brilliantly!) Give yourself a reward (we favor chocolate) and then tackle the following tricky quiz questions.

---

### ☑ Progress Check

If you can do the following, you've mastered this lesson:

❑ Move to a new Web page by using a link.

❑ Move to the preceding page, the next page, or your home page by using the top Toolbar buttons.

❑ Move directly to a page by using the Go menu.

❑ Move directly to a page by using the History window.

# Unit 1 Quiz

For each of the following questions, circle the letter of the correct answer or answers. Remember, each question can have more than one right answer.

1. **Before you can start using Netscape, you need**

   A. Nerves of steel.

   B. A 14,400 bps, 33,600 bps, or 56,000 bps modem.

   C. An account with an Internet Service Provider.

   D. A recent version of the Netscape program.

   E. Happy feet.

2. **The World Wide Web:**

   A. Was created by the U.S. military during the height of the Cold War in the 1950s.

   B. Is currently funded by evil alien spiders.

   C. Consists of electronic pages created by thousands of independent individuals and organizations from all over the globe.

   D. Is often referred to as *the Wide W.*

   E. Is typically accessed with a special program called a *WoWWzer.*

3. **To determine whether a word, phrase, or image on a Web page is a link:**

   A. Ask it politely.

   B. Look for a chain icon to its left.

   C. Check whether it's surrounded by the colors of the rainbow.

   D. Move your mouse pointer over it and see whether the pointer changes to a hand.

   E. Move your hand over it and see whether your fingers change to mouse pointers.

4. **A URL is**

   A. An address indicating the electronic location of something on the Internet, such as a Web page.

   B. The name of a hot Irish rock band.

   C. Internet shorthand for *URban Legend,* meaning a story that may sound plausible but isn't true.

   D. The title of episode 68 of *The X-Files.*

   E. What appears in Netscape's message bar when you point to a link.

*Notes:*

# Unit 1 Exercise

If your setup is typical, you can run Netscape and your dialer program independently of each other. Try it!

1. Run both Netscape and your Internet dialer program at the same time. (**Hint:** Use the Netscape Communicator icon.)

2. Connect to the Internet.

3. Disconnect from the Internet without closing Netscape. (**Hint:** If you use Windows, start by clicking the dialer's button on the Windows 95 Taskbar, or double-clicking its icon in Windows 3.1, to pop up its dialog box and display a disconnect option.)

4. Because you're not being charged for online time now, spend a few leisurely minutes examining the Netscape browser window, including its various menus and buttons. (You'll find using Netscape offline especially helpful when you learn how to create and read e-mail in Unit 5.)

5. Fire up the dialer by itself. (**Hint:** Look for a dialer icon that you can double-click.)

6. Reconnect to the Internet. After you connect, Netscape automatically becomes your window on the Internet again.

7. Click the Netscape window's Close button. This action should exit Netscape but maintain your Internet connection (indicated by your dialer's button still appearing on the Windows 95 Taskbar, or its minimized icon still appearing on your Windows 3.1 desktop, or the program's window still displaying a connection on your Mac desktop). If you had another Internet program, you now could run it instead of Netscape. You'll learn how to get such programs directly from the Web in Lesson 3-2. You can also find Internet programs on the CD-ROM that came with this book; for more information, see Appendix B.

8. Log off from the Internet using your dialer program.

# Searching for Information on the Web

**Prerequisites**

▶ Cruising the Web with
Netscape Communicator
(Lessons 1-2 and 1-3)

## Objectives for This Unit

✓ Using bookmarks to move to Web pages

✓ Creating and deleting bookmarks

✓ Organizing bookmarks

✓ Typing in a URL

✓ Searching a Web page for information

✓ Searching the entire Web for information

on the CD

▶ Exercise file
(Bookmark.htm
for Windows,
Bookmarks.html
for Mac)

The World Wide Web encompasses tens of millions of Web pages — a mind-boggling amount of information. To help you navigate your way through this sea of data, Netscape provides you with several invaluable tools. These include bookmarks, which let you easily create pointers to your favorite Web pages; a Location box that allows you to type in Web addresses directly; a search command that helps you quickly locate information on a Web page; and access to powerful search programs that help you locate information anywhere on the Web. This unit teaches you how to use these tools to cruise the Web like a pro.

| Lesson 2-1 | Cruising the Web by Using Bookmarks |
| --- | --- |

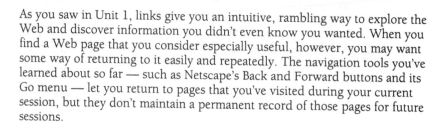

*Notes:*

As you saw in Unit 1, links give you an intuitive, rambling way to explore the Web and discover information you didn't even know you wanted. When you find a Web page that you consider especially useful, however, you may want some way of returning to it easily and repeatedly. The navigation tools you've learned about so far — such as Netscape's Back and Forward buttons and its Go menu — let you return to pages that you've visited during your current session, but they don't maintain a permanent record of those pages for future sessions.

Fortunately, Netscape also provides a nifty feature called *bookmarks.* Just as a physical bookmark helps you quickly go to a particular page in a book, Netscape's bookmarks let you jump to particular Web pages. These electronic bookmarks are stored on your hard disk, and they remain there until you explicitly delete them. Therefore, you can use a bookmark at any time during your Web session to move to a specific Web page.

This lesson shows you how to use predefined bookmarks, create your own bookmarks, and delete bookmarks. By the time you're done, you'll be able to create a Web page library that's tailored to your personal tastes and needs.

## Installing a bookmark file

Bookmarks are normally stored in your Netscape folder in a file named Bookmark.htm (under Windows) or Bookmarks.html (on a Macintosh). The *.htm* and *.html* extensions stand for *HyperText Markup Language,* which is the computer language that both Web pages and bookmarks are written in. (For more information about HTML files, see Unit 8.)

The bookmarks file is typically near-empty until you add bookmarks to it yourself. To jump-start your ability to get around the Web, however, we've created a substitute file crammed with bookmarks for what we consider to be many of the best sites on the Internet. To take advantage of this predefined collection of bookmarks, which is stored on your *Dummies 101* CD-ROM, follow these steps:

**on the CD**

**1** **Insert the *Dummies 101* CD-ROM that came with this book into your CD-ROM drive. If you're using Windows 3.1, you're set.**

Be careful to touch only the sides of the CD-ROM and to insert the CD-ROM with its printed side up.

If you're using Windows 95, the CD-ROM's Installer program is set to run automatically, so after about a minute, you probably see an initial Installer screen. You'll be installing your bookmarks directly from Netscape, though, so follow the on-screen prompts until you see a Do Not Accept or Exit button and then click the button to close the CD-ROM program.

If you're using a Mac, a window will open containing icons for the CD-ROM's various files and folders. Click the window's Close button to exit it.

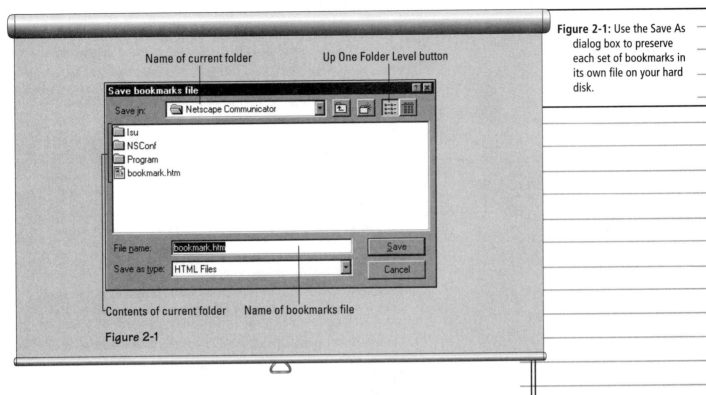

Name of current folder    Up One Folder Level button

Save bookmarks file

Save in: Netscape Communicator

Isu
NSConf
Program
bookmark.htm

File name: bookmark.htm          Save

Save as type: HTML Files          Cancel

Contents of current folder    Name of bookmarks file

Figure 2-1

**Figure 2-1:** Use the Save As dialog box to preserve each set of bookmarks in its own file on your hard disk.

## 2   Run Netscape (but don't connect to the Internet).

You see the Netscape browser window. If you're using Windows, notice that a button in the upper-left section of the browser (directly below the Back and Forward buttons) is named *Bookmarks.* This button lets you access both bookmarks and bookmark commands.

**heads up**

If you're using a Macintosh, you don't have a Bookmarks button. Instead, you have a Bookmarks *menu,* which appears directly to the right of the Go menu and is represented by an icon that looks like a green bookmark. Whenever this book instructs you to click the Bookmarks button, click the Bookmarks icon on your Mac's menu bar instead.

## 3   Click the Bookmarks button.

If you're using Windows, you see a menu with three options at its top: Add Bookmark, File Bookmark, and Edit Bookmarks. If you're using a Mac, you see the single option Add Bookmark.

Below the command(s), you may see a few bookmarks supplied by whichever company provided your copy of Netscape (for example, your ISP or Netscape Communications itself). Before you load the new bookmarks, you should save your current ones so that you have the option of switching back to them later.

## 4   If you're using Windows, click the Edit Bookmarks option. If you're using a Mac, release your mouse button and then press ⌘B.

A Bookmarks window opens that displays all your bookmarks. You can use the Save As option under this window's File menu to save your bookmarks.

**5** **Choose File⇨Save As from the Bookmarks window's menu bar.**

A Save As dialog box like the one in Figure 2-1 appears. The top of the box shows you the name of the folder Netscape is currently set to. Write this folder name down somewhere handy (such as the Cheat Sheet near the front of this book) in case you ever want to return to your old bookmarks.

Also notice that near the bottom of the dialog box is a text box with a blinking cursor and (if you're using Windows) a highlighted filename. This text box lets you assign a new name to your bookmarks file.

**6** **Type the filename** Bookold **(to indicate that these are your old bookmarks) and press Enter.**

Your bookmarks are saved under the name Bookold.htm (if you're using Windows) or Bookold.html (if you're using a Mac). Now switch to the book- marks we created for you, which are stored on your *Dummies 101* CD-ROM. You can do so using the command Open Bookmarks File from the File menu.

*Note:* The Open Bookmarks File command may be grayed out as a result of a bug in some versions of Netscape. If the command isn't available, either obtain a more recent version of Netscape or see the note at the end of this excercise.

**7** **Choose File⇨Open Bookmarks File from the Bookmarks window's menu bar.**

A dialog box opens that looks and operates very much like the Save As dialog box. To load your new bookmarks, first select the appropriate file from the CD-ROM.

**8** **Locate and click the bookmarks file on your CD-ROM.**

- If you're using Windows, click in the Look in box near the top of the dialog box, click the *Dummies 101* CD-ROM icon (which looks like a shiny round disc) from the list that pops down, and then click the filename *bookmark.htm* after it appears in the big list of files in the middle of the dialog box.

- If you're using a Mac, click the Desktop button on the right side of the dialog box, double-click the *Dummies 101* icon (which looks like a shiny round disc) after it appears in the list of files in the middle of the dialog box, and then click the filename *bookmarks.html* after it also appears in the list of files in the middle of the dialog box.

**9** **Press Enter.**

Your new bookmarks appear in the Bookmarks window. There are lots of them (220, to be precise), and you'll have a chance to examine them all shortly. First, though, set Netscape to look for these bookmarks on your hard disk from now on rather than from the CD-ROM. To do so, save the file to your hard disk and then load it from your hard disk.

**10** **Choose File⇨Save As, select any folder on your hard disk, type** Book101 **in the bottom text box, and press Enter. More specifically, after choosing File⇨Save As:**

- If you're using Windows, click in the Save in box near the top of the dialog box, click your hard disk icon — which is probably named Hard Drive (C:) and looks like a sealed disk drive — from the list that drops down, and double-click any folder you see listed in the middle of the dialog box that would be appropriate for storing your new bookmarks file. After you've selected a folder, click in the File name text box near the bottom of the dialog box, type **Book101**, and press Enter. Your new bookmarks are saved to your hard disk in a file named Book101.htm.

- If you're using a Mac, click the Desktop button on the right side of the dialog box, double-click your hard disk icon (which is probably named Macintosh HD and looks like a sealed disk drive) from the list that drops down, and double-click any folder you see listed in the middle of the dialog box that would be appropriate for storing your new bookmarks file. After you've selected a folder, click in the Save bookmarks file text box near the bottom of the dialog box, type **Book101,** and press Enter. Your new bookmarks are saved to your hard disk in a file named Book101.html.

**11** **Reload your new bookmarks by choosing File⇨Open Bookmarks File, clicking the Book101 file listed in your current folder, and pressing Enter.**

Your new bookmarks are loaded again, but this time from your hard disk rather than the CD-ROM.

**12** **Click the Bookmark window's Close box.**

The window exits.

You can also eject your *Dummies 101* CD-ROM now. Be sure to store it in a safe place, though; you'll need it again in Unit 6.

*Note:* If for some reason the preceding exercise doesn't work properly for you, repeat Steps 1 through 9, but for Step 7 choose File⇨Import rather than File⇨Open Bookmarks File. Instead of switching you to a different bookmarks file, this command copies all the bookmarks from the CD-ROM into a folder in your existing bookmarks file.

You now have a bunch of interesting new bookmarks. Proceed to the next section to check 'em out!

## Leafing through bookmarks

To examine the new bookmarks you just installed, follow these steps:

**1** **Launch Netscape (if it isn't already running) and connect to the Internet.**

Your Netscape browser window should be maximized and displaying a Web page.

**2** **Click the Bookmarks button.**

You again see the commands Add Bookmark, File Bookmark, and Edit Bookmarks (or, on a Mac, Add Bookmark) at the top of the menu. This time, however, you also see a long list of bookmark categories (or *folders*) below the commands, as shown in Figure 2-2.

**Figure 2-2:** The Bookmarks menu lets you create and use Web page pointers that are stored on your hard disk.

*Notes:*

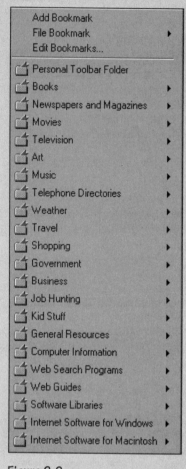

Figure 2-2

**3** **Move your mouse pointer over Books.**

You see the names of book-related Web sites, including The Internet Classics Archive (offers full-text translations of nearly 400 classic Greek, Roman, and Italian works, such as the *Iliad* and the *Odyssey*), The Complete Works of Shakespeare (provides all the plays and sonnets of William Shakespeare), BookWire (supplies book news, reviews, and handy guides to book resources on the Net), and Amazon.com (an online bookstore with more than two million titles in its searchable electronic catalog).

**4** **Move your mouse pointer over Newspapers and Magazines.**

You see the names of more Web sites, including The New York Times on the Web (a searchable version of the daily "newspaper of record"), USA Today (a searchable version of the visually splashy daily newspaper), The Wall Street Journal Interactive Edition (a source for up-to-date stock prices, business news, and other timely financial information), and Time Warner's Pathfinder (which lets you search for and read articles from a variety of Time-Warner publications, including *Entertainment Weekly, Fortune, Money, People, Sports Illustrated,* and *Time Magazine*).

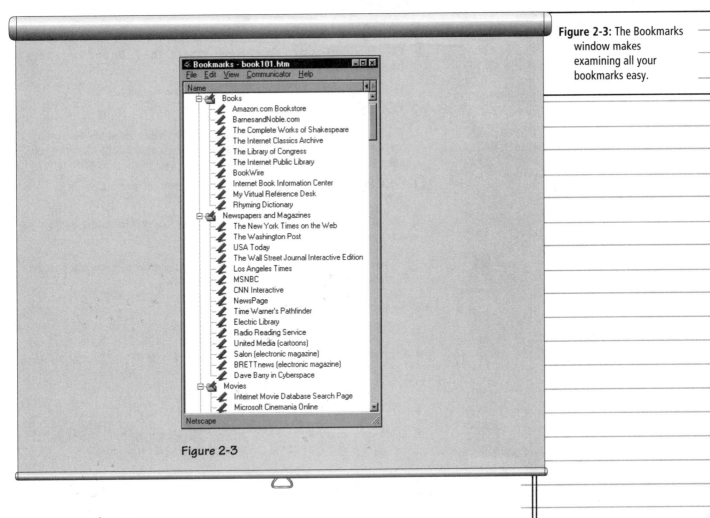

Figure 2-3

**5 Move your mouse pointer over Job Hunting.**

You see the names of additional Web sites, including America's Job Bank (lists over 250,000 jobs from 1,800 state Employment Service offices), CareerPath.com (lets you search through the employment ads of dozens of major newspapers, including *The New York Times, The Washington Post,* and the *Los Angeles Times*), and Online Career Center (lets you search for work by job category and region, and lets you post your resume online).

**6 Move your mouse pointer over Travel.**

You see the names of yet more Web pages, including City.Net (provides extensive information on virtually any city or region in the world), Microsoft Expedia (makes it easy to find and book the best airline ticket, hotel, and car rental for virtually any destination), and Epicurious Travel (helps you locate great vacation spots and gives you tips on how to best enjoy them).

**7 Click the Edit Bookmarks option near the top of the menu. (If you're using a Mac, release your mouse button and press ⌘B.)**

The Bookmarks window you used in the preceding exercise opens again, and you see the names of the bookmarks within each folder, as shown in Figure 2-3. (If you don't see the bookmark names, double-click each folder to display the Web page names that it contains.) Because you have scores of bookmarks, you can't see them all in the window simultaneously.

**8** **Click the vertical scroll bar arrows or press the PgDn and PgUp keys to examine all your bookmarks.**

The window contains 220 bookmarks covering a wide range of topics.

**9** **Click a bookmark.**

The URL the bookmark is associated with is displayed in the window's message bar, similar to the way a URL is displayed in Netscape's message bar when you point to a link on a Web page.

**10** **Click the Bookmarks window's Close button (or press Ctrl+W or ⌘W) to exit.**

The list of bookmarks closes, giving you an unobstructed view of the browser window again.

**heads up**

The Bookmarks window can actually be opened in a variety of ways. If you use Windows, any of the following methods will work:

▶ Press the keystroke shortcut Ctrl+B.

▶ Click the Bookmarks button and click Edit Bookmarks.

▶ Choose Communicator⇨Bookmarks⇨Edit Bookmarks.

If you're on a Mac, you can use either of these techniques:

▶ Press the keystroke shortcut ⌘B.

▶ Choose Communicator⇨Bookmarks. (The Communicator menu is the lighthouse icon directly to the right of the Bookmarks icon.)

Intrigued? Good, because your next step is to use the bookmarks that you just viewed to actually visit some of the best sites on the Web.

## Using bookmarks to sample the best of the Web

Using a bookmark to visit a Web page is just as easy as using a link — you simply point to it and click (unless you're in the Bookmarks window, in which case you need to point and *double*-click).

Keep in mind, however, that everything on the Internet changes rapidly, including Web addresses. Therefore, if a bookmark that you try in the following exercise no longer works, just select a different bookmark.

**1** **Click the Bookmarks button and choose Books⇨The Complete Works of Shakespeare.**

You're greeted with information about the Bard and his works. If you're so inclined, delve deeper into this Web site by choosing to read scenes from a particular play. You don't have to rush; we'll wait for you. (After all, his work *is* timeless. . . .)

**2    Click the Bookmarks button and choose Newspapers and Magazines⇨USA Today.**

You see the latest headline news from *USA Today* (complete with full-color photographs!).

**3    Click the Bookmarks button and choose Travel⇨City.Net.**

You're met by a map of the world and an invitation to click the name of the area in which you're interested. Follow the prompts and click progressively more detailed maps until you zero in on information about the country, state, or city you're seeking.

Pretty cool, huh?

If you enjoyed visiting those Web sites, you may want to take some time to explore a few of the other pages linked to the predefined bookmarks. In each case, move to the page that you want by clicking the Bookmarks button, moving your mouse pointer over the appropriate category, and then clicking the bookmark. After you're done, go on to the next section, which explains how to create your own bookmarks.

## Creating bookmarks

Using predefined bookmarks is a fun and easy way to get started exploring the Web. However, because nobody else can judge which Web pages are of the most interest to *you*, get in the habit of creating your *own* bookmarks. If you do so regularly and thoughtfully, you'll soon build up an extremely useful Web page library tailored to your particular tastes and needs.

**on the test**

Creating a bookmark is easy, and you can do it in a variety of ways. First, move to the Web page that you want to bookmark. You can then click the Bookmarks button and click the Add Bookmark option. Or you can simply press Ctrl+D or ⌘D. In either case, the bookmark is added to the bottom of your list of bookmarks.

If you're using Windows, you also have a slick third option. Notice that to the right of the Bookmarks button is a small icon that looks like a green bookmark. This icon is called the *Page Proxy* because it acts as a stand-in for the Web page being displayed. Specifically, you can click and drag the Page Proxy over to the Bookmarks menu and then "drop" the bookmark into any folder you want; so using the Page Proxy lets you both create and file a bookmark at the same time. (Plus, it's fun!)

to create a bookmark, press Ctrl+D or ⌘D, or click the Bookmarks button and the Add Bookmark option, or drag the Page Proxy to the Bookmarks menu

Page Proxy icon

After you've created a bookmark, you can use it in exactly the same way you use a predefined bookmark — that is, by displaying it via the Bookmarks menu and clicking it.

**1 If you aren't still connected to the Internet, log on again now.**

Your Netscape browser window should be maximized and displaying a Web page.

**2 Locate a link to a Web page that interests you.**

When you point to the link, your mouse pointer turns into a hand and the link's URL appears in the message bar.

**3 Click the link.**

You move to the Web page associated with the link.

**4 Repeat Steps 2 and 3 until you reach a page that you think you'd enjoy visiting repeatedly in the future.**

You're on a Web page that you've reached through a series of links.

**5 Click the Bookmarks button.**

You see the option Add Bookmark as well as a list of bookmark categories. Make note of the last item on the menu's list.

**6 Choose Add Bookmark.**

The menu closes, and (although you can't see it right now) a bookmark pointing to your current page is added to the bottom of the bookmarks list.

**7 Click the Home button to move to a different page.**

You move to your default home page (typically, the Netscape Communications site).

**8 Click the Bookmarks button.**

The menu drops down and shows that the last item on the bookmarks list is the bookmark that you created in Step 6.

**9 Click the bookmark that you created.**

You move to the Web page associated with the bookmark, proving that your bookmark works.

If you're running Windows, now create a bookmark for the same page using the Page Proxy (that it, the small bookmark icon to the right of the Bookmarks button):

**1 Click the Page Proxy and, while keeping your mouse button held down, drag the icon to the Bookmarks button.**

The Bookmarks menu automatically opens.

**2** **Drag the Page Proxy down the menu until the folder most appropriate for your bookmark is highlighted, then release your mouse button.**

Your bookmark is both created and filed in the folder that you selected.

**3** **This time, move to a different page by clicking the Netscape *N* logo in the upper-right section of the window.**

You move to the Netscape Communications page! That's because, in addition to its function as an activity indicator, the logo acts as a bookmark that always points to the Netscape site.

**4** **Click the Bookmarks button and then move your mouse pointer over the folder you selected.**

You see the new bookmark that you created stored inside the folder.

**5** **Click your new bookmark.**

You move to the Web page associated with the bookmark, proving that your second bookmark works perfectly, too.

Nice work! The two bookmarks you've just created will remain on your bookmarks list until you explicitly delete them. You learn how to remove bookmarks that are redundant or have outlived their usefulness in the next section.

Creating bookmarks is quick, easy, and even fun. Therefore, as you continue to cruise the Internet and discover interesting Web pages, don't hesitate to take advantage of this great feature.

*extra credit*

## Creating Web page shortcuts

Creating a bookmark isn't the only way that you can set a pointer to a Web page. If you use Windows 95, you can also create a *shortcut*, which is a file that you can keep directly on your desktop. To do so, simply move to a Web page that you want to access frequently, click the Page Proxy and, while keeping your mouse button held down, drag the Page Proxy to your desktop. Lastly, release your mouse button. The shortcut to the Web page appears as an icon on your desktop.

If you double-click the shortcut when Netscape is running, Netscape responds by moving to the page. More important, if you double-click the shortcut when Netscape *isn't* running, Netscape and your dialer program automatically open and, after you connect to the Internet, Netscape moves to the appropriate Web page. The latter is more efficient than double-clicking the Netscape Communicator icon, clicking the Bookmarks button, and then clicking a bookmark. It's best to avoid cluttering your desktop with a lot of icons, however, so we suggest that you create shortcuts for no more than two or three Web pages that you access constantly.

to delete a
bookmark, first
select it in the
Bookmarks window,
and then choose
Edit→Delete or
press the Del key

☑ **Progress Check**

If you can do the following,
you've mastered this lesson:

❑ Install a file containing
predefined bookmarks.

❑ Display bookmarks from
the Bookmarks menu and
Bookmarks window.

❑ Use bookmarks to move
to Web pages.

❑ Create bookmarks.

❑ Delete bookmarks.

## Deleting bookmarks

As you add more and more bookmarks, your bookmark collection may
become too cluttered for you to use easily. You can reduce the muddle by
eliminating bookmarks that have outlived their usefulness.

**on the test**

To remove a bookmark, highlight it in the Bookmarks window and then either
choose Edit⇨Delete or press the Del key (named Delete on the Mac). For
example, follow these steps to remove the first bookmark that you created in
the preceding exercise:

**1** **Press Ctrl+B or ⌘B.**

The Bookmarks window opens and displays all your bookmarks.

**2** **Press the End key.**

You move to the bottom of the window, which is where the first bookmark that
you created resides. That bookmark should now be highlighted. (If it isn't, click
it to highlight it.)

**3** **Press the Delete key (or choose Edit⇨Delete).**

The bookmark that you selected is eliminated.

**heads up**

After you delete a bookmark, you can bring it back if you immediately choose
Edit⇨Undo or press Ctrl+Z or ⌘Z. Still, it's best to think twice before deleting
to ensure that you don't accidentally remove a bookmark you meant to keep.

---

## Lesson 2-2     Organizing Bookmarks

Just as you should keep your hard disk organized by grouping your files into
folders, you should keep your bookmarks organized by grouping *them* into
folders. Doing so helps to ensure that you can always find the bookmark that
you need quickly and easily.

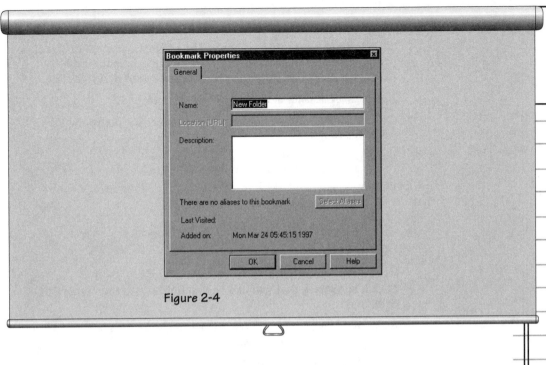

**Figure 2-4:** Use the Bookmark Properties dialog box to create new folders for organizing your bookmarks.

Figure 2-4

*Notes:*

# Copying and moving bookmarks

**on the test**

To put your bookmarks in order, first open the Bookmarks window. You can then use the File menu's New Folder option to create new folders and use your mouse to move bookmarks to and from folders.

For example, to create a Favorites folder and then move some of your favorite bookmarks into it, follow these steps:

**1** **Press Ctrl+B or ⌘B.**

The Bookmarks window opens.

**2** **Press the Home key to move to the top of the window.**

The main bookmark folder, which contains all the other bookmarks and folders, is highlighted.

**3** **Choose File⇨New Folder from the Bookmarks window's menu bar.**

A dialog box like the one in Figure 2-4 appears. Near its top is a Name box that contains the highlighted text *New Folder*.

**4** **Type the name** Favorites **for your new folder.**

The name that you typed replaces the previous text in the Name box.

**5** **Click the OK button.**

The dialog box closes, and a new folder named Favorites appears in the window. The folder is pictured as open to indicate that its contents are displayed automatically.

Notes:

**6** **Click any bookmark that you consider a favorite and, while keeping your mouse button pressed, drag the bookmark up until the Favorites folder is highlighted; then release your mouse button.**

The bookmark instantly moves to your Favorites folder.

**7** **Click and drag another bookmark you especially like to the Favorites folder.**

The second bookmark also moves to your new folder.

If you like, you can continue repeating Step 7 until all your favorite bookmarks are grouped together in your Favorites folder.

Alternatively, you can let bookmarks stay in their original folders and place *copies* of them in the Favorites folder using standard copy and paste commands. Give it a try!

**1** **Click a bookmark that you like to highlight it and then press Ctrl+C or ⌘C.**

A copy of the bookmark is invisibly inserted in your Windows or Mac Clipboard, while the original bookmark is unaffected.

**2** **Click your Favorites folder.**

The folder is highlighted.

**3** **Press Ctrl+V or ⌘V.**

A copy of the bookmark is inserted, or *pasted,* into your Favorites folder.

Placing copies of a bookmark in one or more folders can be useful if the bookmark is important and you want to be sure you can find it easily when you need it.

**heads up**

If, despite your best organizational efforts, you occasionally have trouble locating a bookmark, choose Edit⇨Find, or press Ctrl+F or ⌘F. This action opens a dialog box that lets you find a bookmark based on a word or phrase contained in its name and/or URL.

## Adding and revising bookmarks on the Personal Toolbar

If you expect to use a certain bookmark constantly, you may prefer to access it directly from the browser window rather than have to search for it each time from the Bookmarks menu. For this reason, Netscape allows you to create special bookmark buttons for display on the *Personal Toolbar,* which is the gray bar running directly below the Bookmarks button.

**heads up**

At the time we write this, the Personal Toolbar feature is available only for Windows. If you use a Macintosh and your copy of Netscape doesn't have a Personal Toolbar, skip this section and go directly to Lesson 2-3.

If you use Windows, though, adding a bookmark button to the Personal Toolbar is as easy as creating a conventional bookmark. Simply move to a Web page that you expect to visit often, click the Page Proxy, drag the Page Proxy to the Personal Toolbar (as opposed to the Bookmarks button), and release your mouse button. A button is created on the Toolbar with the name of the Web page. You can then move to the Web page at any time just by clicking the button!

To take advantage of this nifty feature, follow these steps:

**1 If you aren't still connected to the Internet, log on again now.**

Your Netscape browser window should be maximized and displaying a Web page.

**2 Move to a Web page that you expect to visit often (by using an existing bookmark and/or by clicking links).**

**3 Click the Page Proxy and, while keeping your mouse button held down, drag it to the Personal Toolbar (the gray bar running below the Bookmarks button); then release your mouse button.**

A button is automatically created on your Personal Toolbar with the name of the Web page. (Only the first word or two of the name fits on the button, but if you hold your mouse pointer over the button for a second, the entire name is displayed.)

**4 Click the Home button to move to a different page.**

You move to your default home page.

**5 Click the bookmark button you created on the Personal Toolbar.**

You move to the Web page associated with the button, proving that your new bookmark button works.

That's all it takes to add a Toolbar button! To keep your Personal Toolbar useful, however, you should treat it like prime real estate — that is, a space to be kept well-ordered and free of clutter. You can delete obsolete buttons and reorganize buttons through the Bookmarks window. Give it a try:

**1 Press Ctrl+B or ⌘B to open the Bookmarks window and then press the Home key.**

The top section of the Bookmarks window is displayed.

**2 Locate a folder named Personal Toolbar Folder.**

If you don't see the folder right away, scroll through the window until you find it. You should see the name of the bookmark that you just created directly under the folder.

**3 Click the bookmark to highlight it and then press the Delete key.**

The bookmark disappears.

**4 Click the Bookmarks window's Close button.**

The window exits — and the Personal Toolbar no longer displays the button that you created.

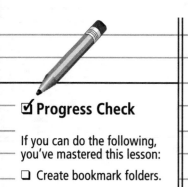

☑ **Progress Check**

If you can do the following,
you've mastered this lesson:

❑ Create bookmark folders.

❑ Move, copy, and paste
   bookmarks.

❑ Add and delete
   bookmark buttons on the
   Personal Toolbar.

In other words, what's displayed on the Personal Toolbar is controlled by what you delete, add, or move in the Personal Toolbar Folder of the Bookmarks window. Therefore, any time that you want to revise the buttons on your Personal Toolbar, simply edit the contents of the Toolbar's folder in the Bookmarks window.

As you've seen in this lesson, you have a lot of freedom in choosing how to organize and reorganize your bookmarks. Play around with different options until you find an ordering scheme that works best for you.

## Recess

You've done a fabulous job of learning how to use cruise the Web with bookmarks, so take some time to brag to your friends about the new skills you've mastered. When you're refreshed, forge ahead to the next lesson, which teaches you how to jump directly to *any* Web page.

---

**Lesson 2-3**     # Entering URLs

---

Cruising the Web using links and bookmarks is fast and fun, but it takes you only so far. For example, if a friend tells you the addresses of some hot new Web pages, or if a favorite magazine prints a list of great Web sites that you'd probably enjoy, how can you get to the Web pages unless you happen to have access to links or bookmarks that point to them? To take advantage of such recommendations, you need to know how to jump directly to a Web page by entering its URL (which, as we explained in Unit 1, is an electronic address that tells browsers such as Netscape precisely where on the Internet a particular Web page is located). By typing a page's URL, you can move straight to the page without passing Go!

*to type a URL, click inside Location box and then enter your text*

**on the test**

Fortunately, typing a URL isn't very hard. To begin, click anywhere inside Netscape's Location box, which is directly below the Navigation Toolbar and to the right of the Bookmarks button (see Figure 2-5). Your click highlights the text in the box, which is typically the URL of your current Web page. Start typing the URL of the new Web page that you're after; the first letter that you type automatically replaces the entire old URL. Finally, press Enter to activate your new URL. If you typed the URL correctly, Netscape jumps to the Web page you want.

The only tricky part is that URLs are about as easy to remember and type correctly as social security numbers. You must remember to type a URL *carefully*. If you get even one number, letter, or punctuation mark wrong, the URL won't work and you end up with an error message rather than a new Web page.

*Note:* Whether you type the characters in a URL in lowercase or uppercase usually doesn't matter, but using the capitalization that you're provided is the safest way to go.

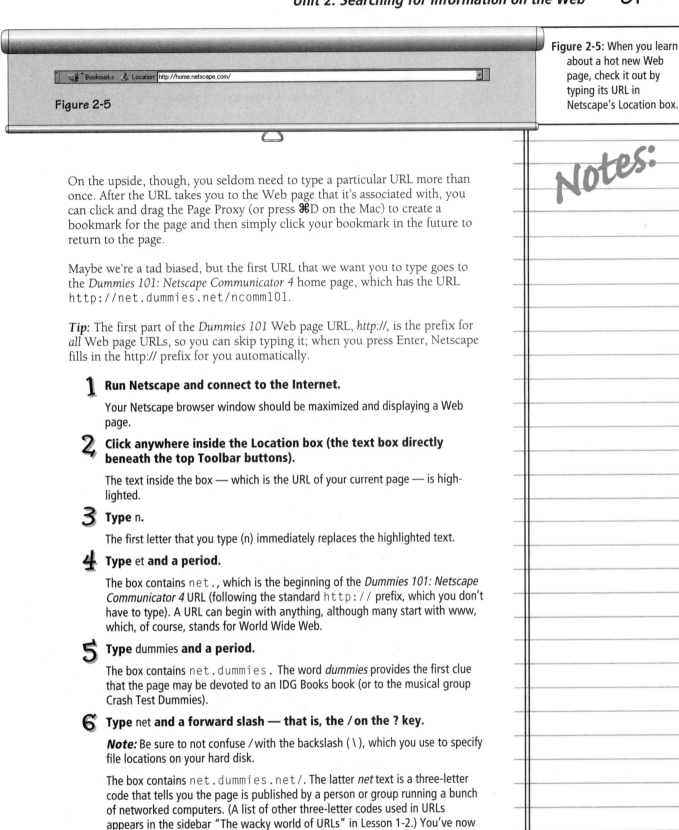

Figure 2-5

**Figure 2-5:** When you learn about a hot new Web page, check it out by typing its URL in Netscape's Location box.

*Notes:*

On the upside, though, you seldom need to type a particular URL more than once. After the URL takes you to the Web page that it's associated with, you can click and drag the Page Proxy (or press ⌘D on the Mac) to create a bookmark for the page and then simply click your bookmark in the future to return to the page.

Maybe we're a tad biased, but the first URL that we want you to type goes to the *Dummies 101: Netscape Communicator 4* home page, which has the URL `http://net.dummies.net/ncomm101`.

*Tip:* The first part of the *Dummies 101* Web page URL, *http://,* is the prefix for *all* Web page URLs, so you can skip typing it; when you press Enter, Netscape fills in the http:// prefix for you automatically.

**1 Run Netscape and connect to the Internet.**

Your Netscape browser window should be maximized and displaying a Web page.

**2 Click anywhere inside the Location box (the text box directly beneath the top Toolbar buttons).**

The text inside the box — which is the URL of your current page — is highlighted.

**3 Type n.**

The first letter that you type (n) immediately replaces the highlighted text.

**4 Type et and a period.**

The box contains `net.`, which is the beginning of the *Dummies 101: Netscape Communicator 4* URL (following the standard `http://` prefix, which you don't have to type). A URL can begin with anything, although many start with www, which, of course, stands for World Wide Web.

**5 Type dummies and a period.**

The box contains `net.dummies.`. The word *dummies* provides the first clue that the page may be devoted to an IDG Books book (or to the musical group Crash Test Dummies).

**6 Type net and a forward slash — that is, the / on the ? key.**

*Note:* Be sure to not confuse / with the backslash ( \ ), which you use to specify file locations on your hard disk.

The box contains `net.dummies.net/`. The latter *net* text is a three-letter code that tells you the page is published by a person or group running a bunch of networked computers. (A list of other three-letter codes used in URLs appears in the sidebar "The wacky world of URLs" in Lesson 1-2.) You've now typed enough to specify the Internet For Dummies Central home page, which

**Figure 2-6:** You can find the *Dummies 101: Netscape Communicator 4* home page at *http:// net.dummies.net/ ncomm101/.*

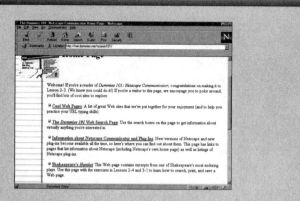

Figure 2-6

*Notes:*

provides information about various *Dummies 101* books and their authors. Internet For Dummies Central is a perfectly nice page and you should be sure to visit it later, but at the moment you want a different page, so you have one more piece of text to type.

**7  Type** ncomm101 **to finish up.**

The box now contains net.dummies.net/ncomm101. The *ncomm101* text tells Netscape that you want the *Dummies 101: Netscape Communicator 4* home page, so you've completed typing the URL.

**8  Press Enter.**

You are on this book's home page, which looks similar to Figure 2-6. If you examine the Location box, you see that Netscape has automatically filled in the prefix and added a final slash so that the URL now reads http:// net.dummies.net/ncomm101/.

***Note:*** If you didn't connect properly, double-check your URL to make sure that you typed it correctly. If you did type the URL exactly as you see it in this book and you still don't reach the page, technical problems with the Dummies site may be blocking your progress — for example, the page may be too busy at the moment to accept your connection request — so just try again a little later until you access the page.

**9  Create a bookmark or bookmark button to access the page easily.**

- If you're using Windows, click the Page Proxy (that is, the small green icon next to the Location box) and, while keeping your mouse button held down, drag the icon to the Personal Toolbar. Finally, release your mouse button. A bookmark button pointing to the *Dummies 101: Netscape Communicator 4* page magically appears on your Personal Toolbar.

- If you're using a Mac, press ⌘D. A bookmark for the page is created at the bottom of your Bookmarks menu.

Congratulations! You successfully typed a URL. You can now take advantage of any recommendation that you receive about the latest and greatest Web pages.

While you're on the *Dummies 101: Netscape Communicator 4* home page, take a few moments to look it over. We use it quite a bit in subsequent exercises, so you may want to take some time to get to know it.

## URL typing tips

If you'd like to practice your newfound URL typing skills, try them on some of the hot Web sites listed on the *Dummies 101: Netscape Communicator 4* page. The list includes most of the Web sites in your bookmarks file (with up-to-date links), as well as exciting new Web sites that have popped up since you created your bookmarks file. Flex your fingers and get typing!

***Tip #1:*** If a Web URL begins with www and ends with com, you can simply type the middle portion of the URL to get to the appropriate page; Netscape fills in the rest of the URL for you automatically! For example, to jump to the first site on this list, www.amazon.com, you can just click in the Location box, type **amazon** and press Enter. Try it!

***Tip #2:*** Netscape checks the History window (which normally stores all the Web pages you've visited within the last day) whenever you type a URL. As a result, if you click in the Location box and begin to type the URL of a page you've recently visited, Netscape will recognize the URL's initial letters and type out the rest of the URL for you! If Netscape guesses incorrectly about the URL you want, just keep typing; the program will automatically withdraw its suggestion in favor of your new Web page address.

## Copying URLs into the Location box

If a URL is printed on paper, you've gotta type it to use it. If a URL appears on your screen, though — say, as a result of a friend e-mailing it to you or the URL appearing in an article that you're reading online — you can simply copy the URL to the Windows or Mac Clipboard and then paste it into Netscape's Location box. Here's how:

1. **Click in front of the first character of the URL that you want to copy.**

2. **While holding down your mouse button, drag the mouse's cursor over the URL until the entire electronic address is highlighted and** then release your mouse button.

3. **Press Ctrl+C or ⌘C to copy the highlighted text to the (invisible) Clipboard.**

4. **Click anywhere inside Netscape's Location box to highlight its current text.**

5. **Press Ctrl+V or ⌘V to paste in your URL.**

6. **Press Enter to activate the URL and jump to its Web page.**

Copying URLs saves your fingers a lot of energy that they can use to do more exploring on the Web.

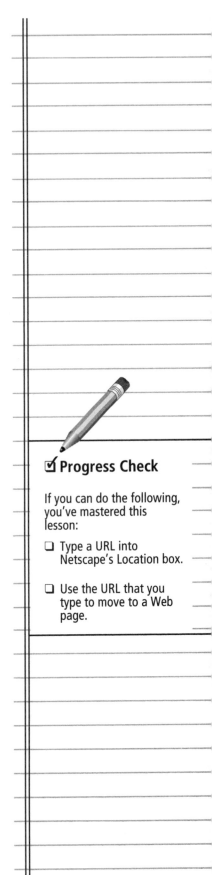

☑ **Progress Check**

If you can do the following, you've mastered this lesson:

❑ Type a URL into Netscape's Location box.

❑ Use the URL that you type to move to a Web page.

## Lesson 2-4    Searching a Web Page for Information

*to search for a word or phrase, choose Edit→Find in Page or press Ctrl+F or ⌘F*

When a Web page consists of only a few paragraphs, you can pick out the facts that you want from it pretty easily. If a page is long and contains lots of text, though, you may appreciate some help locating the information you seek.

**on the test**

That's why Netscape provides a Find command. Like the Find option in a word processor, it lets you search for a word or phrase in an electronic document. To invoke the Find command, choose Edit⇨Find in Page or press the keystroke shortcut Ctrl+F or ⌘F. Any of these actions pops up a Find dialog box. After you type your search text in the dialog box and press Enter, Netscape looks for occurrences of your text on the current Web page.

To try out the Find command, follow these steps to access and search through excerpts from William Shakespeare's classic play *Hamlet*:

**1** **If you aren't still connected to the Internet, dial in again now.**

Your Netscape browser window should be maximized and displaying a Web page.

**2** **Click either the Personal Toolbar button or the bookmark that you created in Lesson 2-3 to move to the *Dummies 101: Netscape Communicator 4* home page.**

You can also jump to the page by clicking inside Netscape's Location box, typing the URL `net.dummies.net/ncomm101`, and pressing Enter.

**3** **Choose Edit⇨Find (or press Ctrl+F or ⌘F).**

A Find dialog box like the one in Figure 2-7 appears. The dialog box contains the following elements:

- A Find what text box (named Find on a Mac) that lets you type the word or phrase you're looking for.

- A Match case option (named Case Sensitive on a Mac) that locates exact uppercase and lowercase matches of your search text.

- Direction buttons to specify whether to search Up or Down from your current position on the Web page. (On a Mac, click the Find Backwards option to search upward.)

- A Find Next button (named Find on a Mac) to execute your search.

For this exercise, accept the default settings. For example, if you use Windows, leave the Match case box unchecked and the Down button selected.

**4** **Drag the Find dialog box to the bottom of the screen so that it doesn't block your view of the page.**

The Find what box and Find Next button should still be visible, but the rest of the dialog box can be hidden behind your Windows 95 Taskbar, or the bottom of your Windows 3.1 or Macintosh desktop.

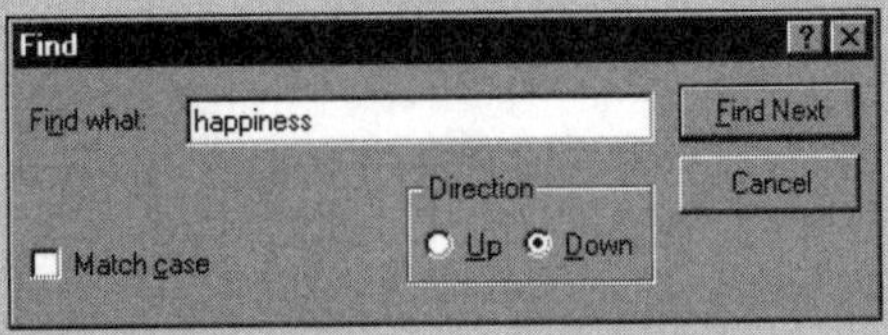

Find

Fi_n_d what:  happiness                              Find Next

                    ┌─ Direction ─┐              Cancel
                    ○ _U_p  ● _D_own
☐ Match _c_ase

Figure 2-7

**Figure 2-7:** Use the Find dialog box to search for a word or phrase on a Web page.

**Notes:**

**5  Type Hamlet in the Fi_n_d what box and then press Enter to execute the search.**

The page jumps to the first (and, in this case, only) occurrence of the word *Hamlet*. This word is part of a link, so you can use it to move to a different page.

**6  Click the Shakespeare's *Hamlet* link.**

The link is activated, and you move to a page containing excerpts from the Bard's immortal drama.

**7  If you're using Windows, double-click in the Fi_n_d what box; on a Mac, press ⌘F.**

The text in the text box is highlighted.

**8  Type life to search for the various ways Shakespeare used this word to weave poetic phrases in *Hamlet*.**

The previous text (Hamlet) is replaced by the word *life*.

**9  Press Enter to execute the search.**

The page jumps to the first occurrence of *life*, which is in Hamlet's bold proclamation concerning his pursuing a ghost: "I do not set my life at a pin's fee,/And for my soul, what can it do to that,/Being a thing immortal as itself?"

**10  Click _F_ind Next or press ⌘G to continue searching.**

The page jumps to the second occurrence of *life*, which is in this terrible revelation by the ghost of Hamlet's father: "But know, thou noble youth,/The serpent that did sting thy father's life/Now wears his crown."

**11  Click _F_ind Next or press ⌘G to continue searching.**

The page jumps to the third occurrence of *life*, which is in Hamlet's fearsome reply, "You cannot, sir, take from me anything that I will more willingly part withal — except my life, my life, my life."

**12  Continue clicking _F_ind Next or pressing ⌘G to locate more matches.**

You should find *life* in several more places, including this section from Hamlet's most famous soliloquy: "To sleep, perchance to dream. Ay, there's the rub,/For in that sleep of death what dreams may come/When we have shuffled off this mortal coil/Must give us pause. There's the respect/That makes calamity of so long life."

## ☑ Progress Check

If you can do the following, you've mastered this lesson:

❑ Open the Find dialog box.

❑ Use the Find dialog box to locate a word or phrase on a Web page.

After you've found all the occurrences of *life*, if you use a Mac, you get beeped at to indicate that your search has been completed. Skip to Step 14.

If you use Windows, a dialog box appears with the message `Search String Not Found!`.

**13** **Press the Esc key to close the dialog box and press Esc again to exit the Find box.**

The message box and Find dialog box disappear.

**14** **Click Netscape's Back button.**

You return to the *Dummies 101: Netscape Communicator 4* home page.

That's all there is to searching for *any* type of text on a Web page. (We should probably add that you'll find most Web material to be considerably cheerier than *Hamlet* . . . though not nearly as well written.) The Find command can save you a lot of time, so make ample use of it when examining text-intensive Web pages.

| | |
|---|---|
| **Lesson 2-5** | # Searching the Entire Web for Information |

**on the test**

Just as you can use Netscape's Find command to search a Web page for a word or phrase, you can use Internet search programs to scour the entire Web for pages dealing with a particular topic. Because literally *tens of millions* of Web pages exist — giving a whole new meaning to the phrase "information overload" — such search programs are indispensable for zeroing in on the data that you need.

Happily, these *Web searchers* (also called *search engines*) are available on the Web itself and can be accessed with just a few mouse clicks. Further, most of them are free! (The publishers of Web searchers generate revenue by selling advertising space on their search sites or by selling related products.)

Because the Web is so enormous and ever-changing, no single search program can do a perfect job of finding the most appropriate pages dealing with your topic. A number of excellent Web searchers are available, though, so if you aren't satisfied with the results that you get from one, you can simply turn to another.

Two different kinds of search programs exist. The first relies on human editors who attempt to bring order to the Web's chaos by organizing Web pages into broad categories (for example, Government, Business, or Arts) and narrower subcategories (for example, Arts⇨Art History⇨Artists⇨da Vinci, Leonardo⇨ Leonardo da Vinci Drawings on Web page `http://banzai.msi.umn.edu/~reudi/leonardo.html`). This type of category-based Web searcher (represented by such programs as Yahoo!) is best when you're researching a broad, popular topic that human editors are likely to have assigned a subcategory.

The second type of search program is *open-ended* — that is, it doesn't rely on any kind of predefined structuring or categorizing of Web pages. Instead, programs such as HotBot and AltaVista try to match your search text to their enormous databases on the fly, and depend entirely on their own intelligence (or, to be more precise, on a number of sophisticated programming tricks) to come up with the most appropriate Web pages for your topic. Using an open-ended search program is best when you're researching a narrow or obscure topic. You'll learn more about the advantages and disadvantages of each approach shortly.

New Web searchers are constantly popping up on the Net. As we write this book, the following are some of the best search programs available:

**on the test**

▶ **AltaVista** (www.altavista.digital.com): Provides extremely fast, accurate searching of more than 40 million Web pages. AltaVista is one of the two most comprehensive Web search programs (the other being HotBot), and it's among our favorites.

▶ **Excite** (www.excite.com): Offers three fine services: a search program named Excite Search, a guide named Excite Web Reviews that lists evaluations of sites organized by topic, and a set of links named Excite NewsTracker that leads you to articles from over 300 newspapers and magazines.

▶ **HotBot** (www.hotbot.com): Provides extremely fast, accurate searching of more than 40 million Web pages. HotBot is one of the two most comprehensive Web search programs (the other being AltaVista), and it's among our favorites.

▶ **InfoSeek** (guide.infoseek.com): Produces highly accurate results within the confines of its database. InfoSeek is excellent at matching your search topic with relatively new Web pages, but sometimes at the price of ignoring older Web sites.

▶ **Lycos** (www.lycos.com): Furnishes sophisticated search options (for example, letting you search for Web pages that mention Dean Martin but *don't* mention Jerry Lewis) and a huge Web page database. Lycos also offers a Web guide organized by category (a2z.lycos.com) and recommendations of top Web sites (point.lycos.com/categories).

▶ **Yahoo!** (www.yahoo.com): The oldest major category-based search program and a great place to start when researching broad topics. Yahoo! isn't as comprehensive as some of the programs in this list, but it's likely to produce more targeted matches. Yahoo! also offers great features such as Picks of the Week (www.yahoo.com/picks), a savvy list of the best of the Web (www.yahoo.com/Entertainment/ Cool_Links), a weekly listing of new Web sites (www.yahoo.com/ weblaunch.html), and a search program devoted to finding Web sites for kids (www.yahooligans.com).

▶ **Savvy Search** (www.cs.colostate.edu/~dreiling/smartform. html): A high-level or "meta-search" program that, instead of scouring the Web directly, plugs your search term into several popular Web searchers and then gives you all the initial matches together on the same page, organized by search program! Use this tool to avoid the time and effort of entering text into each search program separately.

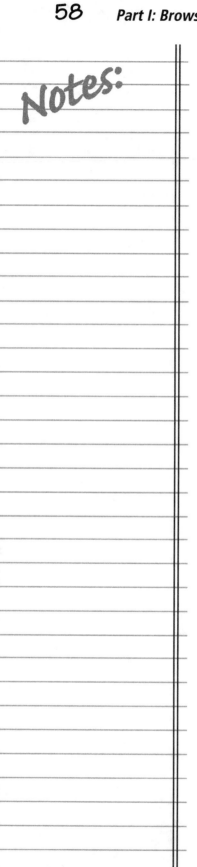

*Notes:*

At this point, you're probably thinking, "Sounds great, but how can I easily get to all these different search programs?" Well, by an amazing coincidence, you can access them with a mouse click from the *Dummies 101: Netscape Communicator 4* home page!

**heads up**

Because there's no way to predict what will change on the Web, a Web searcher that we discuss in this lesson may no longer be available (or available for free) when you try to access it. If a search program becomes unavailable, don't sweat it — simply use a different search program. At the same time, keep an eye on our *Dummies 101: Netscape Communicator 4* Web site for links to fabulous new search programs.

## Using a category-based Web searcher

To get started on your Web research skills, try using Yahoo! — a category-based Web searcher — to find Web sites dealing with movies.

**1 If you aren't still connected to the Internet, dial in again now.**

Your Netscape browser window should be maximized and displaying a Web page.

**2 If you aren't on the *Dummies 101: Netscape Communicator 4* home page, click the Personal Toolbar button or the bookmark that you created in Lesson 2-3.**

You can also jump to the page by clicking inside Netscape's Location box, typing the URL net.dummies.net/ncomm101, and pressing Enter.

**3 Locate and click the link that contains the phrase *Web search*.**

You move to a page with text entry boxes linked to popular Web search programs (see Figure 2-8).

**4 Create a bookmark or bookmark button to access the page easily.**

- If you're using Windows, click and drag the Page Proxy (the small green icon next to the Location box) to the Personal Toolbar and then release your mouse button. A bookmark button pointing to the Searching the Web page pops out of thin air onto your Personal Toolbar.

- If you're using a Mac, press ⌘D. A bookmark for the page is created at the bottom of your Bookmarks menu.

**5 Locate the Yahoo! search box and click inside the box.**

A blinking cursor appears inside the Yahoo! box to indicate that you can now enter your search text.

**6 Type movies to research movie-related Web sites and then press Enter.**

Your search request takes you to a Yahoo! page like the one in Figure 2-9. This page lists the first batch of categories in Yahoo!'s Web catalog that best matches your search phrase *movies*. (You can display additional categories by clicking a link near the bottom of the page that says something like *Next 20 Matches*.)

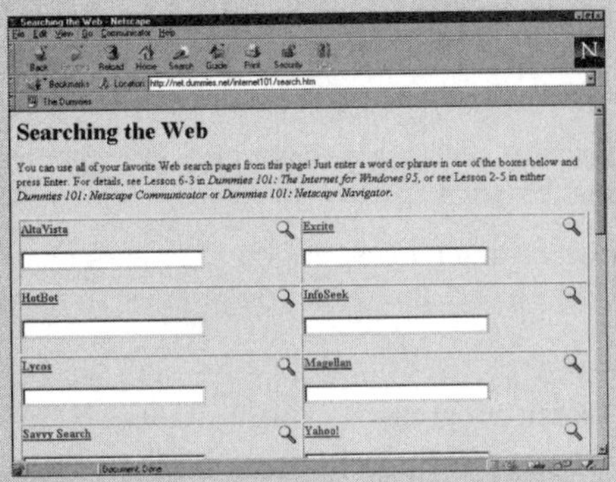

Figure 2-8

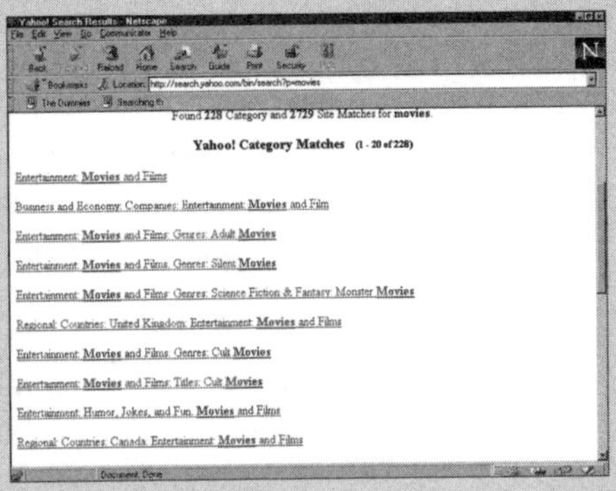

Figure 2-9

**Figure 2-8:** This book's Searching the Web page lets you access many of the best Web search programs. To use a particular program, click in its search box, type your research topic, and press Enter.

**Figure 2-9:** Yahoo! generates a list of Web categories most relevant to your search topic. Scan the list and select appropriate subcategories for your specific topic.

Notice that all the topics listed on the Yahoo! Category Matches page are links. To explore a topic, simply click it.

**7  Locate the Entertainment: Movies and Films category and then click it.**

If you don't see this topic, simply pick out and click a different broad movie category. You move to a subgroup of categories within your selected category. Press PgDn once or twice to view the entire list.

**8  Pick out a listed category that interests you — say, Actors and Actresses, Screenplays, Genres, Box Office Reports, or anything else — and then click it.**

You again move to a subgroup of categories within your selected category.

**9  Continue picking out and clicking categories that interest you until you work your way down to a list of specific Web sites.**

After you're done clicking through subcategories, you find yourself on a page listing the names and descriptions of Web sites that deal with the particular *movies* subtopic that you selected.

**10  Click a listed Web site name (which is a link).**

You arrive at a Web page. (All right!) Explore the page at your leisure and then click Netscape's Back button to return to your Yahoo! list of sites. Continue by clicking any other Web site link that interests you, examining the page, and clicking the Back button to return to your Yahoo! list until you've visited all the Web pages that appeared relevant to what you were searching for.

As you just saw, a category-based guide to the Web such as Yahoo! (or, as another example, Excite's Web Reviews site) is especially useful for kicking off research on a broad topic. That's because the categories let you quickly see what kinds of information are available. Also, human editors make sure that the Web pages listed under each category are directly relevant, thus sparing you from wasting time with false leads.

*Notes:*

However, category-based search programs also have a few disadvantages:

♦ They force you to do some work before arriving at a list of Web pages.

♦ They're less likely to help you discover pages that aren't directly relevant but that you may find interesting anyway.

♦ They're not as helpful for researching narrow or obscure topics because they tend to include fewer Web pages and center on popular subjects.

Because of these shortcomings of category-based searchers, you should also get in the habit of using open-ended search programs — which we discuss in the next section.

## Using an open-ended Web searcher

Open-ended Web searchers don't depend on human editors and don't list categories. Instead, these programs immediately present you with the names of Web sites related to your topic and ordered by relevance (based on a number of clever programming tricks, such as checking how often your search phrase appears on a particular Web page). Because they don't require people to help them organize information, these programs are free to include a lot *more* information; in fact, popular open-ended searchers such as AltaVista and HotBot cover tens of millions of Web pages, making them powerful tools for turning up raw data.

On the other hand, search programs still aren't nearly as smart as humans are, and so may sometimes give you useful and useless sites mixed together, leaving you with the job of sifting through the list and identifying the pages you really need. Open-ended searchers are therefore best when you're looking for a wide range of sites, need information about esoteric topics, or simply want a quick list of Web pages (as opposed to having to first wade through a bunch of categories and subcategories).

To get a feel for how open-ended searches work, use AltaVista to find Web sites devoted to Elvis Presley:

**1** **Click the Personal Toolbar button or bookmark you created in the preceding exercise to return to the Searching the Web page.**

You move back to the page that you used to launch your Yahoo! search. (You can also reach this page by clicking inside Netscape's Location box, typing the URL net.dummies.net/internet101/search.htm, and pressing Enter.)

**2** **Locate the AltaVista search box and then click inside the box.**

A blinking cursor appears inside the AltaVista box to indicate that you can now enter your search text.

**3** **Type Elvis Presley to locate Web sites about the King of rock 'n' roll and then press Enter.**

You move to an AltaVista page that lists an initial batch of Web pages it considers most relevant to your topic (as in Figure 2-10). Notice that each entry in the list includes the Web page's name and URL (both of which are links that

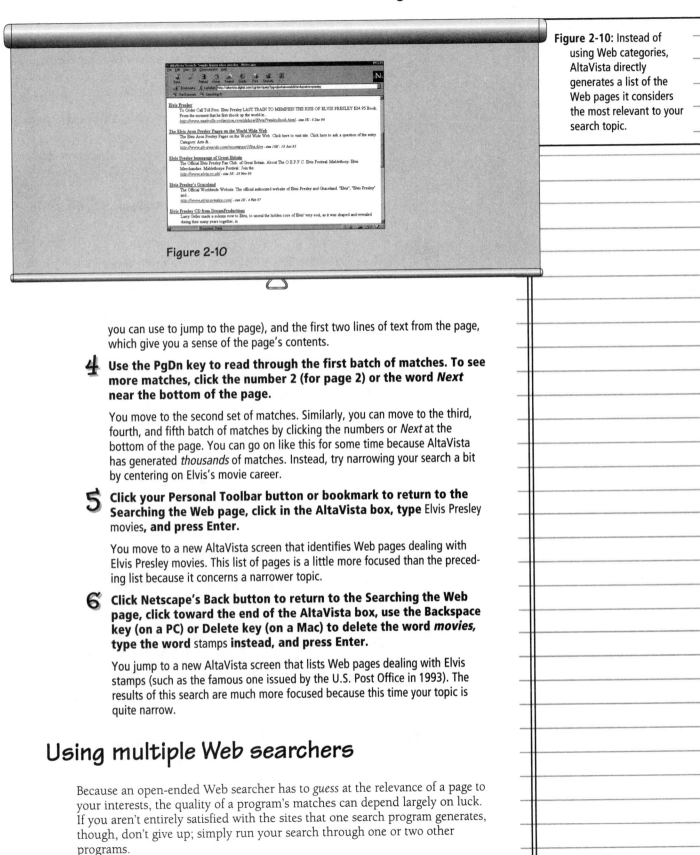

Figure 2-10

**Figure 2-10:** Instead of using Web categories, AltaVista directly generates a list of the Web pages it considers the most relevant to your search topic.

you can use to jump to the page), and the first two lines of text from the page, which give you a sense of the page's contents.

**4 Use the PgDn key to read through the first batch of matches. To see more matches, click the number 2 (for page 2) or the word *Next* near the bottom of the page.**

You move to the second set of matches. Similarly, you can move to the third, fourth, and fifth batch of matches by clicking the numbers or *Next* at the bottom of the page. You can go on like this for some time because AltaVista has generated *thousands* of matches. Instead, try narrowing your search a bit by centering on Elvis's movie career.

**5 Click your Personal Toolbar button or bookmark to return to the Searching the Web page, click in the AltaVista box, type** Elvis Presley movies**, and press Enter.**

You move to a new AltaVista screen that identifies Web pages dealing with Elvis Presley movies. This list of pages is a little more focused than the preceding list because it concerns a narrower topic.

**6 Click Netscape's Back button to return to the Searching the Web page, click toward the end of the AltaVista box, use the Backspace key (on a PC) or Delete key (on a Mac) to delete the word *movies*, type the word** stamps **instead, and press Enter.**

You jump to a new AltaVista screen that lists Web pages dealing with Elvis stamps (such as the famous one issued by the U.S. Post Office in 1993). The results of this search are much more focused because this time your topic is quite narrow.

## Using multiple Web searchers

Because an open-ended Web searcher has to *guess* at the relevance of a page to your interests, the quality of a program's matches can depend largely on luck. If you aren't entirely satisfied with the sites that one search program generates, though, don't give up; simply run your search through one or two other programs.

*Notes:*

**1** **Click your Personal Toolbar button or bookmark to return to the Searching the Web page.**

This time, pick a different search program to use, such as HotBot or InfoSeek.

**2** **Click in the search box of a different search program you'd like to try, type** Elvis Presley**, and press Enter.**

You move to an initial list of Elvis Web pages generated by the program that you selected. Notice that the list is different from AltaVista's initial list (though you may see some overlap).

**3** **Click Netscape's Back button to return to the Searching the Web page.**

Pick another search program to try out, such as Excite or Lycos.

**4** **Click in the search box of another search program you'd like to try, type** Elvis Presley**, and press Enter.**

Again, you move to an initial list of Elvis Web pages that's different from any of the others you've generated. You always get unique results from each Web searcher because each has its own special methods of adding Web sites to its database, matching Web pages to a search phrase, and ranking the pages by relevance.

**5** **Click the Back button to return to the Searching the Web page, and this time use the meta-search program Savvy Search by clicking in its search box, typing** Elvis Presley**, and pressing Enter.**

You move to a list of initial matches from several different Web searchers (typically a mix of category-based and open-ended searchers), organized by program. If you want to delve further, you can click the link to the program that you feel produced the best matches. Doing a search in this way is more efficient than typing the search text yourself for each separate program.

extra credit

## Narrowing your search

Your search results can be affected by more than just which search program you pick; they can vary depending on the syntax you use to specify your topic. For example, in most search programs, the phrase *Princess Diana* matches Web pages that contain either *Princess* or *Diana*. To narrow the results, you can enclose the phrase in quotation marks ("Princess Diana"), which forces the search to match only Web pages that contain the entire phrase *Princess Diana*.

Other ways to zero in on your topic by using syntax exist, but they vary from search program to search program. Therefore, to get the specifics, visit the page of a Web searcher you enjoy and then read about the particular options available for that program.

## Using Netscape's built-in search features

Netscape has its own built-in aids for searching the Web. First, you can click the Search button, which is located directly to the right of the Home button on the Navigation Toolbar. After you do so, you move to a Web page designed by Netscape Communications that has links to a variety of search programs (as well as Web guides and other useful resources).

If you have a search topic that consists of two or more words, you can also simply type the phrase into the Location box!

After you do so and press Enter, Netscape first determines that your text isn't in the format of an Internet URL (because URLs never contain spaces) and then randomly sends your topic to one of several search programs to tackle. Because you don't control which program is used, you won't always get the best results possible; but if you ever get impatient clicking bookmarks and waiting for search pages to appear, this method can't be beat for initiating a search quickly.

To sum up, there's no one right way to search the Web. The program that you use — and whether you should use one Web searcher or several, or a metasearcher such as Savvy Search — depends on how general your search topic is, how comprehensive you need your research to be, how much work you want to do, and your personal tastes.

The main thing is that you don't feel overwhelmed by it all! Although the Web offers a staggering amount of information, so does a library, a museum, or a television set with 50 cable channels. In each case, don't hesitate to follow the advice of author Ken Kesey: "Take what you can use and let the rest go by."

## Recess

You've opened a lot of doors for yourself in this unit. You can now use bookmarks to preserve Web page locations, move to any URL by using the Location box, and find information about virtually anything on the Web. Take a few minutes to contemplate your impressive new powers, and then challenge yourself with the following crafty quiz questions.

☑ **Progress Check**

If you can do the following, you've mastered this lesson:

❏ Research a subject by using a Web search program.

❏ Understand the difference between category-based and open-ended Web searchers.

❏ Use a variety of Web searchers.

❏ Avoid feeling overwhelmed by it all.

# Unit 2 Quiz

For each of the following questions, circle the letter of the correct answer or answers. Remember, each question may have more than one right answer.

1. **To create a bookmark for a Web page, move to the page and:**

   A. Click the Netscape logo.

   B. Press Ctrl+D or ⌘D.

   C. Click the Bookmarks button and click Add Bookmark.

   D. Click and drag the Page Proxy to the Bookmarks menu.

   E. Fasten the page and the Bookmarks menu together by choosing the Glue command.

2. **To remove a bookmark:**

   A. Make it feel unwanted.

   B. Choose Bookmarks⇨Bookworm.

   C. Choose Communicator⇨Bookmarks⇨Edit Bookmarks, click the bookmark, and choose Edit⇨Delete.

   D. Press Ctrl+B or ⌘B, click the bookmark, and press Delete.

   E. None of the above; bookmarks are permanent and can't be removed.

3. **To organize your bookmarks, you can**

   A. Hold up a sign that says *Union!* in front of your screen.

   B. From the Bookmarks window, choose File⇨New Folder to create folders for grouping the bookmarks.

   C. Click and drag bookmarks with your mouse to move them to different folders.

   D. Automatically arrange them by color and pattern using the Bookmarks⇨Fashion option.

   E. Ride them until their wild ways are broken.

4. **If a newspaper article tells you about a great new Web page, you can check it out by:**

   A. Showing the article to Netscape and typing **Go fetch**.

   B. Clicking inside the Location box, typing the Web page's URL, and pressing Enter.

   C. Closing your eyes, breathing deeply, and, like, letting your mind journey to the URL, man.

   D. Using a Web search program to locate the page and then clicking the page's link.

   E. Playing hard to get with the Web page until it eventually comes to you.

5. **To locate a word or phrase on a Web page:**

    A. Use the vertical scroll bar to examine the page carefully.

    B. Use the PgDn and PgUp keys to examine the page carefully.

    C. Use the Web Psychic program to make the desired text float to the front of your screen.

    D. Press Ctrl+F or ⌘F, type your search text, and press Enter.

    E. Click inside the Location box, type your search text, and press Enter.

6. **Some programs that you can use to search the Web are:**

    A. Yahoo!, HotBot, and Lycos.

    B. Yippee, Sneezy, and Dopey.

    C. AltaVista, Excite, and Savvy Search.

    D. Huey, Dewey, and Louie.

    E. Groucho, Chico, and Harpo.

# Unit 2 Exercise

Apply what you've learned about using bookmarks and finding information on the Web by creating a mini-library of Web pages devoted to subjects that interest you.

1. Write down at least three topics that are dear to your heart.

2. Run Netscape and connect to the Internet.

3. Open the Bookmarks window and create an empty folder for each of your three topics.

4. Move to the HotBot home page at www.hotbot.com. (*Tip:* Try typing just hotbot in the Location box and letting Netscape fill in the rest of the URL after you press Enter.)

5. Create a button on the Personal Toolbar for the HotBot page so that you can return to the page easily. (If you're using a Mac, create a bookmark instead.)

6. For each item on your list, search for Web pages devoted to the topic.

7. Whenever you locate a Web page that you feel is interesting, use the Page Proxy to simultaneously create a bookmark for it and file the bookmark in the appropriate menu folder.

8. Repeat Steps 6 and 7 using the Yahoo! site at www.yahoo.com. (*Tip:* Try typing just yahoo instead of the full URL.)

9.  After you're entirely done with your searching, open the Bookmarks window and organize your new bookmarks within each folder, putting your favorites on top.

10. Test out your bookmarks by revisiting some of the Web pages that you've selected.

11. After you're finished, disconnect from the Net and exit Netscape.

# Saving Web Information and Downloading Files

**Prerequisites**

▶ Cruising the Web with Netscape Communicator 4 (Lesson 1-2)

▶ Creating bookmarks (Lesson 2-1)

▶ Entering URLs (Lesson 2-3)

▶ Searching for information on the Web (Lesson 2-5)

### Objectives for This Unit

✓ Printing Web pages

✓ Saving Web pages as text files

✓ Saving Web pages as HTML files

✓ Copying files from the Web

**Y**ou've spent a lot of time on the Web by now, but you've interacted with it in only one way — by viewing Web pages online through your Netscape browser window. In this unit, you'll learn how to read Web pages offline and at your leisure by printing them to paper or saving them to disk. You'll also discover how to access the tens of thousands of programs, electronic images, digital sounds, and other wonderful goodies that are just waiting for you to reach out and pluck from the Web.

## Printing and Saving Web Information                    Lesson 3-1

In Unit 2, you learned how to use Netscape to locate information. If the information is complicated or important, though, you may not want to simply read it on your screen but also preserve it in some way for further study offline.

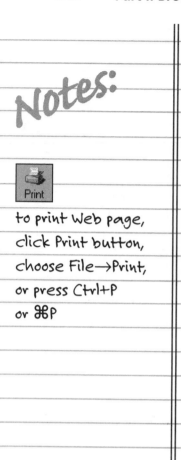

to print Web page,
click Print button,
choose File→Print,
or press Ctrl+P
or ⌘P

Saving Web data allows you to examine the information that you found at your leisure and to organize it, edit it, and reuse it. In addition, perusing text-heavy Web information from paper pages or your favorite word processor gives you the opportunity to mark up the text as you go along and saves you from racking up phone charges while you read.

You can preserve Web data in two ways: by printing it to paper and by saving it to disk. Both methods are quick and easy.

on the test

You can print the contents of your current Web page in any of three ways: by clicking Netscape's Print button, by choosing File⇨Print, or by pressing Ctrl+P or ⌘P. Any of these actions will pop up a Print dialog box with various options. To proceed with standard printing, just click OK.

Similarly, you can save the contents of your current Web page to disk by choosing File⇨Save As or pressing Ctrl+S or ⌘S, which pops up a Save As dialog box. After you type a filename (for example, C:\WebData\NewFile) and press Enter, the file is saved to the hard disk location that you specified.

To try out these convenient features — and also learn about various printing and saving options — work through the next two exercises.

## Printing the contents of a Web page

Although the Internet's electronic mail and World Wide Web pages may ultimately save a lot of trees, paper still has its uses. For example, paper pages are light, portable, and easy to read and mark up. They also can serve as a permanent record, as opposed to Web pages that can disappear overnight or even computer file formats that can become obsolete after a number of years. Finally, printing on paper lets you preserve the whole "look" of a Web page, including its graphics, whereas saving to disk preserves a Web page's text but not its graphics.

In Lesson 2-4, you searched through excerpts from Shakespeare's *Hamlet*. Now follow these steps to print the text on the *Hamlet* Web page:

**1  Run Netscape and connect to the Internet.**

Your browser window should be maximized and displaying a Web page.

**2  Click the Personal Toolbar button or bookmark that you created in Lesson 2-3 to move to the *Dummies 101: Netscape Communicator* home page.**

You can also move to the page by clicking inside Netscape's Location box, typing the URL net.dummies.net/ncomm101, and pressing Enter.

**3  Locate and click the *Hamlet* link that you used in Lesson 2-4.**

You move to the page containing the excerpts from *Hamlet*.

**4  Make sure that your printer is on.**

Also check that your printer is connected to your computer, that its online light is on, and that it has at least ten pages in its paper tray. After you do so, you're ready to print the contents of the Web page.

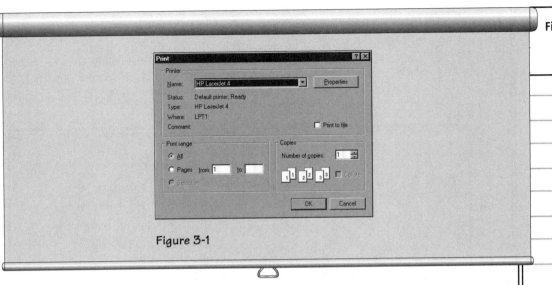

Figure 3-1

**Figure 3-1:** Use the Print
dialog box to print the
contents of a Web page.

**5** **Click the Netscape Print button (or choose File⇨Print or press Ctrl+P or ⌘P).**

A Print dialog box like the one in Figure 3-1 appears. If you're using Windows, the dialog box contains a Print range box that lets you print All the contents of the current Web page, a range of paper Pages (for example, from 1 to 2 prints only the first two paper pages), or a Selection, which lets you print a high-lighted section of the Web page.

The dialog box also lets you switch to a different printer; set the Number of copies to print; Collate your pages (meaning to print them in reverse order, or last page first); and Print to file, in case you want to save the output to disk (for example, if you're using a laptop and won't be able to print until later).

Finally, the dialog box provides a Properties button that lets you set such things as paper size and how fonts and graphics are handled.

If you're using a Macintosh, the contents of the Print dialog box vary depending on which printer you've selected from the Chooser. However, you'll typically see most of the options just mentioned, though their names may be slightly different.

For now, accept the default settings by leaving the Print dialog box as it is.

**6** **Click the Print dialog box's OK button (under Windows) or Print button (on a Mac).**

The Print box is replaced by a Printing Status box, which continually tells you what percentage of the Web page's contents have been processed for printing. When the processing is completed, the box closes and the actual printing of your Web page begins. (***Note:*** If the page doesn't print, double-check both your printer's status and the settings in the Print box.)

**7** **After the page prints, check your pages against the contents of the Web page.**

The text and graphics on your paper pages should look the same as the text and graphics that appear on the electronic page.

*Notes:*

To sum up, you can print the contents of a Web page by performing two simple steps: clicking Netscape's Print button and then clicking the Print box's OK button (under Windows) or Print button (on a Mac). Because printing is relatively effortless, be sure to take advantage of this feature.

**extra credit**

# Changing print settings

If you ever need to adjust Netscape's standard print settings, you can do so in several ways:

▶ Choose File⇨Page Setup to adjust such formatting features as page margins, page numbering, and headers and footers.

▶ Under Windows, choose File⇨Print⇨ Properties to switch to a different paper size, paper tray, and/or paper orientation (Portrait prints across the width of a page, and Landscape prints across the long side of a page). The Properties

dialog box also lets you set how fonts and graphics are printed.

On a Mac, choose File⇨Print⇨ Options to access additional printing options.

▶ Under Windows only, choose File⇨Print Preview to see what your paper pages will look like as a result of the settings you've selected.

Detailing these options is beyond the scope of this book, but you may want to play around with them on your own.

Printing a Web page has many advantages, but it also has drawbacks, such as the cost in paper and ink, the clutter that paper creates, and the difficulty of manipulating paper data (not to mention the possibility of nasty paper cuts). That's why Netscape also lets you save information to disk, which you'll take on next.

## Saving the contents of a Web page to disk

For long-term use, saving Web data to a disk is often better than printing it because electronic text takes up much less space than paper and is significantly easier to search through and organize.

In addition, you can easily manipulate and reuse electronic data. For example, you can save stock prices from a Web page to a disk file and then import the file into a spreadsheet program or other analysis tool to crunch the numbers. As another example, you can periodically dump Web data that's pertinent to your job onto your hard disk and then edit the information in your word processor to produce savvy and timely office reports.

You can save Web data in two file formats: text and HTML. The text format is understood by all PC and Mac programs, but it achieves that universality by ignoring formatting such as underlining, boldfacing, margins, fonts, and colors — basically, anything outside standard words, numbers, and punctuation. Saving information as text allows you to view and edit it in any program, but at the cost of the "look" of the Web page.

Conversely, saving a Web page as an HTML file preserves the look of the page (except for pictures, which are represented in the file by copies of a simple placeholder image). However, you can view HTML files properly only from a Web browser program such as Netscape. If you load HTML files into another type of program instead, you see a messy jumble consisting of Web page text mixed together with confusing-looking formatting codes set in <brackets>. (For more information about HTML, see Unit 8.)

on the test

Because of these technical differences, you typically save Web information in text format so that you can view and edit the data using other programs (such as your favorite word processor). You save in HTML format when you just want archival records of Web pages that you can re-examine at your convenience via Netscape.

## Saving Web data as a text file

To save your data as a text file, turn once again to the Hamlet page.

**1** **If you aren't still on the Hamlet Web page, move there now.**

If you need help finding the page, refer to Lesson 2-4.

**2** **Choose File➪Save As (or press Ctrl+S or ⌘S).**

A Save As dialog box like the one in Figure 3-2 appears. You use this box to select the format that you want to use for your disk file and to specify where on your hard disk you want to save the file.

The dialog box's large middle section is a *file list* that shows you the files in your current disk folder. To display the contents of a different folder, you can click inside the Save in box (above the file list) to display all your drives, click the drive that you want, and then double-click the folder that you want. Alternatively, you can click in the box below the file list — labeled File name under Windows and Save as on a Mac — type a new drive letter and folder name (for example, C:\MyFolder), and press Enter.

If you're using Windows 95, the dialog box also contains four buttons in its upper-right corner. You can use these buttons to move up one folder level (that is, to move from your subfolder to its parent folder); to create a new folder; to list files by name only (which lets you see more of them at a time); or to list each file followed by its size, type, creation date, and creation time. On a Macintosh, buttons on the right side of the dialog box let you Eject the current floppy disk or CD-ROM, switch to the Desktop, and create a New folder.

Finally, you should notice the box at the bottom, which is labeled Save as type under Windows and Format on a Mac. This box lets you specify the format that Netscape uses to save your Web page. Under Windows, this box's settings also determine the type of files that you see in the file list.

**3** **Move to a folder that's appropriate for storing Web data.**

For example, if you have a folder named Data on your C drive, double-click inside the File name box, type **C:\Data,** and press Enter. Your folder name appears in the Save in box.

*to save contents of Web page, choose File→Save As, or press Ctrl+S or ⌘S*

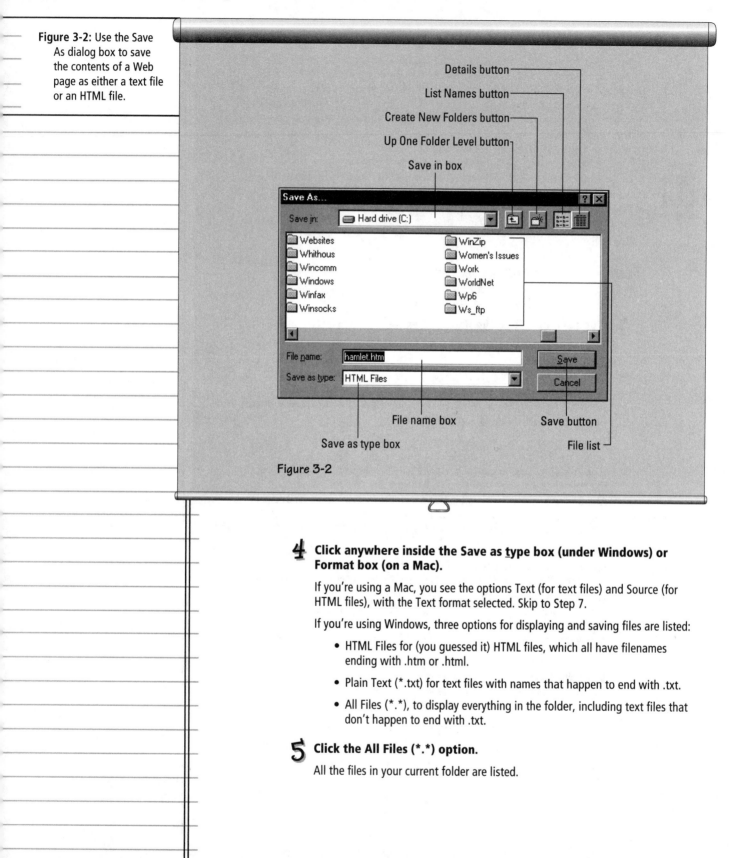

**Figure 3-2:** Use the Save As dialog box to save the contents of a Web page as either a text file or an HTML file.

Details button

List Names button

Create New Folders button

Up One Folder Level button

Save in box

File name box

Save button

Save as type box

File list

Figure 3-2

**4  Click anywhere inside the Save as type box (under Windows) or Format box (on a Mac).**

If you're using a Mac, you see the options Text (for text files) and Source (for HTML files), with the Text format selected. Skip to Step 7.

If you're using Windows, three options for displaying and saving files are listed:

- HTML Files for (you guessed it) HTML files, which all have filenames ending with .htm or .html.

- Plain Text (*.txt) for text files with names that happen to end with .txt.

- All Files (*.*), to display everything in the folder, including text files that don't happen to end with .txt.

**5  Click the All Files (*.*) option.**

All the files in your current folder are listed.

**6** **Click inside the Save as type box again and, this time, click the Plain Text (*.txt) option.**

Only files in your current folder with names ending in .txt are listed. Use this setting to save your Web page as a text document named Hamlet.txt.

**7** **Double-click inside the File name box (under Windows) or Save as box (on a Mac) to highlight any text that's already there and then type Hamlet.txt.**

Your filename Hamlet.txt is entered in the box.

**8** **Press Enter or click Save.**

The text of your Web page is saved to the current drive and folder in the file Hamlet.txt, and the Save As dialog box closes.

**9** **Press Ctrl+S or ⌘S.**

The Save As dialog box reopens. If you're using a Mac, scroll through the file list; you should see the file you just saved listed.

**10** **If you're using Windows, click inside the Save as type box and click the Plain Text (*.txt) option.**

You should now see the file Hamlet.txt listed, verifying that your text save was successful.

## Saving your data as an HTML file

Next, perform a similar operation to save your Web page as an HTML file. The Save As dialog box should still be open.

**1** **If you're using Windows, click inside the Save as type box and click the HTML Files option. If you're using a Mac, click inside the Format box and click the Source option.**

If you're using Windows, only files with names ending in .htm or .html in the current folder are listed. Use this setting to save your Web page as an HTML document.

**2** **If you're using Windows, double-click inside the File name box to highlight any text that's already there and then type Hamlet.htm. If you're using a Mac, double-click inside the Save as box and then type Hamlet.html.**

Your filename is entered in the box.

**3** **Press Enter or click Save.**

Both the text and formatting of your Web page are stored to the current drive and folder in the file Hamlet.htm (under Windows) or Hamlet.html (on a Mac), and the Save As box closes.

## Checking your saved text and HTML files

You've now finished saving your Web page in both text and HTML versions, so check out the files that you created.

*Notes:*

*Notes:*

to view HTML file,
choose File→Open
Page, or press
Ctrl+O or ⌘O

**1  Open Notepad, WordPad, or some other word-processing program.**

Both your word processor and Netscape should be running, with your word processor in the foreground.

**2  Load the file Hamlet.txt into the word processor that you're using.**

Specifically, for most word processors, choose File⇨Open; specify the appropriate drive letter, folder name, and filename (for example, type C:\Data\Hamlet.txt); and press Enter.

You should see a plain, all-text version of the current Web page. (If you notice any extraneous pieces of text, they're probably leftover HTML codes, which you should delete.) You can now use this Web data in the same way that you would any other word-processing document.

**3  Save any revisions you made to the document (for example, by choosing File⇨Save) and exit your word processor.**

Both the document and the word processor close, returning the Netscape window to the front of your screen. Now examine the HTML file that you created, which you can do by using Netscape's Open Page option. If you're using a Macintosh, skip to Step 6.

**4  Choose File⇨Open Page or press Ctrl+O.**

An Open Page dialog box appears, prompting you to enter the name of the file.

**5  Specify the appropriate drive letter, folder name, and filename (for example, type C:\Data\Hamlet.htm).**

Notice that the dialog box also gives you the option of opening the file in a Navigator window or a Composer window. The latter lets you create your own Web pages, and you'll learn all about it in Unit 8. For now, though, make sure that the Navigator option is selected and then skip to Step 8.

**6  On your Mac, choose File⇨Open⇨Page in Navigator or simply press ⌘O.**

An Open dialog box appears that lets you select a file.

**7  Scroll through the file list until you see Hamlet.html and then click the file to select it.**

The Hamlet.html file is highlighted.

**8  Press Enter or click the Open button.**

The HTML file that you created appears in the Netscape window. The file looks very similar to the Web page that generated it. In place of the graphics on the Web page, however, the file has only copies of a simple placeholder image to represent the missing graphics.

**9  Click the Back button.**

You move back to the *Hamlet* Web page.

Whew! These file-saving exercises took a while to get through because they contain a lot of new material. Now that you have it all under your belt, though, you should have no trouble saving Web data. If you're using Windows, you'll typically press Ctrl+S to open the Save As box, set the format to Plain Text (*.txt), type an appropriate filename in the File name box, and press Enter. And on a Mac, you'll typically press ⌘S, type an appropriate filename in the Save as box, and press Enter. Easy as pie.

## Saving Web page text using the Clipboard

One other way that you can save Web data is by highlighting it and then copying it to the Windows or Mac Clipboard. This technique is especially handy when you're interested in only a portion of the Web page, because it spares you from having to save the entire document. Here's how to manage it:

1. **Click the beginning of the Web text that you want to copy.**

2. **While holding down your mouse button, drag over the section of text until all of it is highlighted and then release your mouse button.**

3. **Press Ctrl+C or ⌘C to copy the highlighted text to the (invisible) Clipboard.**

4. **Open a document in a word processor or other program where you want to use the text.**

5. **Click the spot where you want to insert the text and then press Ctrl+V or ⌘V to paste it in.**

    You can now work with the text.

6. **After you're done editing the data, save your document.**

You may also find it easier to save an entire Web page using the Clipboard because the whole operation can be accomplished with a few keystrokes. Specifically, press Ctrl+A or ⌘A (or choose Edit⇨Select All) to select all the text on the page; press Ctrl+C or ⌘C to copy the text; click the spot in the window where you want to insert the text; and press Ctrl+V or ⌘V to paste. Finally, after you've edited the text, save it from its new window.

## Keeping copyright issues in mind

As this lesson demonstrates, you can print or save to disk virtually any information you find on a Web page. However, that doesn't mean you're free to use the information without restraint. The text and pictures on Web pages are owned by the authors of those pages, and they're protected by U.S. copyright laws in the same way that the contents of books and magazines are protected (even if the pages don't display copyright notices). For example, you can't publish large portions of text from a Web page without obtaining permission from the author, just as you can't publish long sections from a book or magazine article without permission.

If you need more information about U.S. copyright laws, a good place to start your research is the United States Copyright Office. To visit the Web site of the Copyright Office, click inside Netscape's Location box, type the URL `lcweb.loc.gov/copyright`, and press Enter.

☑ **Progress Check**

If you can do the following, you've mastered this lesson:

❑ Print a Web page's contents.

❑ Save a Web page's contents as a text file.

❑ Save a Web page's contents as an HTML file.

❑ Open text and HTML files that you've created.

Using some discretion when preserving Web information is necessary, because cluttering your desk or disk with nonessentials hinders you from locating the facts you really need. (Comedian Steven Wright made this point succinctly when he observed, "You can't have everything. Where would you put it?") But as long as you restrict printing and saving to genuinely useful data, you'll find these features to be great aids on your journey along the Web.

## Lesson 3-2     Downloading Files from the Web

In Lessons 2-5 and 3-1, you learned how to search Web pages for text information and save the data to disk. You can also search for and copy *files* from the Web to disk. The files may be programs (such as a new version of Netscape), pictures (ranging from the Mona Lisa to a Madonna poster), digital sounds (ranging from a Mozart sonata to the theme from *The Twilight Zone*), digital video (such as a clip of Neil Armstrong's famous first steps on the moon), or any other kind of data that you can use on your computer.

**on the test**

Getting files from another computer is called *downloading*, because the data is typically loaded from a much larger computer system down to the hard disk of your PC or Mac. (Similarly, sending files from your PC or Mac to another computer is called *uploading*.)

**downloading = transmitting files to your computer**

**uploading = transmitting files from your computer**

To locate files to download, you can employ the same Web search programs that you used in Lesson 2-5 for text research. Alternatively, if you aren't sure what's available, you can cruise over to one of the many Web sites that specialize in distributing the latest and greatest program, picture, and sound files.

After you locate a file that you want, you can initiate copying it to your hard disk by clicking the file's link. If the file ends in a three-letter extension that Netscape recognizes — for example, .txt for text or .exe for a program — a Save As dialog box appears. You can then specify the hard disk location and name for the file and press Enter to execute the download.

On the other hand, if the file ends in a three-letter extension that Netscape does *not* recognize, you have to perform one extra step. Specifically, Netscape first displays an Unknown File Type dialog box that includes a Save File button. After you click the button, Netscape displays the Save As dialog box, which you can then use to download the file.

Most files on the Internet are *compressed* — that is, via special programming tricks, they're shrunken by up to 90 percent of their normal size — to cut down on the amount of space needed to store them and, more important, the amount of time needed to download them. After you transfer a file to your hard disk, you therefore typically need to restore it to its normal size to make it useable. Decompressing a file usually isn't a big deal, though; in most cases, all you have to do is double-click the file, which will then either decompress itself or automatically activate a decompression program on your hard disk.

*Notes:*

The most popular decompression programs are WinZip for Windows and Stuffit Expander for the Mac, and they're both provided on your *Dummies 101* CD-ROM. (If you haven't already installed WinZip or Stuffit Expander, we recommend that you do so now by following the instructions in Appendix B.)

This downloading process may seem complicated, but it really isn't — as we hope the next section demonstrates.

## Searching for and downloading a file

You can find thousands of fun and useful files on the Internet. For example, one of the hottest programs around as we write this is PointCast Network (from PointCast, Inc.), which "broadcasts" information to your computer from such distinguished sources as *The New York Times,* the *Los Angeles Times, The Boston Globe,* the *Chicago Tribune, Time Magazine, People Magazine, Money Magazine, Reuters, BusinessWire, Sportsticker,* and *Accuweather.* After you choose which services you want, PointCast Network uses your Internet connection to transmit the latest headline news, stock market prices, local weather forecasts, sports scores, and so on directly to your screen whenever your computer is idle. This approach is called *push technology* because it pushes data at you, and it's an important alternative to the *pull technology* represented by browsers such as Netscape's Navigator program, which make you actively seek out and travel to Web sites to obtain information. Even nicer, everything that PointCast Network provides to you is *free* — its services are supported entirely by advertising.

To learn more about the downloading process and get the latest version of PointCast Network, follow these steps:

**1** **If you aren't still connected to the Internet, dial in again now.**

Your browser window should be maximized and displaying a Web page.

**2** **Click the Personal Toolbar button or bookmark that you created in Lesson 2-3 to move to the Web search page.**

You also can reach this page by clicking inside Netscape's Location box, typing the URL `net.dummies.net/internet101/search.htm`, and pressing Enter.

**3** **Locate the HotBot search box and then click inside the box.**

A blinking cursor appears inside the box to indicate that you can enter your search text.

**4** **Type** Pointcast Network **and press Enter to find the Web site of the publisher of this program.**

You jump to a HotBot list of Web pages that distribute — or, at minimum, mention — the PointCast Network program. The PointCast home page (which, at the time of this writing, has the URL `http://pioneer. pointcast.com`) should be listed at least once among the first batch of matches. (If you don't see the PointCast home page at first, try looking at additional matches by clicking the right-pointing arrow near the bottom of the page.)

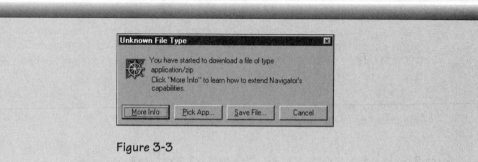

Figure 3-3

**Figure 3-3:** When you activate a link leading to a file type Netscape doesn't recognize, it displays the Unknown File Type dialog box. Click the Save File button to download the file.

**5  When you locate a link to the PointCast home page, click the link.**

If you can't locate the link, just click inside Netscape's Location box, type the URL `pioneer.pointcast.com`, and press Enter. You should move to the PointCast site.

**6  Locate the link that leads to the PointCast Network file (for example, a Download the PointCast Network button or graphic) and click the link.**

You move to another page that offers narrower options leading to the file.

**7  Continue clicking appropriate options until you work your way to the link that lets you download the latest version of PointCast Network for either Windows or the Macintosh and then click the link.**

If you're using a Macintosh, the file may immediately start to download to your Desktop. If this occurs, you see a Save dialog box, with the name of the file at its top, that continually shows you what percentage of the download is completed. After the download is finished, use the Finder to switch to the Desktop, locate the file, and then skip to Step 11.

Alternatively, a Save As dialog box may appear that lets you specify which folder you want to use to store the file. If this happens, skip to Step 9.

Otherwise, an Unknown File Type dialog box like the one in Figure 3-3 appears. Notice that among its options is a Save File button.

**8  Click the Save File button.**

A Save As dialog box (just like the one that you used in Lesson 3-1 to save Web page data) appears. Notice that the name of the file you want has been entered for you automatically in the File name box.

**9  Use your mouse to select a folder for temporarily storing the compressed file (or accept whatever folder is currently selected), write down the folder location and filename (for example, jot it down in the margin of this book), and press Enter or click Save to initiate the download.**

The file is copied to your hard disk. A Saving Location dialog box that continually tells you how much data has been transmitted and how much time is left for the transfer appears. After the entire file has been copied, the dialog box goes away.

**10** **Using Windows Explorer, the Windows 3.1 File Manager, or the Macintosh Finder, switch to the folder that contains your down-loaded file.**

Locate your file, which is actually a collection of many compressed files packaged with an installation program. To make PointCast Network useable, first run the current file.

**11** **Double-click the file that you just downloaded.**

At the time we write this, the initial PointCast Network file is capable of decompressing itself, so you probably first see a message from a setup program. Follow the instructions that the program gives to complete your installation of PointCast Network. If you need any additional help, return to the PointCast Web site for more information about installing and using the program.

**12** **Enjoy your cool new program.**

Congratulations! You've successfully downloaded one of the hottest programs on the Internet. Just as important, you can use the same procedure to find and download thousands of *other* popular files.

*Note:* If you like PointCast Network, be sure to explore Netscape's own Netcaster program, which also broadcasts information to your computer. You can read more about Netcaster at the end of Unit CD-5, which is a bonus unit on your *Dummies 101* CD-ROM. (For instructions on how to view and print bonus units, see Appendix B.)

## Poking around Web sites for files

As efficient as Web searchers are, you shouldn't rely on them entirely to find files. That's because new kinds of files that you may not even dream exist, let alone think to search for, come out all the time. Therefore, you should also occasionally nose around Web sites devoted to program and data files and see whether anything new catches your fancy. In fact, why not try that now?

**1** **If you aren't still connected to the Internet, dial in again.**

Your browser window should be maximized and displaying a Web page.

**2** **Click the Bookmarks button and choose Software Libraries⇨ Clicked.Com Top 20 Shareware Gallery (which is at URL** www.clicked.com/shareware**).**

You move to what this site considers to be the top 20 Windows programs in each of several categories, including Internet, graphics, multimedia, and games. As of this writing, the site includes the versatile graphics viewer/editor L-View Pro, the business flowchart and diagram generator SmartDraw, the cutting-edge music and words player RealAudio, and the classic game Duke Nukem 3D. Explore the site at your leisure and download any files that you think would be genuinely useful (but avoid cluttering your disk with files that you don't really need).

**Notes:**

**3** **Click the Bookmarks button and choose Software Libraries⇨ SHAREWARE.COM (which is at URL** www.shareware.com**).**

You move to the SHAREWARE.COM site, which offers thousands of different kinds of files, including word processors, electronic spreadsheets, database programs, picture files, sound files, and more. Snoop around the site's many different areas, including its Most Popular list.

**4** **Click the Bookmarks button and choose Software Libraries⇨ JUMBO! (which is at URL** www.jumbo.com**).**

You move to JUMBO!, a lighthearted site that also offers tens of thousands of files. Poke around its nooks and crannies, and download any files that you feel may bring you joy.

**5** **Click the Bookmarks button and choose Software Libraries⇨Happy Puppy Games (which is at URL** www.happypuppy.com**).**

You move to Happy Puppy Games, a site devoted to games that (presumably) will make you as happy as a playful puppy. Sniff around until you're satisfied.

These four sites are by no means the only ones with interesting files available for downloading. For example, arguably the best Internet-related software library is The Ultimate Collection of Winsock Software (www.tucows.com), which reviews, rates (on a scale of one to five cows), and lets you download fabulous Windows and Macintosh programs that help you exploit the many resources available on the Net.

And if all those sites still don't fulfill your craving for data, you can use links, magazine articles, and the advice of friends to find more. In addition, be sure to check in periodically with the *Dummies 101: Netscape Communicator 4* home page (net.dummies.net/ncomm101) for recommendations of new software distribution sites as they pop up!

**heads up**

As you download programs and other files, you should keep in mind that many of them are *not* free. Instead, they're *shareware,* which means that these programs are available to you for an evaluation period (typically, anywhere from 30 to 90 days). If you decide that you like a shareware program and want to keep using it, you're expected to send its publisher a registration fee, which entitles you to technical support and notifications about new versions.

Most shareware operates on an honor system, so the programs continue working even if you don't register them. However, it's a good idea to support the shareware concept and encourage the continued production of quality low-cost software by sending in your payment for the programs you use. For more information about paying for your shareware software, see the registration information that's included with each program.

**heads up**

One last thing to keep in mind when downloading a program is the tiny risk that running it will infect your hard disk with a computer virus. Contrary to the hype from the popular press, the odds of encountering a virus are very low, especially if you stick to well-maintained Web sites that test each program before offering it for downloading. Still, viruses that can infect and destroy your hard disk's data *do* exist, so running a virus-detection program before launching any new software is sensible. You can buy a virus checker from a software store, or you can download one from the Web. Alternatively, you can simply install ThunderBYTE Anti-Virus for Windows or Disinfectant for the Macintosh, which are both supplied on your *Dummies 101* CD-ROM (as detailed in Appendix B).

**extra credit**

---

# Netscape's Security button

Viruses aren't the only threat on the Net. Another danger is that when you transmit sensitive information — for example, when you supply your credit card number to purchase a product through a Web page — there's a small chance the data will be intercepted by high-tech criminals. You can avoid such risks by never providing personal information via your modem, but that means sacrificing genuine conveniences such as online shopping. Fortunately, another approach is nearly as safe: rely on Netscape's built-in security features, which can scramble, or *encrypt*, your information so that no one can decipher it except for your intended recipient.

For encryption to work, the Web site you're dealing with must be able to support Netscape's security features. Most Web sites let you know whether they do before

asking for a credit card number or other sensitive data; but if a site neglects to bring up the issue, or if you want to verify that a site is secure, you can click Netscape's Security button, which appears on the browser window's Navigation Toolbar. After you click, a dialog box pops up that tells you the security status of the Web page you're on.

The Security dialog box also provides other options, such as encrypted e-mail (for extra-sensitive messages) and password-protecting the use of Netscape (if you work in an area where others can get access to your computer). Covering these features are beyond the scope of this book, but you can learn more by choosing Help⇨Security from the menu bar of any Netscape window.

---

# Recess

Before you start downloading scores of programs and multimedia files that will keep you at your computer for hours, go out and get some fresh air, smell some flowers (even if you have to walk to a florist to do so), visit some local trees, and feed a squirrel. When you're rejuvenated, return to tackle the following quirky quiz questions.

Netscape's
Security button

☑ **Progress Check**

If you can do the following, you've mastered this lesson:

❑ Find files on the Web.

❑ Download files from the Web.

❑ Understand the importance of paying for shareware that you use regularly.

# Unit 3 Quiz

*Notes:*

For each of the following questions, circle the letter of the correct answer or answers. Remember, each question may have more than one right answer.

1. **Printing a Web page is helpful because:**

    A. The Web is constantly changing, and there's always a chance that the information on a given Web page will disappear suddenly.

    B. Printing preserves the look of a Web page, including its graphics.

    C. Reading from paper pages is often easier on the eyes than reading from a computer screen.

    D. You can carry paper pages anywhere and read them at any time, even when you don't have access to a computer.

    E. All of the above.

2. **To print a Web page:**

    A. You must first obtain a printing license.

    B. You press Ctrl+P or ⌘P and press Enter.

    C. You must have Netscape Communicator Professional, which is the only version of Netscape that includes the printing feature.

    D. You choose File⇨Print and click OK (under Windows) or Print (on a Mac).

    E. You click the Print button and click OK or Print.

3. **Saving Web page information to disk is helpful because:**

    A. Limiting paper usage saves both money and trees.

    B. Electronic data is easier to analyze, edit, and reorganize than paper data.

    C. Storing electronic data requires much less space than storing paper data.

    D. Your computer will start acting up if you don't appease it by regularly feeding it interesting new data.

    E. All of the above (except for D).

4. **To save a Web page:**

    A. Pray for it nightly.

    B. Click the Save button and click OK.

    C. Choose File⇨Save As, select a file type by using the Save as type box, type a filename in the File name box, and press Enter.

    D. Keep it away from direct sunlight.

    E. Sock away a little bit of Web data every day and be patient.

5. **To get, or download, a file from the Web:**

    A. Swipe it when nobody's looking and hope that you don't get caught.

    B. Offer one of your own files to the Web and try to work out a trade.

    C. Choose File⇨Download, enter a filename in the Download To box, and click OK.

    D. You don't get down from a load — you get down from a duck.

    E. Click the file's link, click the Save To Disk button on the Unknown File Type dialog box, select an appropriate folder by using the Save As dialog box, and press Enter.

# Unit 3 Exercise

In this exercise, apply what you've learned about finding and downloading files.

1. Run Netscape and connect to the Internet.

2. Click the Personal Toolbar button or bookmark that you created in Lesson 2-5 to move to this book's Searching the Web page (or just use the Location box to go to net.dummies.net/internet101/ search.htm).

3. Use a Web searcher (for example, AltaVista or HotBot) to locate the Web site of a shareware program you've heard about and would like to own. After you do so, go to the site.

4. Find a page on the Web site that describes the program and save or print the page.

5. Download the program.

6. Disconnect from the Internet; decompress and install the program you've downloaded; and have fun exploring the program!

7. You've now tackled all the exercises that require you to have buttons on your Personal Toolbar for the *Dummies 101: Netscape Communicator 4* home page and Searching the Web page. If you're using Windows and would like to remove these buttons, press Ctrl+B to open the Bookmarks window, locate the Personal Toolbar Folder (which is typically near the top of the window), delete the two *Dummies 101* bookmarks under the folder, and close the Bookmarks window.

8. Exit Netscape.

Notes:

# Fine-Tuning the Browser

## Objectives for This Unit

✓ Cruising the Web without viewing pictures to speed up performance

✓ Using multiple Netscape windows to speed up performance

✓ Hiding Netscape window elements to expand the Netscape Web page display

✓ Using menu options in place of the Toolbar buttons and the Location box

✓ Changing the appearance of the Toolbar, links, and fonts

## Prerequisites

▶ Cruising the Web with Netscape (Lesson 1-2)

▶ Using bookmarks (Lesson 2-1)

▶ Entering URLs (Lesson 2-3)

▶ Using Navigation Toolbar buttons (Lessons 1-2, 2-4, and 3-1)

Now that you're an expert at getting around the Web, you're ready to take a closer look at the program you're using to do your cruising. This final section on the Web therefore concentrates on special features of Netscape Communicator.

In this unit, you'll learn how to change Netscape's settings to help you get to Web pages more quickly. You'll also find out how to adjust Netscape's appearance to make it more attractive and more efficient for your particular needs.

**Lesson 4-1**              # Enhancing Netscape's Performance

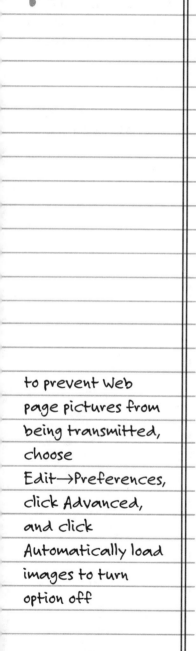

*Notes:*

If you haven't been frustrated by how *l-o-n-g* Web pages take to be transferred to your screen, you're probably using a super-fast computer system and don't have much need for this lesson (although we recommend that you at least skim it to see whether any of the options discussed interest you).

If Web pages *do* take an awfully long time to appear on your screen, though, your system may have some limitations. For example, your modem may be slower than the current standard speed of 33,600 bits per second (or *bps*), which puts a ceiling on how rapidly your computer can receive data.

Another possibility is the amount of electronic memory in your system. Modern PCs and Macs tend to come with 16MB, 32MB, or 64MB of memory. If your system has less memory, your computer operates less efficiently, and that affects its performance on the Web.

A third factor is the speed of your computer's "brain," which is called a *central processing unit* chip, or *CPU*. Modern PC CPUs include the Pentium and the Pentium Pro, which are faster than such older models as 486 and 386 CPUs; and modern Macintosh CPUs include the PowerPC 604 and 604e.

Upgrading your computer system isn't your only option for boosting performance, though; you can choose to take advantage of some special Netscape features. The next two sections tell you how.

## Cruising without pictures

If you don't care to spend lots of money making your computer system faster, you can still improve your cruising speed on the Web dramatically by making one simple adjustment to Netscape: Tell it to skip the pictures.

**on the test**

Specifically, you can choose Edit⇨Preferences, click an Advanced category from the dialog box that appears, and click an Automatically load images option to tell Netscape to *not* transmit any images that appear on a Web page and instead show only a simple "placeholder" graphic for each image. This setting makes transfers go a lot faster because text can move rapidly over the Web. Delays are caused almost entirely by graphics, which require much more data to be displayed on a computer than text does (proving once again that a picture is worth a thousand words).

When the Automatically load images command is turned off, you still have the option of seeing the pictures on a Web page, but only when you explicitly *force* Netscape to get the data. You accomplish that by clicking the Netscape Images button or choosing View⇨Show Images, which causes the graphics of the current Web page to be sent to your screen.

to prevent Web
page pictures from
being transmitted,
choose
Edit→Preferences,
click Advanced,
and click
Automatically load
images to turn
option off

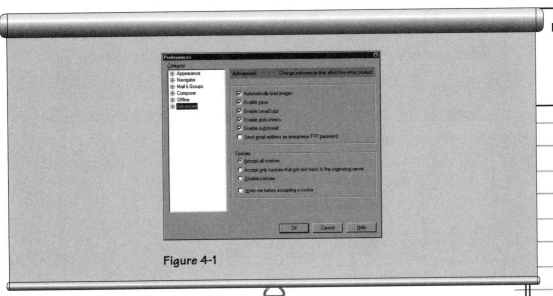

Figure 4-1

**Figure 4-1:** Use the Preferences box's Advanced settings to turn the Automatically load images option off or on.

Follow these steps to see whether you prefer cruising the Web without pictures:

**1 Connect to the Internet and run Netscape.**

Netscape should be maximized and displaying a Web page.

Notice that the Navigation Toolbar currently lacks an Images button. This omission makes sense because you're currently set to receive *all* Web page images automatically, so having a button that lets you receive images would be redundant right now.

**2 Choose Edit⇨Preferences.**

A Preferences dialog box appears. Notice that the left side of the box displays different categories of settings you can adjust.

**3 Click the Advanced category.**

You see the options in Figure 4-1. Notice that the first option is named Automatically load images and has a check mark to its left to indicate that it's currently turned on.

**4 Click Automatically load images to turn the option off.**

The check mark to the left of the option disappears to indicate it's been turned off and that Web pictures will now be blocked from being transmitted to your computer. (***Note:*** Your setting will prevent Netscape from downloading any *new* pictures from the Web. If you go to a Web page you recently visited, however, you might still see the page's pictures; Netscape temporarily stores recent Web images on your hard disk so they can be redisplayed quickly.)

**5 Click the OK button at the bottom of the dialog box.**

Your change is saved, and the dialog box goes away. In addition, an Images button now appears on your Navigation Toolbar! (If you don't spot it immediately, look near the Guide button.) Now move to a Web page to try out your new setting.

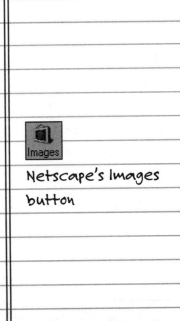

Netscape's Images button

**Figure 4-2:** When you turn off the Automatically load images option, Netscape substitutes a placeholder image for a Web page's actual pictures.

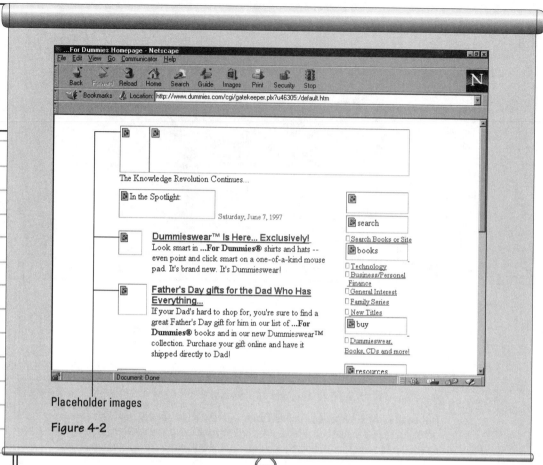

Placeholder images

Figure 4-2

Netscape's standard placeholder image

to force transmission of Web page's images, click Images button or choose View→ Show Images

**6  Click anywhere inside Netscape's Location box.**

The text inside the box is highlighted.

**7  Type the URL** www.dummies.com.

The highlighted text is replaced by your URL.

**8  Press Enter.**

You move to the home page of Dummies Press, an imprint of IDG Books Worldwide that publishes many wonderful books (including, by a remarkable coincidence, the one you're reading!). Notice that the Web page was transferred to your computer unusually quickly. Also notice that no graphics are on the page except for a standard placeholder image that Netscape substitutes for the page's actual pictures (as shown in Figure 4-2).

**9  Click the Images button (or choose View⇨Sho̲w Images).**

The Web page is retransmitted, but this time with its pictures included. Unless you have a very fast system, the data transfer takes noticeably longer to complete this time. On the other hand, the Web page is now much more lively and attractive (see Figure 4-3).

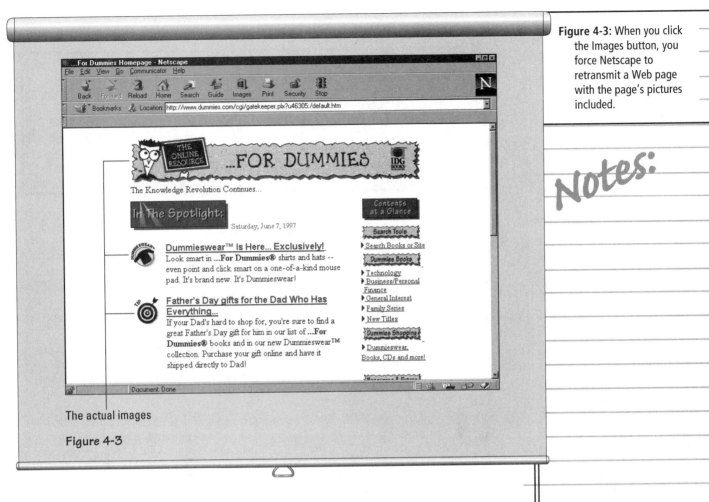

**Figure 4-3:** When you click the Images button, you force Netscape to retransmit a Web page with the page's pictures included.

The actual images

Figure 4-3

*Notes:*

**10** **Explore the Dummies Press Web site by clicking links that interest you; whenever you move to a page that you find especially intriguing, click the Images button to see the page's graphics.**

If you find that moving from page to page without having to wait for pictures to be copied over is a lot easier, consider keeping the Automatically load images option turned off in the future. To perform the remaining exercises in this unit, however, turn the option back on.

**11** **Choose Edit⇨Preferences, click the Advanced category, click the Automatically load images option, and click the OK button to turn automatic picture loading back on.**

The dialog box closes, and the Images button disappears to indicate that you're once again set to accept Web page pictures as well as text.

To sum up, the Automatically load images command lets you choose between the pleasure of Web graphics and the pleasure of speedy cruising. Which you opt for depends in part on the reason that you're using the Web — for example, pictures aren't as important for research as they are for entertainment — and on just how exasperated you are by the amount of time Web pages take to appear on your screen. If you *do* decide to run with the Automatically load images option turned off, don't forget that you can still display the pictures on a Web page by clicking the Images button.

extra credit

## Displaying a single picture

Sometimes you aren't interested in seeing *all* the pictures on a Web page, but just a *particular* picture. Rather than click the Images button and wait for the whole page to be retransmitted, you can simply click the placeholder for the picture you're curious about. Doing so causes the data for that single picture to be transmitted, which typically takes much less time than reloading the entire page.

## Using multiple browsers

People say that two heads are better than one. After reading this section, you may decide that the same is true of browsers! That's because you can increase your efficiency by using two (or more) Netscape browser windows at the same time.

Running multiple browsers allows you to study the information on one Web page while Web data is being transferred in the background to a different Netscape window. It also lets you switch between several Web pages without having to wait for any of the pages to reload.

**on the test**

Opening a new browser is a snap; just choose File⇨New⇨Navigator Window, or press Ctrl+N or ⌘N. You can do so as often as you like (up to the limits of your computer's memory); but it's generally best to avoid running more than two or three browsers at a time to avoid confusion.

After you open your browser windows, you can quickly switch between them by using the *Component Bar,* which resides in the lower-right corner of virtually every Netscape window and houses icons for Netscape's four major programs. The first icon in the bar is named Navigator, and clicking it when you're running only one browser window makes Netscape open a second window — in other words, it has the same effect as choosing File⇨New⇨ Navigator Window. If you have two or more browser windows open, however, clicking the Navigator icon switches you from one browser window to another.

To explore the advantages of using multiple browser windows, follow these steps:

**1    If you aren't still connected to the Internet, dial in again now.**

Your Netscape browser window should be open and displaying a Web page. If you're running Windows 95, notice that the Netscape Communicator icon (a ship's navigation wheel) appears as a button on the Window 95 Taskbar to represent your current window.

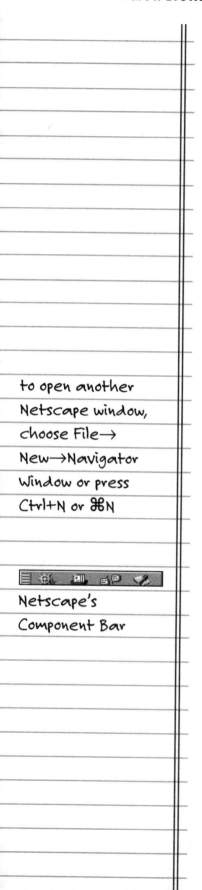

to open another
Netscape window,
choose File→
New→Navigator
Window or press
Ctrl+N or ⌘N

Netscape's
Component Bar

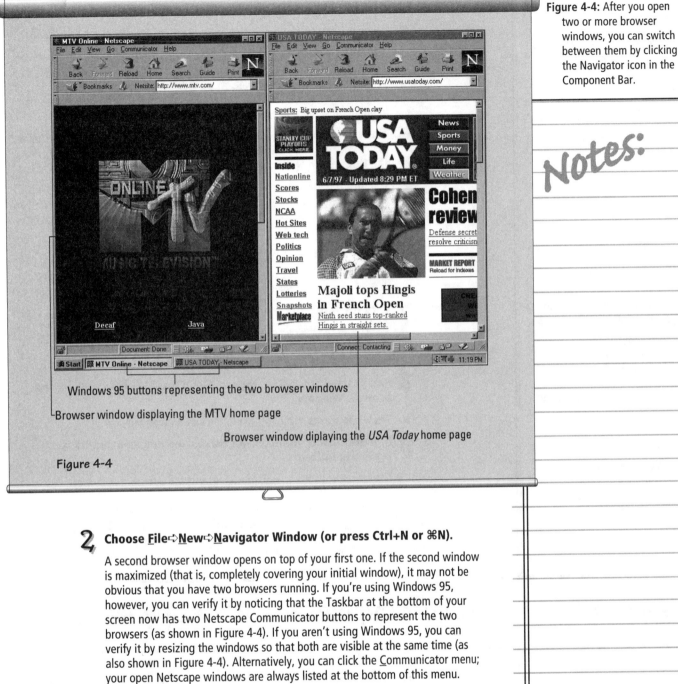

*Notes:*

**Figure 4-4:** After you open two or more browser windows, you can switch between them by clicking the Navigator icon in the Component Bar.

Windows 95 buttons representing the two browser windows

Browser window displaying the MTV home page

Browser window diplaying the *USA Today* home page

Figure 4-4

**2** **Choose File⇨New⇨Navigator Window (or press Ctrl+N or ⌘N).**

A second browser window opens on top of your first one. If the second window is maximized (that is, completely covering your initial window), it may not be obvious that you have two browsers running. If you're using Windows 95, however, you can verify it by noticing that the Taskbar at the bottom of your screen now has two Netscape Communicator buttons to represent the two browsers (as shown in Figure 4-4). If you aren't using Windows 95, you can verify it by resizing the windows so that both are visible at the same time (as also shown in Figure 4-4). Alternatively, you can click the Communicator menu; your open Netscape windows are always listed at the bottom of this menu.

**3** **Access the home page of *USA Today* (which gives you the day's news) by clicking anywhere inside Netscape's Location box, typing the URL** www.usatoday.com, **and pressing Enter.**

In your second browser window, you move to the *USA Today* Web site.

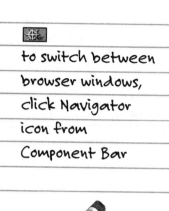

to switch between
browser windows,
click Navigator
icon from
Component Bar

☑ **Progress Check**

If you can do the following,
you've mastered this lesson:

❑ Prevent Web page
pictures from being
transmitted.

❑ Use the Images button to
receive Web page
pictures.

❑ Open and use multiple
Netscape browser
windows.

**4** **Click the Navigator icon, which is the first icon in the Component Bar (the bar in the lower-right corner of the window).**

You switch to your first browser window, which still displays your initial Web page, proving that your two Netscape windows are operating independently of each other. Now that you have two browser windows open, you can read the information in one while transferring Web data to the other.

**5** **Access the home page of MTV (a Web site that typically contains a lot of graphics) by clicking inside Netscape's Location box, typing the URL www.mtv.com, and pressing Enter.**

Your first browser connects to the MTV site and begins transmitting its Web page data. MTV typically crams lots of pictures on its pages, though, so instead of waiting for the process to complete, make good use of your time by switching to your second browser window.

**6** **Click the Navigator icon from the Component Bar.**

The *USA Today* home page is displayed again. Spend a minute or two scrolling through the page to read today's headlines and see what articles are available.

**7** **Click the Navigator icon from the Component Bar.**

You should see the complete MTV home page. While you were reading today's news, all the data on this Web page was transmitted in the background. Examine the MTV page until you're ready to exit it.

**8** **Press Ctrl+W or ⌘W (or choose File⇨Close) to close your second browser window.**

The window exits, returning you to the first browser window.

**9** **If your browser window isn't maximized any longer, click its Maximize button.**

The window fills the screen, providing you with a large Web display.

This exercise demonstrates only one use of multiple browsers. As you become comfortable juggling several browser windows simultaneously, you're likely to find additional uses suited to your particular work habits that help you save time and avoid frustrating waits.

---

**Lesson 4-2**

# Adjusting Netscape's Appearance

Netscape is extremely flexible in the ways that it lets you display both itself and Web data. For example, you can hide and expand parts of its window, adjust how links appear, select different fonts and colors, and even choose to operate in a different language! This lesson shows you how to use such options to tailor Netscape's appearance to your personal tastes.

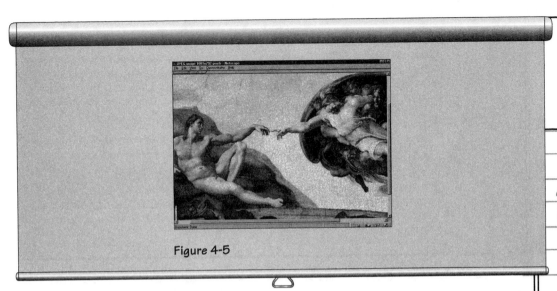

Figure 4-5

*Notes:*

# Hiding the browser window's Toolbars

Only about three-quarters of your Netscape browser window is normally available for displaying Web pages. The rest of the window is taken up by such elements as the Navigation Toolbar, which displays Netscape buttons such as Back, Forward, and Home; the Location Toolbar, which you use to type in Web page URLs; and the Personal Toolbar, which displays links you've created to your favorite Web pages.

on the test

Although these elements in your Netscape window are convenient, they are *not* necessities. That's because the functions they provide are all duplicated in Netscape's menu options. As a result, you may want to consider eliminating some or all of these Toolbars to make more room in the window for your Web page display. Here's how:

**1 If you aren't still connected to the Internet, dial in again now.**

Your Netscape window should be maximized and displaying a Web page.

Notice that Netscape's Toolbars are displayed near the top of the window. Also notice that a tab appears in the left side of each Toolbar.

**2 Click the left tab of the Personal Toolbar.**

The Toolbar collapses, hiding your personal links. Also, the Web page display expands to take advantage of the additional space you created in the window.

**3 Click the left tab of the Navigation Toolbar.**

The Toolbar collapses, hiding Netscape's browser buttons. Also, the Web page display expands again to take advantage of the extra space.

**4 Click the left tab of the Location Toolbar.**

The Toolbar collapses, hiding the Location box. Also, the Web page expands to take up most of the window (see Figure 4-5).

click leftmost area of Netscape window Toolbar to collapse or expand Toolbar

to open temporary
Location box, click
Open button,
choose File→
Open Location, or
press Ctrl+O or ⌘O

Running Netscape this way doesn't require sacrifices in functionality, because you can still access all the usual commands by using menu options. For example, instead of using a constantly available Location box, you can choose File⇨Open Page, or press Ctrl+O or ⌘O, to open a temporary Location box that exits after you type a URL and press Enter. As another example, instead of clicking the Back button, you can choose Go⇨Back or press Alt+← (that is, Alt and the left arrow key) or ⌘[ (that is, the Command key and the left bracket key). You can also do without the Search and Guide buttons (which simply take you to sites offering Web search programs or Web guides) and your Personal Toolbar buttons (which take you to Web pages you've personally selected) by creating a bookmark for each pertinent Web page and then using the Communicator⇨Bookmarks option. A complete list of Toolbar button equivalents appears in Table 4-1.

| Table 4-1 | Browser Toolbar Button Equivalents | | |
|---|---|---|---|
| **Toolbar Button** | **Menu Option** | **PC Keystroke** | **Mac Keystroke** |
| Back | Go⇨Back | Alt+← | ⌘[ |
| Forward | Go⇨Forward | Alt+→ | ⌘] |
| Reload | View⇨Reload | Ctrl+R | ⌘R |
| Home | Go⇨Home | None | None |
| Search | Communicator⇨Bookmarks and then click appropriate bookmark | | |
| Images | View⇨Show Images | None | None |
| Guide | Communicator⇨Bookmarks and then click appropriate bookmark | | |
| Print | File⇨Print | Ctrl+P | ⌘P |
| Security | Communicator⇨ Security Info | Ctrl+Shift+I | None |

| Toolbar Button | Menu Option | PC Keystroke | Mac Keystroke |
|---|---|---|---|
| **Stop** | View⇨Stop Page Loading | Esc | ⌘. (Command key+period) |
| Location: http://www.hotbot.com/ | File⇨Open Page | Ctrl+O | ⌘O |
| Personal  Toolbar | Communicator⇨Bookmarks and then click appropriate bookmark | | |

extra credit

# The Reload button

The one item on the Navigation Toolbar that we haven't discussed yet is the Reload button. As its name implies, Reload forces your current Web page's contents to be retransmitted, or *reloaded,* to your Netscape window. This button is useful because the Web transfers only a "snapshot" of a page at the moment you access it, so what you're viewing doesn't reflect subsequent changes that occur on the Web page. If you're connected to, say, a page of stock quotes that's updated every minute, you need to click Reload periodically to get the latest information from the page.

Another reason that you may be viewing old Web data is that Netscape uses a portion of your hard disk, called a *disk cache,* to temporarily store pages you've recently traveled to. When you tell Netscape to return to a page that you've visited, it checks its storage area and, if the page is

there, loads the page from your hard disk immediately instead of making you wait for it to be recopied from the Web. This is a great time-saver when you're accessing Web pages that don't change frequently. If you suspect that a page has changed since your last visit, though, clicking Reload makes Netscape check for changes and, if it finds them, retransmit the page from the Web. If Netscape doesn't find any changes, though, it reloads the page's contents from your disk cache. (***Note:*** If you want Netscape to skip checking for changes and immediately start retransmitting your page from the Web, hold down your PC's Shift key or your Mac's Option key before clicking Reload.)

Finally, if a Web page that you cruise to doesn't transfer properly for some reason, you can click Reload to make Netscape resend the page to your computer.

Although you don't *need* to include Netscape's Toolbars in your browser window, you may prefer having their options displayed conveniently in place of having a larger Web page display. Happily, you can always restore any Toolbar quickly by just clicking its tab again. Try it now:

**1   Click the third tab near the top of your window.**

The Web page display shrinks to provide some extra room in the window, and the Personal Toolbar reappears.

**2** **Click the second tab near the top of your window.**

The Web page display shrinks some more, and the Location box comes back.

**3** **Click the remaining tab near the top of your window.**

The Web page display returns to its standard size, and the Navigation Toolbar buttons reappear.

Whether you decide to devote a larger area of your window to the Web page display or accept the standard browser window is entirely a matter of taste. Therefore, simply choose a display that you're comfortable with and that pleases your eye.

## Rearranging the browser window's Toolbars

If you're using Windows, then in addition to deciding whether the browser's Toolbars appear, you can choose the *order* in which they appear. Even better, you can do so with just a few clicks and drags of your mouse! Here's how:

**1** **Click any blank portion of the Navigation Toolbar (that is, the top Toolbar that displays the Back and Forward buttons); while holding your mouse button down, drag the Toolbar down as far as it will go and then release your mouse button.**

The Navigation Toolbar, which is normally the top Toolbar, slides down to become the bottom Toolbar!

**2** **Click any blank portion of the Personal Toolbar (which is now the middle Toolbar); while keeping your mouse button held down, drag the Toolbar up as far as it will go and then release your mouse button.**

The Personal Toolbar, which is normally the bottom Toolbar, slides to the top.

**3** **Click any blank portion of the Location Toolbar (which is now the middle Toolbar); while keeping your mouse button held down, drag the Toolbar down as far as it will go and then release your mouse button.**

The Location Toolbar, which is normally the middle Toolbar, slides to the bottom.

**4** **Click any blank portion of the Personal Toolbar again, drag it all the way to the bottom, and release your mouse button.**

The three Toolbars revert to their usual order.

So if you ever get bored with the way your Toolbars look, don't hesitate to give them a makeover. All it takes is a few mouse clicks.

Figure 4-6

**Figure 4-6:** Netscape's Component Bar lets you open a Navigator window, an e-mail Mailbox, an online Discussions window, or a Web page Composer window with a mouse click.

# Moving the Component Bar

**on the test**

One other element that you can move around is the Component Bar (shown in Figure 4-6), which you were introduced to in Lesson 4-1. This bar houses four icons, each of which you can activate with a mouse click:

▶ **Navigator:** Opens a second browser window or, if you've already opened multiple browsers, switches you from one browser window to another (as you saw in Lesson 4-1).

▶ **Mailbox:** Opens the Netscape Messenger window, which lets you receive and read electronic mail, and compose and send your own e-mail (covered in Units 5 and 6).

▶ **Discussions:** Opens the Netscape Message Center window, which lets you access both e-mail and newsgroup messages (covered in Unit 7).

▶ **Composer:** Opens the Netscape Composer window, which lets you create your own Web pages (covered in Unit 8).

In other words, the Component Bar provides you with a one-click method of accessing any of Netscape's four major program components.

The Component Bar typically resides, or is *docked,* in a Netscape window's bottom-right corner. However, you can move the bar anywhere on your screen by choosing Communicator➪Show Component Bar or by simply clicking the tab on the bar's left.

To experiment with moving the Component Bar, follow these steps:

**1** **Locate the Component Bar in the bottom-right corner of your browser window and then click the tab on its left.**

If you don't see the bar, choose Communicator➪Dock Component Bar to move the bar to its usual corner and then click the tab.

After you've clicked, the small, static Component Bar turns into a larger bar that floats above your current window.

**2** **Click any blank spot on the Component Bar's title bar (that is, the strip running across its top); while holding your mouse button down, drag the Component Bar around your screen.**

Notice that you can move the bar anywhere, including areas outside of your current window.

**Notes:**

**3**  **If you're using Windows 95, right-click the title bar; if you're using Windows 3.1, click the Control-menu box in the Component Bar's upper-left corner.**

A menu appears that includes the option Vertical or Horizontal, depending on the current orientation of the bar; and the option Always on Top which, when selected, keeps the bar displayed above all your other windows. (If you're on a Mac, you can make the bar switch orientations by clicking the button in its upper-right corner; the bar always floats above other windows when not docked.)

**4**  **Try out each menu option by clicking it; then restore each setting by reopening the Component Bar's menu and clicking the option again.**

You should see the Component Bar switch orientations from horizontal to vertical (or vice versa). In addition, when you turn on the Always on Top option, you should see the Component Bar remain visible no matter where you place it or what other windows you switch to.

**5**  **When you're done experimenting, return the bar to its usual size and location by clicking its Close button (or by choosing Communicator⇨Dock Component Bar).**

The bar returns to the Netscape window's bottom-right corner.

You'll be using the Component Bar in later sections of this book to access Netscape's other Internet programs. If you get in the habit of clicking the Component Bar frequently, you may prefer to have its larger, moveable version constantly displayed on top of all your other windows. Otherwise, you can still access it quickly by simply clicking it from the bottom-right corner of virtually any Netscape window.

## Changing fonts, colors, and other Netscape settings

on the test

In addition to rearranging the elements in your browser window, you can adjust how links appear, what colors and fonts you see in your Web display, which Web page pops up when you run Netscape — even which Netscape program is launched! You can revise any or all of these options by choosing Edit⇨Preferences and then selecting the appropriate settings category. To discover the many varied and astounding choices that Netscape offers you, follow these steps:

**1**  **Choose Edit⇨Preferences.**

The Preferences box in Figure 4-7 appears. Notice that a tree appears on the box's left side that's organized into settings categories and subcategories. Also notice that settings appear on the box's right side that correspond to the category currently selected.

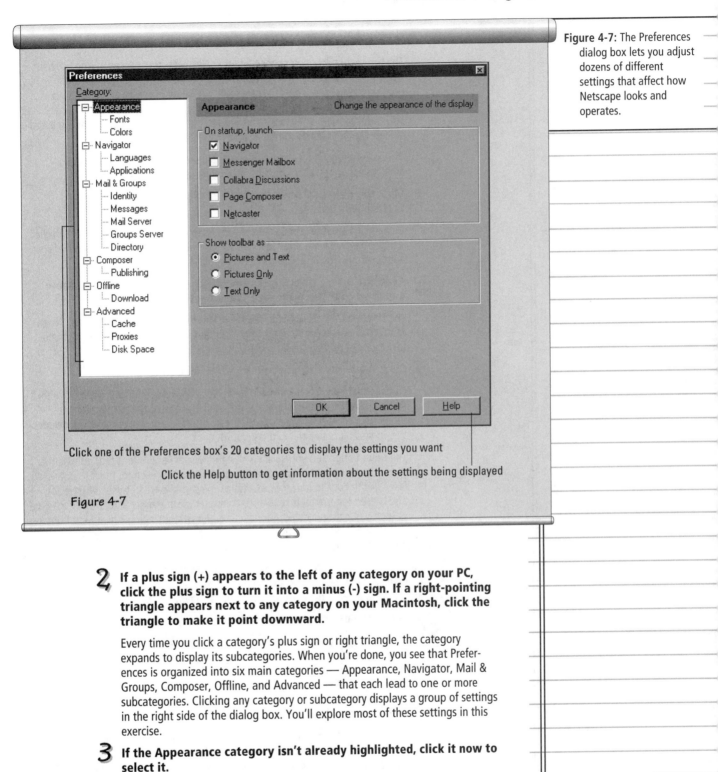

Figure 4-7: The Preferences dialog box lets you adjust dozens of different settings that affect how Netscape looks and operates.

Click one of the Preferences box's 20 categories to display the settings you want

Click the Help button to get information about the settings being displayed

Figure 4-7

**2** **If a plus sign (+) appears to the left of any category on your PC, click the plus sign to turn it into a minus (-) sign. If a right-pointing triangle appears next to any category on your Macintosh, click the triangle to make it point downward.**

Every time you click a category's plus sign or right triangle, the category expands to display its subcategories. When you're done, you see that Preferences is organized into six main categories — Appearance, Navigator, Mail & Groups, Composer, Offline, and Advanced — that each lead to one or more subcategories. Clicking any category or subcategory displays a group of settings in the right side of the dialog box. You'll explore most of these settings in this exercise.

**3** **If the Appearance category isn't already highlighted, click it now to select it.**

In the right side of the Preferences box, you see Appearance settings, which are divided into two sections (see Figure 4-7).

*Notes:*

The top section lets you choose whether Netscape starts up as a Web browser (Navigator, which is the default), an e-mail window (Messenger Mailbox, a program covered in Unit 5), a newsgroup window (Collabra Discussions, a program covered in Unit 7), a Web page editor (Page Composer, a program covered in Unit 8), an information broadcaster (Netcaster, a program discussed in Unit CD-5), or some combination of the five.

The bottom section lets you display the Netscape Toolbars as all text or all pictures, or both text and pictures (which is the default).

**4** **Click the Help button in the bottom-right corner of the Preferences box.**

Detailed information about the current group of settings appears. You can click Help while displaying any settings category, so be sure to do so whenever you aren't certain how to use a particular option.

**5** **Read the information that currently appears in the Help window and then click the window's Close button.**

The Help window disappears, returning you to the Appearance settings. Now that you understand the options in this dialog box, adjust the settings to your tastes or simply leave them as they are.

**6** **Click the Fonts category on the Category tree.**

Options that let you select which fonts Netscape uses to display Web page text appear. The top option lets you select the language of the font letters and offers such choices as Japanese, Chinese, Korean, and Western (which includes the English alphabet and is the default).

The other options let you select a Variable Width Font (a font that adjusts the spaces between letters to enhance readability and is used for most text) and a Fixed Width Font (a font that maintains the same space between each letter and is used for special text such as computer programming code). For each type of font, you can specify the font's name (the defaults being Times New Roman and Courier New, respectively) and size (the defaults being 12 points and 10 points, respectively).

Click inside each box you're interested in to drop down a list of choices and then click the new setting that you want to try. On the other hand, if you're comfortable with the current font settings, simply let them stand.

**7** **Click the Colors category on the Category tree.**

Options appear that let you choose the Text and Background colors of your Netscape windows, the default being whatever colors Windows is set to (on a PC) or black text against a gray background (on a Mac). You can also tell Netscape whether to always use your colors or to accept the colors of documents you encounter that already have their own color scheme (such as Web pages on the Net), which is the default.

In addition, you can select the colors that Netscape uses to display links you haven't clicked (the default is blue) and links you have clicked (the default is purple); and you can select whether links appear as underlined (which is the default). Make any changes that you want or leave the settings as they are.

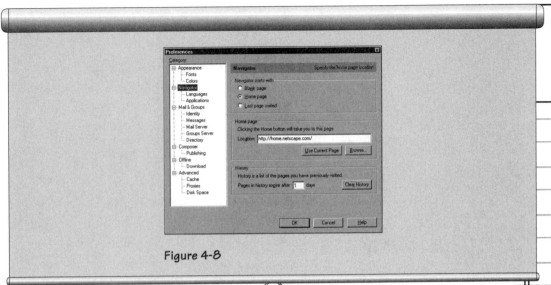

Figure 4-8

**Figure 4-8:** The Preferences box's Navigator settings let you specify which Web page you go to when you start Netscape.

**8 Click the Navigator category on the Category tree.**

You see settings that are divided into three sections (as shown in Figure 4-8).

The top section lets you choose whether the browser window starts off by displaying a blank page, the last Web page you visited, or the assigned home page (which is the default).

The middle section lets you specify the URL to use for your browser's home page — in other words, the Web page that you'll normally go to when you start Netscape! Unless your Internet provider changed it, the default is `http://home.netscape.com/`, which is the URL for the Netscape Communications home page. If you're not happy with that, you can double-click anywhere inside the Location text box and then type in the URL of your favorite Web page instead.

Lastly, the bottom section lets you set the number of days that the History window will store the URLs of Web pages you've visited before deleting them (the default being one day). This section also lets you purge the contents of the History window immediately by clicking a Clear History button (on a PC) or Expire Now button (on a Mac). Make any changes that you desire, or leave the settings alone.

**9 Click the Languages category on the Category tree.**

You're asked to specify which languages Netscape should display (that is, in addition to the one you're using). This feature is useful if you expect to access Web pages written in other languages. If you want to learn more about this feature, click the Help button, read the detailed explanation, and then click the Help box's Close button.

The next two major settings categories, Mail & Groups and Composer, deal with programs that you'll learn about in Units 5 through 8. We recommend that you return to these categories after you've read those units, but for now skip to the Offline category.

**Figure 4-9:** The Preferences box's Advanced settings let you control whether Netscape automatically loads Web images, runs Java and JavaScript programs, and allows data about your Web page choices to be saved to your hard disk.

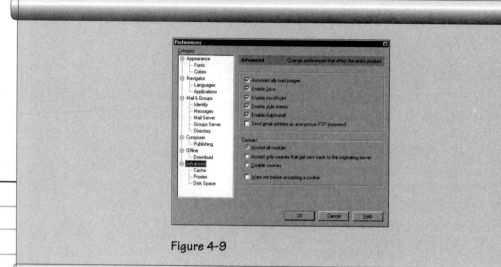

Figure 4-9

Notes:

## 10 Click the Offline category on the Category tree.

You're given the option of having Netscape automatically try to connect to the Internet every time you run it (Online Work Mode), never automatically connect (Offline Work Mode), or ask you each time it's launched whether you want to connect right away or not (Ask Me). If you're in the habit of connecting to the Internet and then running Netscape, accept the Online Work Mode option, which is the default. If you prefer to first work offline with Netscape and then connect to the Net, click Offline Work Mode (which requires you to choose File⇨Go Online when you're ready to connect), or choose the Ask Me option (which pops up a dialog box every time you run Netscape asking whether you want to connect right away or first work offline).

## 11 Click the Advanced category on the Category tree.

You see the options in Figure 4-9. As explained in Lesson 4-1, the first option in this category lets you turn automatic image loading off or on.

The next three options let you control Netscape's ability to run *Java* and *JavaScript,* which are the main programming languages used on the Internet, and *style sheets,* which is a related feature that's new to this version of Netscape. The default is to allow Java, JavaScript, and style sheet programs to run automatically whenever you encounter a Web page that includes them, because they can make Web browsing a lot more fun. However, if you'd rather not be slowed down by such programs, or if you're nervous about the security aspects of having programs run automatically (even though Java programs have safeguards built-in), you can turn the Enable Java, Enable JavaScript, and Enable style sheets options off.

You're also asked whether you want your copy of Netscape to be automatically updated when newer versions become available via your office's local area network (a setting typically determined by your company's computer administrator) and whether your e-mail address should be transmitted automatically when you log on to a public File Transfer Protocol, or *anonymous FTP,* site. The latter is an old-fashioned type of site (created before the World Wide Web existed) that's devoted to transferring files.

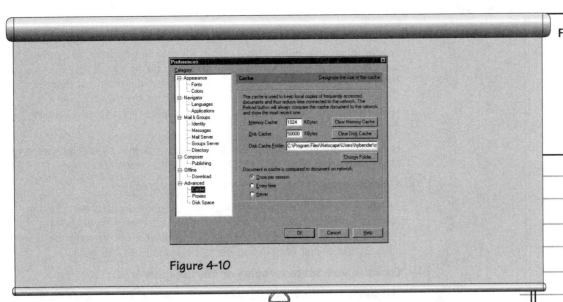

Figure 4-10

**Figure 4-10:** The Preferences box's Cache settings let you set the size of Netscape's temporary storage areas on your hard disk and in your system's electronic memory.

Finally, you're asked how you want to handle cookies. On the Net, *cookies* are small bits of information that help Web sites remember previous choices you've made. For example, if you were visiting an online mall, you might select several items to place in your electronic shopping basket but then go to another Web site to compare prices before actually making your purchases. Your first Web site would ordinarily store your shopping basket selections as cookies on your hard disk so that they'd be waiting for you when you returned to the site. Unless you're concerned about the security aspects of Web sites that you visit writing data to your hard disk, let stand the default selection of Accept all cookies. (Needless to say, this option is also the appropriate choice if you have a sweet tooth.)

**12  Click the Cache category on the Category tree.**

Options appear for setting the size of Netscape's *disk cache* and (if you're using Windows) Netscape's *memory cache,* which are both temporary storage areas (see Figure 4-10).

The *disk cache* is a portion of your hard disk that Netscape uses to store recent data, such as the text and graphics of the last few Web pages you've visited. Whenever you revisit a Web page, Netscape checks to see whether the page is already present in its cache. If it is, Netscape displays the page immediately from your disk instead of making you wait for the page to be retransmitted from the Internet. Unless you tend to visit Web pages that change frequently, we recommend that you allocate around 5000K — that is, around five megabytes — for your disk cache so that you can bring up previous pages quickly.

Similarly, the *memory cache* is a portion of your electronic memory that Netscape uses to store recent data. If you later return to the data, Netscape can retrieve it from its memory cache about five to ten times faster than from your hard disk, and many times faster than from the Net. Unless you have lots of electronic memory to spare, the default size of 1024K (which is one megabyte) will probably do fine.

*Notes:*

☑ **Progress Check**

If you can do the following,
you've mastered this lesson:

❑ Hide and restore
  Netscape Toolbars.

❑ Move and adjust the
  Component Bar.

❑ Pop up the Preferences
  dialog box.

❑ Adjust Netscape's dozens
  of different settings by
  using the Preferences
  box's Category tree.

Internet information may change between the time that it's stored in a cache and the time you next visit it, so you're also given the options of having Netscape check its cache data against Net data Every time (which is slowest), Never (which is fastest), or Once per session (which is the default). Even if you select Never, keep in mind that you can always update a Web page by clicking the Reload button.

Finally, you can click the Clear Disk Cache and Clear Memory Cache buttons to purge your caches of old data and start them from a clean slate.

**13 Click the Proxies category on the Category tree.**

Technical options appear for specifying how your computer is connected to the Internet. The typical setting is Direct connection to the Internet (which is the default). If you have a different connection, consult your office's computer administrator or your Internet provider for the appropriate settings.

**14 Click the Disk Space category on the Category tree.**

You see options that let you set the maximum size of e-mail messages you'll accept, when Netscape should automatically use compression techniques on message folders, and if and when Netscape should automatically delete old messages. These options are especially useful if you find yourself frequently running out of disk space.

**15 If you're satisfied with all the settings changes that you've made, click the Preferences box's OK button; otherwise, click the box's Cancel button to abandon your changes.**

The box closes and, if you clicked OK, your changes go into effect. If you aren't satisfied with the way everything turned out, simply choose Edit⇨Preferences again, adjust your settings as needed, and click OK again.

Wow! We haven't seen so many choices since Ben and Jerry started making ice cream! All these options may be a little overwhelming at first, but as you continue to work with Netscape, you'll probably come to appreciate the flexibility it offers. You can always simply accept the default settings — many people do — but if you find yourself dissatisfied with an aspect of Netscape's appearance or performance, don't hesitate to use the Preferences box to tailor the browser to your personal tastes and needs.

## Recess

You've just completed this book's course on the World Wide Web, and you've done it superbly! You can now impress your friends by slinging around intimidating phrases like *URL* and *Web link* and *Yahoo! Web searcher*, and by saying cool things like, "Hey dudes, wanna cruise on down to my fave home page?" Relax a spell by taking a long, leisurely walk, going for a swim, or riding your bike. When you're fully refreshed, fly through these quiz questions on fiddling with Netscape.

# Unit 4 Quiz

For each of the following questions, circle the letter of the correct answer or answers. Remember, each question may have more than one right answer.

1. **To access Web pages more quickly, you can**

   A. Lure the pages toward you with sweets.

   B. Say the magic words "open sez me" five times fast.

   C. Upgrade your system by adding memory, installing a speedier modem, and/or buying a machine with a faster CPU.

   D. Choose Edit⇨Preferences, click the Advanced category, and click Automatically load images to turn this option off.

   E. Type faster.

2. **If the Automatically load images option is turned off, you can still view a Web page's pictures by:**

   A. Wearing those crazy 3-D glasses that are now packaged with all new computers.

   B. Clicking the Images button.

   C. Clicking the Hubba Hubba button.

   D. Choosing View⇨Show Images.

   E. Choosing Images⇨Load Thousand Words.

3. **To open another Netscape browser window:**

   A. Buy another computer, install another copy of Netscape, place your second computer next to your first one, and go wild.

   B. Choose File⇨New⇨Navigator Window or press Ctrl+N or ⌘N.

   C. Click the Navigator icon on the Component Bar.

   D. Trick question; you can't open more than one Netscape window at a time.

   E. You *can* open more than one Netscape window at a time, but doing so makes your computer explode.

4. **Elements that you can adjust on Netscape windows include**

   A. The lace curtains.

   B. The Toolbars.

   C. The Component Bar.

   D. The Location box.

   E. The purple screens.

5. **The Preferences dialog box lets you:**

    A. Select the fonts that Netscape uses to display its text.

    B. Choose which Web page you move to when you start up Netscape.

    C. Choose which Netscape windows open when you start up Netscape.

    D. Set the size of Netscape's disk cache and memory cache.

    E. Change the Netscape logo's streaking comets to flying toasters.

6. **A new scene that appears in the revamped Star Wars trilogy is**

    A. Jabba the Hut walking and talking in the first film.

    B. Luke Skywalker initially blowing up the wrong Deathstar.

    C. Yoda reminiscing about his early days working for a furniture moving company.

    D. Han Solo revealing that he's really Chewbacca's father.

    E. Miss Piggy's light saber battle with Darth Vader.

# Unit 4 Exercise

1. Run Netscape and connect to the Internet.

2. Open a second browser window.

3. In the second window, prevent Web pictures from being transmitted automatically.

4. In the second window, eliminate the Navigation Toolbar and Personal Toolbar.

5. Cruise the Web by using your first window, then do the same by using your second window, and see which you prefer.

6. Enlarge the size of Netscape's disk cache and memory cache, and then cruise the Web again to see whether you notice a significant speed increase.

7. When you're done, exit both browser windows and disconnect from the Internet.

# Part I Review

## Unit 1 Summary

▶ **Preparing to go online with Netscape Communicator:** Make sure that you have the right equipment (primarily a fast computer, a 14,400 bps or faster modem, and a phone line to connect to the modem), sign up for an account with an Internet service provider, and get a recent copy of the Netscape program.

▶ **Starting Netscape:** Double-click the Netscape Communicator icon on your desktop or in your Netscape folder. If you use Windows 95, you can also click the Start button, choose Programs, click Netscape Communicator from the second menu that appears, and click Netscape Navigator from the third menu that appears.

▶ **Moving on a Web page:** Click the arrows, drag the scroll box of the vertical scroll bar, or press the PgDn and PgUp keys.

▶ **Identifying a link:** Move your mouse pointer over an area that's marked in some special way (for example, underlined text that's colored blue or purple) and see whether the pointer's shape changes into a hand.

▶ **Identifying a link's electronic address:** Point to the link and look at the message bar at the bottom of the browser window, which will display the link's URL.

▶ **Switching between a few Web pages:** Click the browser's Back, Forward, and/or Home buttons.

▶ **Switching between many Web pages:** Click the Go menu and click the page you want or press Ctrl+H or ⌘H to open the History window and then double-click the page you want.

## Unit 2 Summary

▶ **Using a bookmark to move to a Web page:** Click the Bookmarks button (on a PC) or Bookmarks menu (on a Mac) and click the bookmark you want. Alternatively, press Ctrl+B or ⌘B to open the Bookmarks window and then double-click the bookmark you want.

▶ **Creating a bookmark:** Move to the Web page that you want to bookmark and press Ctrl+D or ⌘D. Alternatively, click the Bookmarks button or menu and choose the Add Bookmark option. If you're using Windows, you also can drag the Page Proxy (the icon directly to the left of the Location box) to the Bookmarks button, position your mouse pointer in the folder where you want to store the bookmark, and then release your mouse button to add the bookmark.

▶ **Deleting a bookmark:** Press Ctrl+B or ⌘B to open the Bookmarks window, click the bookmark that you want to delete, and press Delete.

▶ **Organizing bookmarks:** From the Bookmarks window, choose File⇨New Folder to create new folders, click and drag bookmarks with your mouse to move them from one folder to another, and use the keystrokes Ctrl+C and Ctrl+V (on a PC) or ⌘C and ⌘V (on a Mac) to copy bookmarks from one folder to another.

▶ **Typing in and activating URLs:** Click anywhere inside Netscape's Location box to highlight the current text, type your URL to replace the text, and press Enter to move to the Web page located at the URL.

▶ **Searching for information on a Web page:** Choose Edit⇨Find in Page or press Ctrl+F or ⌘F to open the Find dialog box. Type an appropriate word or phrase in the Find what text box and then click the Find Next button until you locate what you're after.

# Part I Review

- **Searching for information across the Web:**
  Move to a page that lets you access a Web
  search program — for example, click the
  browser's Search button or go to this book's
  Searching the Web page at net.dummies.net/
  internet101/search.htm. Type an appropriate word or phrase in the program's text box
  and press Enter to generate a list of topic
  categories or Web pages.

- **Searching for a broad popular topic:** Use a
  category-based Web searcher such as Yahoo!

- **Searching for a narrow or obscure topic:** Use
  an open-ended Web searcher such as HotBot or
  AltaVista.

- **Searching via several different programs:** Use
  a "meta-search" program such as Savvy Search
  that plugs your text into several popular Web
  searchers and then gives you all the initial
  matches together on the same page and organized by program.

# Unit 3 Summary

- **Printing the contents of a Web page:** Make
  sure that your printer is ready to print, click the
  browser's Print button to pop up the Print
  dialog box, adjust any settings that you need to
  change, and click OK.

- **Saving the contents of a Web page:** Choose
  File⇨Save As to open the Save As dialog box.
  On a PC, click inside the Save as type box and
  click the Plain Text (*.txt) option (to save as
  text) or the HTML Files option (to save the
  "look" of the Web page); double-click inside the
  File name box to highlight the current text (if
  any); type the drive letter, folder name, and
  filename you want to use (for example,
  C:\WebData\HotNews); and press Enter. On a
  Mac, click in the Format box and click the Text
  option (to save as text) or the HTML Files
  option (to save the "look" of the Web page), use
  your mouse to switch to the folder you want,
  double-click inside the Save as box to highlight
  the current text (if any), type the filename you
  want to use (for example, HotNews), and press
  Enter.

- **Downloading a file from the Web:** Locate a
  link to the file and click the link. If the file
  begins downloading immediately, you're set. If
  an Unknown File Type dialog box appears
  instead, click the Save File button to open the
  Save As dialog box. Otherwise, the Save As
  dialog box will appear immediately. In either
  case, accept the filename in the Save As dialog
  box, switch to the folder that you want to use to
  store the file, and click the Save button.

# Part I Review

## Unit 4 Summary

- **Preventing Web page pictures from being transmitted:** Choose Edit⇨Preferences, click the Advanced category, click Automatically load images to turn the option off, and click the OK button. Repeat these steps to turn the option back on.

- **Receiving Web page pictures when the Automatically load images option is turned off:** Click the browser's Images button to receive all the pictures on your current Web page. Click a picture's placeholder to receive only that picture.

- **Opening additional browser windows:** Choose File⇨New⇨Navigator Window, or press Ctrl+N or ⌘N. You can open as many browser windows as you want (up to the limits of your computer's memory).

- **Switching between multiple browser windows:** Click the Navigator icon, which is the first icon in the Component Bar that typically resides in the lower-right corner of every Netscape window. Alternatively, click the window that you want from the list at the bottom of the Communicator menu; or simply click each window directly.

- **Eliminating Toolbars:** Click the tab at the left edge of any Netscape Toolbar to hide the toolbar. Click the tab again to make the Toolbar reappear.

- **Moving the Component Bar:** Click the tab at the left edge of the Component Bar to make it expand and float above windows. On a PC, right-click the title bar to display various options; on a Mac, click the Zoom box to switch the Component Bar from vertical to horizontal. Click its Close button to return the Component Bar to its usual spot in the lower-right corner. Alternatively, choose Communicator⇨ Show Component Bar to expand it and choose Communicator⇨Dock Component Bar to return it to its corner.

- **Forcing the current Web page to be retransmitted:** Click the Reload button or choose View⇨Reload to update the page. Hold down the Shift key (on a PC) or Option key (on a Mac) while clicking the Reload button to force Netscape to skip checking whether changes have occurred and immediately start retransmitting the page from the Web.

- **Adjusting various Netscape settings:** Choose Edit⇨Preferences to bring up the Preferences dialog box and click any plus (+) sign or right-pointing triangle that appears next to any of the six main categories you're interested in to display the subcategories. Click a category that you're after to display its settings in the right side of the dialog box, and adjust whatever settings you want to change. (If you aren't sure what a setting does, click the Help button.) Continue clicking categories and changing settings until you're satisfied; then click the OK button to save your changes and close the dialog box.

# Part I Test

The questions on this test cover all the material presented in Part 1, Units 1-4.

## True    False

T    F    1. Netscape Communicator combines several programs in one, including a Web browser (Navigator), an e-mail manager (Messenger), a newsgroup reader (Collabra), and a Web page editor (Composer).

T    F    2. Popular national Internet service providers include AT&T WebNet, America CruiseLine, and CompuSurf.

T    F    3. The World Wide Web didn't even exist until 1990, but it now provides access to tens of millions of Web pages from around the globe.

T    F    4. To find a link on a Web page, click Netscape's Find button, type **link**, and press Enter.

T    F    5. To use a link, simply click it. Netscape will then use the link's URL to move you to the appropriate Web page.

T    F    6. If you want to return to your current Web page during future sessions, you can create a bookmark for it by pressing Ctrl+D or ⌘D, choosing the Add Bookmark option, or (on a PC) dragging the Page Proxy icon to the Bookmarks button.

T    F    7. You can get information about virtually any subject by using a Web search program to list sites that cover the subject.

T    F    8. If you don't mind skipping the pictures, you can move to Web pages more quickly by choosing Edit⇨Preferences, clicking the Advanced category, and clicking Automatically load images to turn the option off.

T    F    9. You can run no more than three browser windows at the same time.

T    F    10. The Component Bar lets you access any of Netscape's four major programs with a mouse click via its icons named Navigator, Mailbox (for Messenger), Discussions (for Collabra), and Composer.

# Part I Test

## Multiple Choice

For each of the following questions, circle the correct answer or answers. Remember, each question may have more than one right answer.

11. **Netscape Communicator allows you to:**

    A. Cruise the colorful and fascinating World Wide Web.

    B. Find information about virtually any topic in minutes.

    C. Send e-mail messages to and receive e-mail from friends and colleagues around the globe.

    D. Participate in any of thousands of ongoing discussion groups covering virtually every topic under the sun.

    E. All of the above.

12. **The World Wide Web:**

    A. Was predicted by HAL 2000 in the film *2001: A Space Odyssey*.

    B. Is run by an international committee headed by the Duke of URL.

    C. Is just another name for the Internet, and the two terms can be used interchangeably.

    D. Is a subset of the Internet, along with other Internet features such as electronic mail and newsgroups.

    E. Is owned by no one and available to virtually everyone, which is why the Web is so chaotic, enormous, and fascinating.

13. **Links:**

    A. Was the character played by Clarence Williams III on *The Mod Squad*.

    B. Display URLs in the message bar when you point to them.

    C. Was the symbol used in the 1950s to identify Iron Curtain Web sites.

    D. Are a great tool for rambling around the Web and discovering pages that you might not have even thought to look for.

    E. Is a wild cat inhabiting the northern U.S. that has thick soft fur, a short tail, and tufted ears.

14. **The best way to handle the vast amount of information on the Web is to:**

    A. Hide your head under the blankets and hope it all goes away.

    B. Tell endless stories about the good old days when people just watched TV.

    C. Stay on the Web every waking hour so that you miss as little as possible.

    D. Save it all to disk because tomorrow it may be gone.

    E. Take what you can use and let the rest go by.

15. **If you want to preserve a Web page, you can**

    A. Print it.

    B. Save it to disk as a text file.

    C. Save it to disk as an HTML file.

    D. Print it or save it but not both.

    E. Rub moisturizer on it daily.

# Part I Test

16. **Files that you can download from the Web include**

    A. Business programs such as spreadsheets, database managers, and presentation software.

    B. Fun programs such as games and educational software.

    C. Attractive pictures, including illustrations, paintings, and photographs.

    D. Sound, music, and video clips.

    E. Steel tools with hardened ridged surfaces used for smoothing, grinding down, and boring.

17. **You *can't* use the Preferences dialog box to specify**

    A. Whether links are underlined.

    B. Which colors to use for links.

    C. Which fonts to use for text.

    D. Which letter to display above the planet in the Netscape logo.

    E. Which Web page Netscape jumps to when you launch it.

18. **Famous personalities who probably would have used the Web if given the chance include**

    A. Cleopatra.

    B. Michaelangelo.

    C. James Joyce.

    D. Little Miss Muffet.

    E. All of the above; the Web is for everyone (though Little Miss Muffet would probably have been a little put off by its name).

## Matching

19. **Match the following Navigation Toolbar buttons with the corresponding commands:**

    A.      1. View⇨Show Images

    B.      2. File⇨Print

    C. (Print)     3. Communicator⇨Security Info

    D.      4. Go⇨Back

    E. (Images)     5. Edit⇨Search Internet

# Part I Test

20. Match the descriptions with the buttons on the Navigation toolbar:

A. Moves you to the next Web page.

1.  Home

B. Forces a Web page's pictures to be transmitted.

2.  Reload

C. Cuts off data being transmitted from a Web page.

3.  Forward

D. Returns you to your initial Web page.

4.  Images

E. Forces an entire Web page to be retransmitted.

5.  Stop

21. Match the following keyboard shortcuts with the corresponding feature:

A. Ctrl+D or ⌘D

1. Open the History window.

B. Esc or ⌘.

2. Open the Bookmarks window.

C. Ctrl+P or ⌘P

3. Create a bookmark for the current Web page.

D. Ctrl+B or ⌘B

4. Print the contents of the current Web page.

E. Ctrl+H or ⌘H

5. Stop transferring data from a Web page.

22. Match each navigator/explorer with the land he's best known for reaching:

A. Christopher Columbus  1. Moon.

B. Eric the Red  2. Florida.

C. Robert Edwin Peary  3. Southwest coast of Greenland.

D. Juan Ponce de Léon  4. America.

E. Neil A. Armstrong  5. North Pole.

# Part I Lab Assignment

Create your own list of cool Web sites by following these steps:

## 1. Run Netscape and connect to the Internet.

# Part I Lab Assignment

## 2. Peruse Web guides to uncover cool Web pages.

You can start with Yahoo's guide at www.yahoo.com/Entertainment/Cool_Links, Cool Central's guide at www.coolcentral.com, Netscape Communication's guide at home.netscape.com/home/whats-cool.html (which you can jump to by clicking the Guide button on the Navigation Toolbar and then clicking the What's Cool option), and this book's own guide at net.dummies.net/internet101/sites.htm. Preserve each list by printing it and/or saving it to disk.

## 3. Discover more Web guides.

Use some Web search programs, such as Yahoo! or AltaVista, or a "meta-searcher" such as Savvy Search. Again, preserve each list by printing it and/or saving it to disk.

## 4. Compile a list of the most promising-looking Web pages.

Study the paper pages and/or files you've generated to do so.

## 5. Investigate each Web page on your list by moving to it.

Visit each page by either clicking its link or typing its URL. If you decide that you like the page and will want to return to it in the future, create a bookmark for it.

## 6. When you've worked your way through your list, organize your new bookmarks.

Create a folder with the name of your topic and then move all your new bookmarks into the folder.

## 7. Visit some of the most interesting sites that you've discovered, and enjoy yourself!

## 8. After you've finished, disconnect from the Internet.

And give yourself a treat as a reward for mastering the World Wide Web.

Communicating via E-Mail, Newsgroups, and Web Pages

Part II

## In this part . . .

**N**ow that you know how to browse the Web with Netscape's Navigator program, you can explore the other key use for the Internet: electronic mail. In Units 5 and 6, you'll learn to use the Netscape Messenger window to compose and send e-mail, receive and read e-mail, reply to and file messages, maintain an electronic address book, and send and receive data files by e-mail. After you're through, you'll be able to transmit messages in seconds to friends and colleagues around the world for the price of a local call.

Another way to communicate with people on a global scale is by joining some of the tens of thousands of online discussion groups that take place in Usenet newsgroups. Unit 7 tells you how.

Finally, in Unit 8 we explain how you can communicate through the World Wide Web by creating your own Web pages. Using the Netscape Composer program, you'll learn how to create a home page for yourself and then spruce it up with headings, links, bulleted lists, and pictures. You'll also learn how to go about publishing your page so that it can be seen by the millions of people who cruise the Web.

# Receiving and Sending E-Mail

**Prerequisites**
▶ Running Netscape
(Lesson 1-1)
▶ Adjusting Netscape
(Lesson 4-2)

## Objectives for This Unit

✓ Setting up Netscape to send and receive e-mail

✓ Sending your first e-mail message

✓ Reading e-mail messages

✓ Replying to e-mail messages

✓ Forwarding messages

✓ Printing messages

✓ Deleting messages

✓ Following the rules of e-mail etiquette

Netscape is famous as a Web browser (as you learned in the first part of this book), but the single most-used Internet service is still e-mail. *E-mail* (or *electronic mail*) allows you to type messages on your computer, connect to the Internet, and send the messages to anyone with an Internet e-mail address. While you're connected, you can receive e-mail messages from other people. Netscape comes with an excellent e-mail program named *Messenger,* so you've already got everything you need to start sending and receiving e-mail.

In this unit, you'll set up Netscape to handle your e-mail. You'll then use the Netscape Composition window to create, spell-check, and send an e-mail message; and you'll use the Netscape Messenger window to read, reply to, forward, delete, and print messages.

use the Netscape Messenger window to send and receive e-mail

**Lesson 5-1**

# Telling Netscape How to Get Your Mail

## Notes:

ISP = Internet
Service Provider

server = computer
that provides a
service to a
number of people

POP server =
computer that
stores e-mail until
you collect it

SMTP server =
computer that
accepts outgoing
messages for
delivery over
Internet

Mailbox

to both open
Messenger window
and pick up e-mail,
click Mailbox icon
in Component Bar

Netscape doesn't require any unique information from you to browse the Web, because Web pages are a public resource that anyone can access. But your e-mail account is private; the only one who can use it is you. As a result, Netscape needs to know a few things about your particular account before it can handle your e-mail.

If you got your copy of Netscape directly from your Internet Service Provider, or *ISP*, the program may already be set up to use your e-mail account. Otherwise, we'll guide you through entering the necessary information yourself. Either way, by the end of this lesson, Netscape will be ready to receive and send your e-mail.

To do e-mail, Netscape needs four pieces of information. First, it has to know your e-mail address, which identifies your electronic mailbox, and your password, which is the secret code word that you use to *unlock* your mailbox. In addition, Netscape needs to know the names of two computers, or *servers*:

▶ The computer at your ISP that stores incoming mail for you to pick up. This is called a *POP* or *POP3* server, which stands for Post Office Protocol, Version 3.

▶ The computer at your ISP that accepts outgoing mail from you and sends it along to its intended destination. This is called an *SMTP* server, which stands for Simple Mail Transfer Protocol.

To find out whether your copy of Netscape already has the e-mail information that it needs, do the next exercise.

## Can Netscape get your mail?

The best way to find out whether your copy of Netscape knows how to get your e-mail is to try it! Follow these steps:

**1** **Run Netscape and connect to your Internet Service Provider.**

See Unit 1 if you aren't sure how. After the browser window opens, locate the Component Bar, which is typically in the lower-right corner of the window (as you learned in Lesson 4-2). The second icon in this bar is the Mailbox icon, and clicking it both opens the Messenger e-mail window and makes Messenger retrieve your e-mail.

**2** **Click the Mailbox icon, which is the little envelope-and-inbox picture in the Component Bar.**

Netscape tries to activate the Netscape Messenger window and collect your mail.

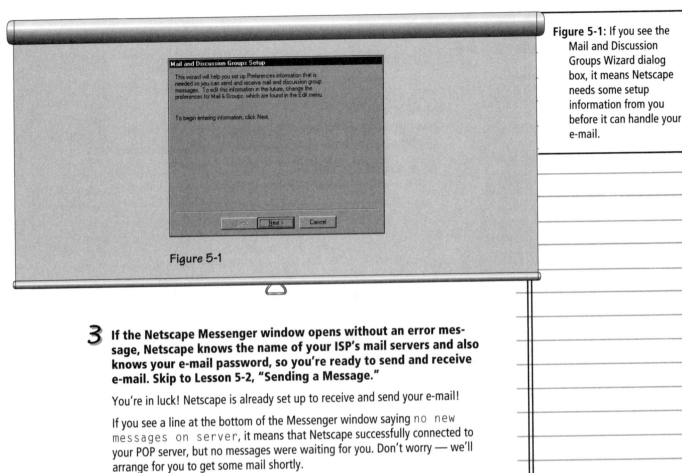

Figure 5-1

**3** **If the Netscape Messenger window opens without an error message, Netscape knows the name of your ISP's mail servers and also knows your e-mail password, so you're ready to send and receive e-mail. Skip to Lesson 5-2, "Sending a Message."**

You're in luck! Netscape is already set up to receive and send your e-mail!

If you see a line at the bottom of the Messenger window saying no new messages on server, it means that Netscape successfully connected to your POP server, but no messages were waiting for you. Don't worry — we'll arrange for you to get some mail shortly.

**4** **If you see a dialog box asking for your POP password, skip forward to the section "Telling Netscape your e-mail password."**

Netscape knows how to get your mail, but it doesn't know your password. If you don't remember your e-mail password, take a look at the information your ISP gave you when you signed up for your account.

**5** **If you see the dialog box in Figure 5-1, or if you see an error message, then Netscape needs some information from you before it can handle your e-mail. Click the Cancel button to make the dialog box go away or click the OK button to make the error message disappear.**

Netscape doesn't know how to contact your POP and SMTP servers, so you're going to have to tell Netscape their names.

**6** **Disconnect from the Internet while you obtain the information that Netscape requires.**

Hang up on your Internet account for now because you may need to use the phone line to call your ISP's technical support number. Leave Netscape running, though, because you'll be using it again soon.

Notes:

# Finding out where your mail is

If the dialog box in Figure 5-1 appeared when you tried to open the Netscape Messenger window, Netscape is missing information that it needs to check for mail on your ISP's computer. Don't panic! Here's the information that you need to get:

> ▶ **Your e-mail address:** The address that you choose (or are assigned) through your ISP to establish the name of your electronic mailbox. For example, if you choose the user name *janedoe* for an AT&T WorldNet e-mail account, your e-mail address is janedoe@worldnet.att.net. This means that everyone who wants to send you e-mail can do so by addressing messages to janedoe@worldnet.att.net; and all the e-mail *you* send displays this address near the top of each message to identify you.

> ▶ **Your e-mail password:** The secret code that, like a key, unlocks access to your e-mail account (so that you can pick up your messages and send messages) and simultaneously locks everyone else out of your e-mail account. Your e-mail password may be the same as the password that you use to log onto the Internet, or it may be different.

> If you don't already know your password, your ISP's staff may not be willing to tell you what it is over the phone for security reasons. (Makes sense — how do they know it's really you?) If necessary, they may mail it to you (using paper mail, of course), and you'll have to wait until you receive it to use e-mail.

> ▶ **Your Internet Service Provider's POP (Post Office Protocol) server:** The computer that stores your incoming mail; its name is a series of words separated by periods. Many ISPs use the word *pop* followed by the provider's Internet name, such as pop.sover.net for SoVerNet (Margy's ISP in Vermont). Others use the word *mail*, like mail.tiac.net for TIAC (an ISP in Boston).

> ▶ **Your Internet Service Provider's SMTP (Simple Mail Transfer Protocol) server:** The computer that handles your outgoing mail; its name is also a series of words separated by periods. Your provider's SMTP server may have the same name as its POP server; it's not uncommon for both server programs to run on the same computer. However, many providers use separate computers for incoming and outgoing mail; for example, the AT&T WorldNet POP server is named postoffice.worldnet.att.net, and its SMTP server is named mailhost.worldnet.att.net.

> ▶ Your Internet Service Provider's NNTP (Network News Transfer Protocol) server: The computer that stores the messages of Usenet newsgroups. (You won't use newsgroups until Unit 7, but you may as well get this information at the same time you're getting the e-mail data.)

You can probably find what you need by reading the information your ISP sent you when you signed up for an account. If you never received this information or can't find it, call your ISP and ask. Write down the answers in Table 5-1 and on the Cheat Sheet in the front of this book. Write your e-mail password on a separate sheet of paper and store the sheet in a safe place.

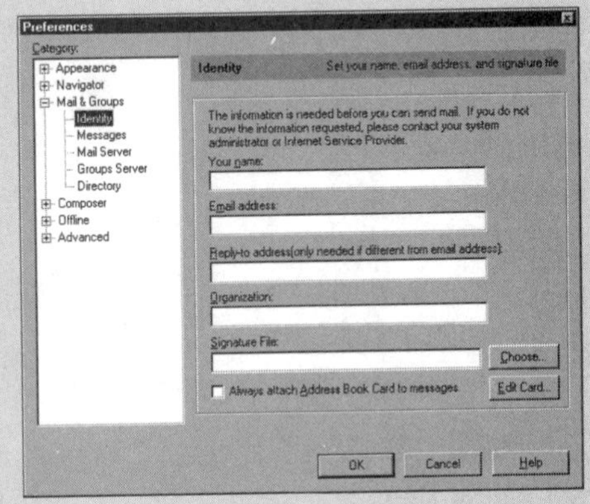

**Figure 5-2:** Use the Preferences box's Mail & Groups categories to enter your e-mail and newsgroup setup information.

Figure 5-2

### Table 5-1   Information from Your Internet Service Provider

| What You Need to Know | Write Your Information Here |
| --- | --- |
| E-mail address | _____ |
| E-mail password | (write on separate sheet of paper) |
| POP server | _____ |
| SMTP server | _____ |
| NNTP server | _____ |

*Note:* Don't try to use the POP or SMTP server of an Internet Service Provider for which you haven't established an e-mail account. If you do, you just end up with an error message.

## Setting up Netscape to handle your e-mail

Great! Now that you have all the information you need, follow these steps to set up Netscape for your e-mail account (refer to Table 5-1 or the Cheat Sheet at the front of this book as needed):

**1** If Netscape isn't already running, launch it now.

**2** Choose Edit⇨Preferences (the bottom option on the Edit menu).

You see a Preferences dialog box like the one in Figure 5-2. Notice that the left side of the box displays a Category tree with different categories of settings you can adjust. Also notice that one of the categories is named Mail & Groups.

*to set up Netscape to handle e-mail, choose Edit→Preferences*

**Figure 5-3:** Identify the
POP and SMTP
computers of your
Internet Service
Provider for handling
incoming and outgoing
e-mail.

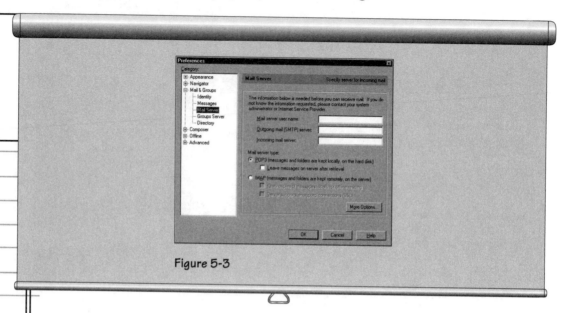

Figure 5-3

**3**  **If a plus (+) sign (under Windows) or a right-pointing triangle (on a
Mac) appears to the left of the Mail & Groups category, click the
plus sign to turn it into a minus (-) sign or click the triangle to make
it point downward.**

The category listing expands, and five categories appear under the Mail &
Groups category (as in Figure 5-2). For this exercise, you'll use the Identity,
Mail Server, and Groups Server categories.

**4**  **Click the Identity category.**

In the right side of the dialog box, you see the Identity options in Figure 5-2.
Notice that the first two text boxes are Your name and Email address. These
boxes will identify you to both your ISP and the people to whom you send
messages.

**5**  **Click anywhere in the Your name box and type your actual name;
then press Tab.**

For example, if you were Elvis, you'd type *Elvis Presley*. If you make a mistake,
press the Backspace key (on a PC) or Delete key (on a Mac) to correct the error
and then type the correct text. After you're done, pressing Tab moves you to the
Email address box.

**6**  **Type your e-mail address.**

For example, if you were Elvis and had an e-mail account with the Internet
Service Provider MindSpring, you'd type *elvis@mindspring.com*. Your name and
e-mail address are all the identification you need to provide here, so move on to
the Mail Server category, which lets you identify the computers to handle your
incoming and outgoing e-mail.

**7**  **Click the Mail Server category on the Category tree.**

You see the Mail Server options shown in Figure 5-3. The first text box is
labeled Mail server user name, which refers to the first portion of your e-mail
address.

*Notes:*

**8** **Click inside the Mail server user name box and then type only the portion of your e-mail address that appears before the @ sign; then press Tab.**

For example, if your e-mail address was elvis@worldnet.att.net, you'd type *elvis* for your user name. After you press Tab, you move to the Outgoing mail (SMTP) server box, which tells Netscape which Internet computer will handle your outgoing messages (that is, the e-mail you send).

**9** **Type the name of your Internet provider's SMTP server and then press Tab.**

You move to the Incoming mail server box, which tells Netscape which Internet computer will handle your incoming messages (that is, the e-mail you receive).

**10** **Type the name of your Internet provider's POP server.**

The next option specifies which type of server is used for your incoming mail. If you're using a standard e-mail account, POP3 should be selected.

You're also given the option of leaving copies of your messages on the server after you've picked them up. This option can be handy under special circumstances, such as when you're using a laptop that doesn't have enough disk space to store your messages, because it lets you read your mail right away but then reread it later from your desktop. Generally, though, this option should be turned off.

**11** **If the POP3 option isn't already selected, click it to make a black dot appear to its left; and if the Leave messages on server after retrieval option isn't already turned off, click it to make the check mark to its left disappear.**

This dialog box also has a button in its lower-right labeled More Options, which leads to additional choices — such as telling Netscape whether to remember or forget your password.

**12** **Click the More Options button.**

Extra options appear, including one that lets you choose which folder on your hard disk stores your e-mail and another that tells Netscape how often to automatically check for new e-mail messages (with the default being every zero minutes, meaning never check automatically). You can adjust these settings on your own later, if desired.

Notice that one option is named Remember my mail password. If you're the only one who has access to your computer, make sure that this option has a check mark on its left because it will spare you from having to type your password every time you want to pick up your e-mail or send e-mail. On the other hand, if you work with other people around and are concerned about them being able to read your mail when you're away from your desk, turn this option off so that anyone who wants to access your e-mail account must first type in the password.

**13** **If necessary, click the Remember my mail password option to turn it on or off; then click the OK button of the smaller dialog box to close it.**

Finally, enter the name of the computer your ISP uses to store Usenet newsgroup messages. (You won't work with newsgroups until Unit 7, but you may as well get Netscape set up for them now.)

**Figure 5-4:** Before you can pick up your e-mail messages for the first time, you must type your e-mail password.

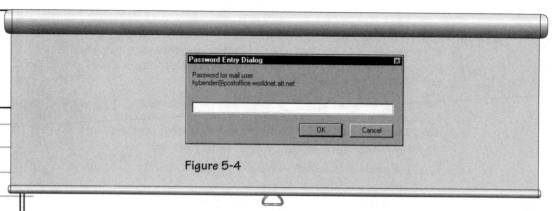

Figure 5-4

**14** **Click the Groups Server category on the Category tree.**

You see a text box named Discussion groups (news) server.

**15** **Click in the Discussion groups (news) server box and type the name of your Internet provider's NNTP server.**

Congratulations; you've finished supplying virtually all the e-mail and newsgroups setup information that Netscape needs!

**16** **Click the OK button in the Preferences box.**

The information that you've entered is saved, and the dialog box disappears. You're ready to try getting your mail again.

**17** **Connect to the Internet and then click the Mailbox icon from the Component Bar.**

This time, Netscape should successfully open the Messenger window. It should also successfully contact your Internet provider's POP server and try to get your e-mail. Before it can do the latter, though, it needs one more piece of information.

You should now see a dialog box asking for your password. Perform the next exercise to finish setting up Netscape.

## Telling Messenger your e-mail password

When you tell Netscape Messenger to get your mail, it connects to your Internet provider's POP server and transmits your e-mail name. However, it also needs to send your password. That's why the first time you connect to the POP server, you see a message like the one in Figure 5-4. If Messenger is set to remember your password (see Steps 12 and 13 of the preceding exercise), this is the only time that you'll need to type it in; Messenger will save the password in encrypted form on your hard disk and supply it automatically in the future.

Do the following to tell Netscape your password:

**1** **Carefully type your e-mail password, paying attention to lowercase and uppercase differences.**

As you enter your password, only asterisks appear so that anyone who may be glancing over your shoulder can't read what you're typing.

**2** **Click the OK button.**

Messenger tells the POP server your password. If you gave the right password, Messenger succeeds in connecting to the POP server and copies all your incoming e-mail to your computer. You see a list of messages in the upper portion of the Messenger window (you learn how to read them in Lesson 5-3). You're all set!

If you see a line at the bottom of the window saying `no new messages on server`, Messenger succeeded in connecting to your provider's incoming mail computer and checking your e-mail, but you didn't have any messages waiting. Even though getting messages is more fun, this is still good news — it means that Messenger is now ready and able to handle your e-mail.

**3** **If you didn't type the right password, Messenger repeats its request; try typing your password again and clicking OK.**

The asterisks can make it hard to type accurately, so retype your password slowly and carefully before clicking OK. If that doesn't work, try typing the password that lets you log onto the Internet (as opposed to the password specific to your e-mail account). If that doesn't work either, call your ISP to ask how to find out what your e-mail password is.

After you successfully type your password and click OK, Netscape is ready to tackle your e-mail.

> ☑ **Progress Check**
>
> If you can do the following, you've mastered this lesson:
>
> ❑ Check whether Netscape is set up for handling e-mail.
>
> ❑ If necessary, gather and type the setup information that Netscape requires to access your e-mail account.
>
> ❑ Click the Mailbox icon to open the Messenger window and pick up your mail.

# Sending a Message

Lesson 5-2

on the test

Now that Netscape is ready to do e-mail, the first thing we'd like you to do is to send us a message. Not surprisingly, when you send e-mail, you must know the *e-mail address* of the person to send it to. E-mail addresses look like this:

    username@computername

The *username* part is the person's user name on the computer system that he or she uses. The *computername* part is the name of the computer on which the person's mail is stored. For example, the product information department at Netscape Communications Corp. has this e-mail address:

    info@netscape.com

The user name is *info,* and the computer that stores the mail is named *netscape.com.*

on the test

To create an e-mail message, you use the Netscape Composition window. First, click the New Msg button on the Messenger Toolbar (or choose File⇨New⇨ Message, or press Ctrl+M or ⌘M) to open a blank Composition window. Next, type in the appropriate e-mail address, a subject heading, and the text of your message. After checking your message for errors (such as typos), click the Send button on the Composition Toolbar to transmit the

*e-mail address
format =
username@
computername*

Notes:

message to your ISP, which sends it out over the Internet to the party that you're trying to reach. In the case of your very first e-mail message, you're trying to reach us, the authors of this book!

In this lesson, you open the Netscape Messenger window, create a test e-mail message, spell-check the message, and send the message. You also learn the best way to get someone's e-mail address.

## Composing, spell-checking, and sending a message

To test that your e-mail is working, and to make sure that you have e-mail to read in Lesson 5-3, send a message to Internet For Dummies Central, where a tireless mail robot (a program that automatically responds to messages) stands ready to reply to your e-mail message. (Thanks to John Levine, King of the Internet Dummies, for providing this service!) The address to use is:

ncomm101@dummies.net

We set up this address especially for readers of this book!

**1** **Launch Netscape (if it isn't already running); you don't have to connect to the Internet yet.**

You're ready to open the Messenger window again.

In the previous lesson, you ran Messenger and retrieved your e-mail by clicking the Mailbox icon in the Component Bar. This "double action" is convenient when you want to check for new messages. When you simply want to create your own messages, though, you don't have to be connected to the Internet and so may prefer to just open the Messenger window (that is, without also picking up your e-mail). You can do so by choosing Communicator➪Messenger Mailbox or pressing Ctrl+2 or ⌘2.

**2** **Click the Communicator menu and the Messenger Mailbox option (or press Ctrl+2 or ⌘2).**

You see a Messenger window like the one in Figure 5-5. Notice that directly below the menu bar is a Toolbar containing buttons such as Get Msg (which tells Messenger to get your e-mail messages) and New Msg (which opens a blank window for creating your own messages).

**3** **Click the New Msg button (the second button on the Toolbar) to start composing a new message.**

Alternatively, you can choose File➪New➪Message from the menu bar or press Ctrl+M or ⌘M. After you do so, Netscape opens a blank Composition window like the one in Figure 5-6. The top portion of the window contains the header lines for the message. The bottom portion of the window will hold the text of your message. Your cursor is on the To line.

to open Messenger window without retrieving e-mail, choose Communicator→ Messenger Mailbox or press Ctrl+2 or ⌘2

to create new message, click New Msg button on the Messenger Toolbar, press Ctrl+M or ⌘M, or choose File→ New→Message

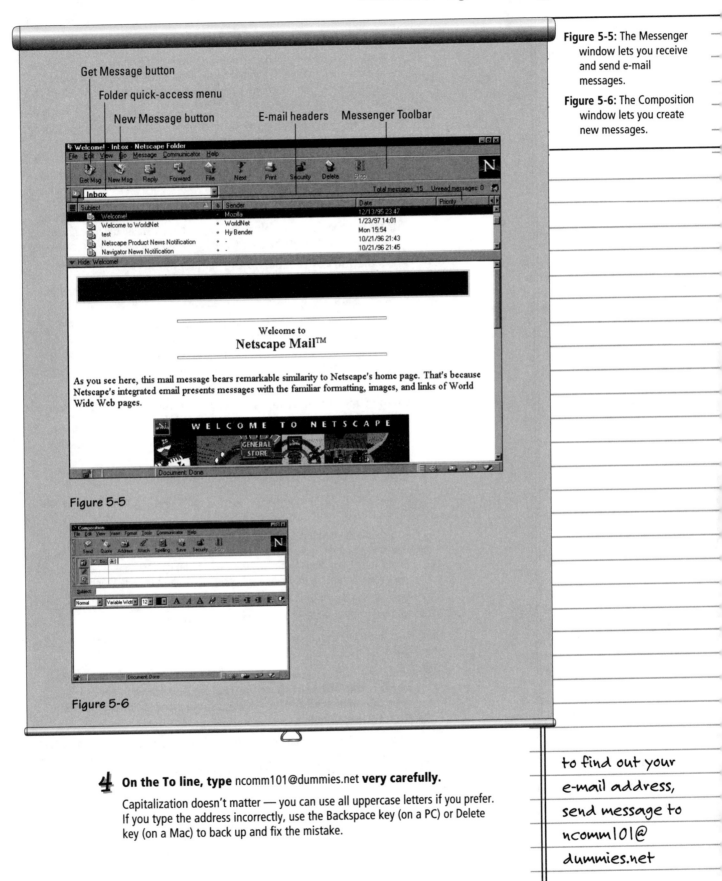

**Figure 5-5:** The Messenger window lets you receive and send e-mail messages.

**Figure 5-6:** The Composition window lets you create new messages.

Get Message button

Folder quick-access menu

New Message button    E-mail headers    Messenger Toolbar

Figure 5-5

Figure 5-6

4 **On the To line, type** ncomm101@dummies.net **very carefully.**

Capitalization doesn't matter — you can use all uppercase letters if you prefer. If you type the address incorrectly, use the Backspace key (on a PC) or Delete key (on a Mac) to back up and fix the mistake.

to find out your
e-mail address,
send message to
ncomm101@
dummies.net

Notes:

press Tab to move
to next header
line and Shift +
Tab to move to
previous header
line

press Enter only at
end of each
paragraph

Spelling

to spell-check your
message, click
Spelling button on
Composition Toolbar
or choose
Tools→Check
Spelling

**Note #1:** If you want to send your message to several people, you can type one address after another, separated by commas. Alternatively, you can press Enter after each address to create a new address line and type each address on its own line. You can create as many To lines in a message as you want.

**Note #2:** Not every address has to be on a To line. When sending a message to several people, it's common to place the main person you're addressing on the To line and to place others on a Cc line (*Cc* stands for carbon copy, and refers to a method of copying messages used back in the Stone Age). You can also put someone on a Bcc (blind carbon copy) line, which hides the person's e-mail address from the other people receiving the message. To change a To line to a Cc or Bcc line, simply click the To button to display a list of headings and then click the heading that you're after. Just as you can create an unlimited number of To lines, you can create as many Cc and Bcc lines in a message as you want.

**5** **Press the Tab key to move to the Subject line.**

You can always move to the next header line by pressing Tab and to the previous header line by pressing Shift+Tab.

Don't press Enter to move to a header line; rather than move the cursor forward, Enter creates an entirely new header line. If you press Enter by mistake, you can remove the new line by pressing the Backspace key (on a PC), or by clicking the line's icon to highlight it and then pressing the Delete key (on a Mac).

**6** **On the Subject line, type** Test Message **or whatever you'd like the subject of the message to be; then press Tab.**

This message is going to a mail robot, but we authors read these messages, too, so be polite. The cursor jumps to the message area.

**7** **Type a message to the mail robot and to the authors of this book.**

How about saying how you like (or don't like) this book? The message can be as long as you want.

Notice that the Composition window behaves like a simple word processor. For example, you don't have to press Enter at the end of each line — your cursor moves to the beginning of the next line as you fill up each line. As a result, you must press Enter only at the ends of paragraphs and to create blank lines.

Similarly, you can erase mistakes using the Backspace or Delete key, and undo your last editing change by pressing Ctrl+Z or ⌘Z.

Also, like a word processor, the Composition window lets you check your spelling. Try it!

**8** **After you're done writing your message, click the Spelling button, which is the fifth button on the Toolbar and shows a check mark over the letters *ABC*; alternatively, choose Tools⇨Check Spelling from the menu bar.**

A Check Spelling dialog box like the one in Figure 5-7 appears. If the Word box is blank and a Done button appears in the upper-right corner, the checker didn't find any questionable words. In this case, skip to Step 10.

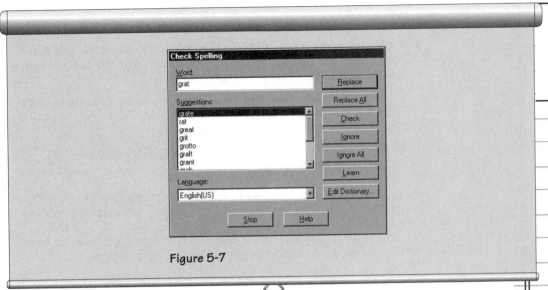

**Figure 5-7:** Use the Check Spelling dialog box to catch and correct your message's typos and misspellings.

Figure 5-7

**9** **Spell-check your message by responding to each word that the spelling checker doesn't recognize.**

When the checker finds a word that isn't in its dictionary (such as *grat* or *sykology*), it displays the word in the Word text box and also lists suggested alternatives (such as *great* or *psychology*).

If a suggested word is the one you want, click it to select it, and then click the Replace button to replace that one word. Alternatively, click the Replace All button if you want to replace *all* occurrences of the word in your message.

On the other hand, if you want to leave the word as it is, click the Ignore button (to skip over that one word), or the Ignore All button (to skip over all occurrences of the word in your message), or the Learn button (to permanently add the word to the spelling checker's dictionary). You can also simply click in the Word text box and edit the word manually.

**10** **After you've dealt with all the words flagged by the spelling checker, click the Done button in the upper-right corner of the dialog box.**

The dialog box disappears, letting you see how your message has been changed by the spelling checker.

There's just one thing left to do — send your message! You can do so byclicking the Send button on the Toolbar, by choosing File⇨Send Now, or by pressing Ctrl+Enter or ⌘Enter.

*Tip:* If you're not ready to send a message right away — for example, if you'd like to create several messages offline and then send them all simultaneously, or if you'd like to give a message more thought before shipping it off — choose File⇨Send Later. This command saves your message in an e-mail folder named Outbox. When you're ready, you can either send the message by connecting to the Internet and choosing File⇨Send Unsent Messages from the Messenger menu bar or delete the e-mail by switching to the Outbox folder, clicking the message to select it, and pressing the Del key (labeled *Delete* on a Macintosh).

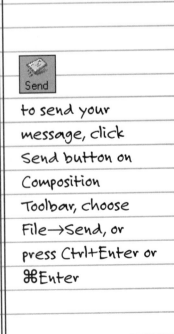

to send your message, click Send button on Composition Toolbar, choose File→Send, or press Ctrl+Enter or ⌘Enter

*Notes:*

**11** Connect to the Internet (if you aren't already connected) and then click the Send button (which is the first button on the Toolbar and has a picture of a flying envelope on it).

Alternatively, choose File⇨Send Now. Within a few seconds, you see a series of status messages flash by, such as `assembling message`, `contacting host`, and (finally) `mail message sent`.

Poof! Netscape has sent your message! The Composition window, having completed its job, disappears.

Congratulations! You just sent your first e-mail. It's pretty exciting, we must admit. But eventually, you'll want to send messages to other people besides us, and when you do, you'll encounter a variety of e-mail addresses. Taking a quick look at the structure of e-mail addresses is worthwhile so that you know what to expect when you start sending e-mail all over the Internet.

**on the test**

All the major online services as well as ISPs are connected to the Internet, so you can send e-mail to people with accounts on America Online, AT&T WorldNet Service, CompuServe, Concentric, IBM Internet Connection, Microsoft Network, MindSpring, Prodigy, and just about anyplace else. See Table 5-2 for how to write to friends belonging to some of the most popular national online services and ISPs.

| Table 5-2 | Internet Addresses of Online Services and Internet Service Providers |
| --- | --- |
| **Service or Provider** | **E-Mail Address Format** |
| America Online | Add *@aol.com* to the screen name; if someone has the screen name *SteveCase*, address mail to `SteveCase@aol.com` |
| AT&T WorldNet Service | Add *@worldnet.att.net* to the user name; if someone has the user name *Michaelangelo*, address mail to `Michaelangelo@worldnet.att.net` |
| CompuServe | Change the comma in the user ID to a period and add *@compuserve.com* to the end; if someone has the user ID *76543,210*, address mail to `76543.210@compuserve.com` |
| Concentric | Add *@cris.com* to the end; if someone has the user name *BruceWayne*, address mail to `BruceWayne@cris.com` |
| IBM Internet Connection | Add *@ibm.net* to the user name; if someone has the user name *BigBlue*, address mail to `BigBlue@ibm.net` |
| Microsoft Network | Add *@msn.com* to the user name; if someone has the user name *BillGates*, address mail to `BillGates@msn.com` |

| Service or Provider | E-Mail Address Format |
|---|---|
| MindSpring | Add *@mindspring.com* to the user name; if someone has the user name *RockNRoll*, address mail to `RockNRoll@mindspring.com` |
| Prodigy | Add *@prodigy.com* to the service ID; if someone has the service ID *ABC123*, address mail to `ABC123@prodigy.com` |

*extra credit*

# How to find out someone's e-mail address

You hear that your aunt has an e-mail address and you want to send her a message. Here's the best way to find out your aunt's address:

### Call and ask.

True, this method is neither zoomy nor high-tech, but it is by far the quickest and easiest way.

But what if you don't know your aunt's phone number or address? A number of e-mail directories have sprung up on the World Wide Web. Using the Netscape browser window, try searching for an e-mail address at such sites as WhoWhere (`www.whowhere.com`), Switchboard (`www.switchboard.com`), Four11 (`www.four11.com`), and Bigfoot (`www.bigfoot.com`).

## Exiting the Messenger window

When you're done sending messages, here's how to leave both the Messenger window and Netscape:

**1** **Choose File⇨Exit or press Ctrl+Q (on a PC) or choose File⇨Quit or press ⌘Q (on a Mac).**

Netscape asks whether you want to close all Netscape windows.

**2** **Click Yes.**

Netscape disappears.

**3** **If you're still connected to the Internet, follow your usual procedure to disconnect.**

Alternatively, if you're done with e-mail but want to keep using other Netscape windows, choose File⇨Close from the Messenger menu bar (or press Ctrl+W or ⌘W). The Messenger window closes, but any other open Netscape windows remain open.

---

### ☑ Progress Check

If you can do the following, you've mastered this lesson:

❑ Open the Netscape Composition window.

❑ Enter the e-mail address of a person to whom you want to send a message.

❑ Compose, edit, and spell-check the text of your e-mail message.

❑ Send your e-mail message.

❑ Exit the Netscape Messenger window.

*Notes:*

Now you know how to get in and out of the Netscape Messenger window — mission control for e-mail. And you've sent an e-mail message to Internet For Dummies Central. (You'll receive a reply in the next lesson.) Good work!

## Recess

You've sent your first e-mail out over the Internet. Take a walk around the block while your e-mail message winds its way back to you. First, though, if you haven't already disconnected from the Internet, consider doing so now. (Hanging up on your ISP is a good idea whenever you'll be away from your desk for more than a few minutes, especially if you pay by the hour.) When you return, you can reconnect to your Internet account.

## Lesson 5-3       Reading E-Mail Messages

Reading messages is a lot easier than sending them because you don't have to do any typing. When you receive e-mail messages over the Internet, your ISP holds them for you until you pick up your mail. It then copies the messages to your hard disk, allowing you to read the messages, compose replies, and file any messages that you want to keep.

To retrieve your messages, you can simply click the Mailbox icon in the Component Bar, which both opens the Messenger window and tells Messenger to pick up your mail. If you're already in Messenger, you can get your messages by clicking the Get Msg button (the first button on the Toolbar), or by pressing Ctrl+T or ⌘T.

*e-mail folder holds group of messages*

After Messenger gets your e-mail, it stores it in a *folder* — that is, a group of messages. Messenger comes with a folder named Inbox, where incoming messages wait for you to read them. Messenger also provides other folders, such as a Trash folder for messages that you delete and a Sent folder for messages that you've sent. In addition, you can create your own folders to organize your messages more precisely (for example, a *Joe* folder for storing messages from your friend Joe).

*folder quick-access menu lets you switch between folders*

You can list your e-mail folders by clicking in the *folder quick-access menu,* which is the box in the upper-left corner residing directly below the Messenger Toolbar. You can then switch to the folder you want simply by clicking its name. After you do so, the messages in the folder that you've selected are listed in the upper portion of the Messenger window. Finally, you can read each message by clicking it; the contents of the message appear in the lower portion of the Messenger window.

In this lesson, you use the Messenger window to download and read your mail.

# Picking up and reading your e-mail

Here's how to get your e-mail and read it:

**1** **Launch Netscape and connect to the Internet.**

**2** **Open the Messenger window by clicking the Mailbox icon in the Component Bar (which is typically in the lower-right corner of any Netscape window).**

Messenger opens and automatically checks your mailbox for new messages. While Messenger is retrieving your mail, messages flash by such as `contacting host` (*host* referring to your ISP), `host contacted`, `sending login information`, and (if you have mail) `receiving message`. When all your mail has been collected, the bottom line of the window tells you how many messages have been picked up — or, if you didn't have any mail, that there were `no new messages on server`.

In this case, you should have received a reply to the message that you sent in Lesson 5-2. You may have also received messages from anyone to whom you've revealed your e-mail address. (***Note:*** If you didn't get mail, you may want to wait an hour and try again. If you wait several hours and still don't receive a reply to your previous message, send a message to yourself and then work with that mail instead.)

After your mail has been collected, the Messenger window looks like Figure 5-8, with the first message displayed in the lower portion of the window.

**3** **If you want as much space as possible for reading your mail, maximize the Messenger window.**

If you're using Windows 95, click the Maximize button, which is the middle of three buttons residing in the window's upper-right corner. If you're using Windows 3.1 or a Macintosh, click the Maximize button or Zoom button in the window's upper-right corner. The Messenger window expands to fill the screen.

Notice the box in the upper-left corner residing directly below the Toolbar. This is the folder quick-access menu, which lets you switch among your various e-mail folders. It should currently display the word *Inbox,* meaning that Messenger is set right now to show the messages in your Inbox folder.

**4** **If the folder quick-access menu does *not* currently display the word *Inbox*, click anywhere inside the quick-access menu to list all your e-mail folders and then click the Inbox option to switch to the Inbox folder.**

The messages that you just received were filed in your Inbox, so you should see them listed in the upper part of the Messenger window (which is called the *message list*). You can tell how many messages are in the folder, and how many of those messages are unread, by looking at the numbers on the far right of the folder quick-access menu.

You can also scroll through the list of messages by clicking the arrows on the vertical scroll bar along the right edge. Notice that each message is represented by one line that tells you the message's subject, who sent it, when it was sent, and (if the sender bothered to set it) the message's priority. The messages you haven't read yet appear in boldface, with a green gemlike thingy between the Subject and Sender columns.

*new mail is filed in your Inbox folder*

**Figure 5-8:** New messages are stored in the Inbox folder and listed in the upper portion of the Messenger window. The contents of the selected message are displayed in the lower portion of the window.

The folder quick-access menu lets you switch among different folders and tells you which folder is currently selected.

The divider sets the size of the message list and message area.

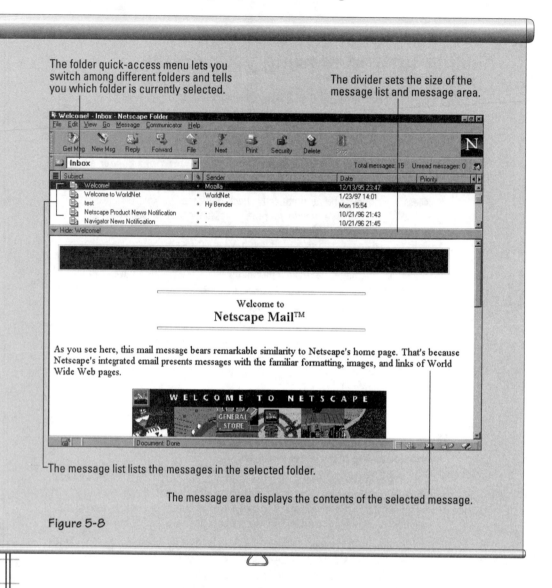

The message list lists the messages in the selected folder.

The message area displays the contents of the selected message.

Figure 5-8

**5** **Click a listed message that you want to read.**

The contents of the message appear in the lower portion of the Messenger window (which is called the *message area*). The message starts with header lines that tell you who the message is from, the subject of the message, and when your ISP received the message.

**6** **Click another listed message you're interested in (if you have another e-mail message).**

The contents of the message that you've selected replace the previous one in the message area. You can read any message you like by simply clicking its line on the message list.

If a message is longer than the message area, you can scroll through its contents by clicking the vertical scroll bar along the right edge. You can also click anywhere inside the message area to select it and then move through the message using your arrow keys or PgUp and PgDn keys.

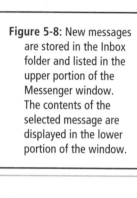

*to read long messages, scroll through message area using arrow keys or mouse*

**7** **For each message in your Inbox, first select the message from the message list and then read the message from the message area.**

When you reach the message that you received from Internet For Dummies Central, notice that it tells you your official Internet e-mail address, in case you weren't sure what it was. (And you know that the address works because this message arrived!)

*Note:* If you don't receive a reply from the mail robot, you may instead get a message saying that your mail was undeliverable. Such messages are generated automatically by your ISP's own mail robot whenever an e-mail address can't be located. Study the e-mail address that the message reports as being incorrect. If the address is something other than ncomm101@dummies.net, then repeat the message composition exercise in Lesson 5-2, making sure to get every character in the e-mail address exactly right.

**extra credit**

# Adjusting how the message list is displayed

Messenger gives you lots of flexibility in determining how messages are listed.

To list your messages in a particular order, simply click the appropriate header in the message list. For example, to sort your messages from most recent to least recent, click the Date header. To sort your messages from least recent to most recent (that is, the reverse order), just click Date again. You can follow the same procedure to sort messages alphabetically by Sender or Subject, or numerically by Priority.

You can also adjust the width of each header's column. To do so, click the divider at either side of the column and, while holding your mouse button down, drag the divider to make the column wider or narrower and then release your mouse button. (Alternatively, rest your mouse pointer over any text too big to fit into its column; in a moment, the entire text is displayed!)

You can rearrange the order in which the headers appear, too. To do so, simply click a header and, while holding your mouse button down, move it to where you want it. (Cool!)

You can even display more or fewer columns at a time. To do so, notice that two arrowheads are at the right end of the headers. Every time you click the first arrowhead, an additional column is added

to the display; each time you click the second arrowhead, a column is hidden (providing more room for the remaining columns).

Finally, you can adjust the size of the message list using the gray horizontal divider between the list and the message area. To expand the message list, click the divider and, while holding your mouse button down, drag the divider down. This also makes the message area contract, so you must balance having a longer message list with having a shorter message area. (To restore the divider to its default position, just drag it up as high as it will go.)

Alternatively, click the triangle on the left end of the divider (which, on a PC, is next to the word *Hide*). This makes the message area disappear entirely, allowing the message list to fill the Messenger window. To read a message, double-click it from the list; the message's contents appear in a separate window! Some people like this arrangement because it provides the maximum amount of space for both listing and reading messages. If you prefer the convenience of having the message list and message area in the same window, though, click the triangle that now appears in the lower-left corner of the window (or choose View⇨Show Message) to return to a standard display.

**Notes:**

☑ **Progress Check**

If you can do the following, you've mastered this lesson:

❏ Pick up your new e-mail messages.

❏ Read your e-mail messages.

to pick up e-mail
while in Messenger
window, click Get
Msg button on
Messenger Toolbar
or press Ctrl+T
or ⌘T

## Checking your e-mail from the Messenger window

If you've just launched Netscape, you can open the Messenger window and check your mail by clicking the Mailbox icon. If you're already in Messenger, though, you can check your mail by clicking the Get Msg button (the first button on the Toolbar) or by pressing Ctrl+T or ⌘T. Try it!

**1** **Click the Get Msg button on the Toolbar (or press Ctrl+T or ⌘T).**

Messenger contacts your ISP to collect your messages. The bottom line of the window tells you whether you have new mail.

**2** **If you have new messages, go ahead and read them!**

**3** **After you're done, close Netscape by pressing Ctrl+Q or ⌘Q.**

All Netscape windows close.

---

**Lesson 5-4**

# Replying to, Forwarding, Printing, and Deleting Messages

Some messages are destined for oblivion; others demand a reply or need to be passed along to someone else. In this lesson, you'll learn how to reply to messages, forward messages to other people, print messages, and delete unwanted messages.

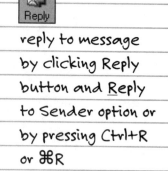

reply to message
by clicking Reply
button and Reply
to Sender option or
by pressing Ctrl+R
or ⌘R

quoted text
appears with blue
vertical line or > at
beginning of each
line

## Replying to a message

Personal messages deserve a reply, and composing one is easy. First, make sure that the message you want to respond to is selected. Next, press Ctrl+R or ⌘R or click the Reply button and click Reply to Sender. A Composition window opens that is already pre-addressed to the person who sent you the message. In addition, the subject text of the message is copied to the Subject line.

Also, the content of the message is *quoted* in the new message; that is, the text appears with each line preceded by either a blue vertical line or a > character (see the "HTML and e-mail" sidebar that appears later in this lesson). Quoting the interesting parts of the original text is a good way to help you and the person you are writing to remember what the heck you were both talking about. Deleting the boring parts or the parts to which you aren't replying is polite.

**heads up**

## HTML and e-mail

Whether you see blue lines or > characters when quoting a message depends on the format you're set to. The Composition window normally creates your message using a formatting language called *HTML*, which (as explained in Lesson 3-1) allows you to include special effects such as colors, fonts, graphics — and horizontal blue lines for marking quoted text. If this feature is turned off, the Composition window uses ASCII instead, which is a plain text format that can't handle special effects but that, unlike HTML, all programs understand.

You can turn HTML formatting off by choosing Edit⇨Preferences, clicking the Messages category (under the Mail & Groups category), clicking the By default send HTML messages option to turn the check mark off, and clicking OK. Keeping HTML formatting on is generally a good idea, however. If all you're sending is quoted text, the blue lines will automatically show up as > characters in e-mail programs that don't support HTML. And if you're sending e-mail that contains significant HTML formatting, Netscape will remind you that the person who will receive the message may not be able to handle HTML and ask you whether you want to transmit the message in HTML format, plain text format, or *both* (with the HTML message sent as a file that's attached to the plain text message).

To learn how to reply to an e-mail message, send a reply to the Internet For Dummies Central message.

**1** **Fire up Netscape and choose Communicator⇨Messenger Mailbox.**

You see the Messenger window.

**2** **If the window isn't already set to list the messages in your Inbox, click the folder quick-access menu and click Inbox.**

You see the messages that you've received, including the message from Internet For Dummies Central.

**3** **Click the header for the message from us, which says "Automated response."**

The text of the message appears. If you'd rather reply to a different message you've received, feel free.

**4** **Press Ctrl+R or ⌘R (or click the Reply button and click Reply to Sender).**

You see the Composition window again. Instead of a blank window this time, though, Messenger has created a new message addressed to us because you're replying to a message from us (the address is `Automated response <ncomm101@dummies.net>`). The subject of the message is the same as the subject of the original message, with *Re:* added to the front. (*Re* is short for the Latin *in re*, in case you were wondering, which means *about the thing*.) You can change this subject, if you like, by clicking in the Subject box and revising the text.

If you scroll up to the top of the message area of the new message, you see a line like this:

`Automated response wrote:`

Netscape thinks that you're replying to a message from someone named Automated Response, which is how our mail robot signs messages. Then you see the quoted text of the original message.

**Note:** If the quoted text of the message doesn't appear, choose Edit⇨Preferences, click the Messages category (under the Mail & Groups category), click the Automatically quote original message when replying option to make a check mark appear to its left, and click OK. This setting tells Netscape to always include the original message when you create a reply.

**5** **With your cursor at the top of the message area, press Enter once to leave a blank line and then type a message to us (such as *Thanks for the nice message*).**

While you're at it, tell us how long it took for our first message to get to you. (Days? Hours? Minutes? Just a rough idea is fine.)

When you reply to a message, deleting all but the interesting parts is considered polite. If the quoted text includes salutations, lots of blank lines, or other unnecessary text, eliminate the excess verbiage by highlighting it with your mouse and pressing the Del key.

**6** **Delete most or all of the original message.**

If you're replying to the message from Internet For Dummies Central, you can delete the whole message because we are already familiar with what it says.

**7** **Connect to the Internet.**

Now that you're ready to send your message, you'd better be online!

**8** **Click the Send button to send your reply.**

Netscape sends your message. In addition, it files a copy of the message in your Sent folder so that you have a record of your outgoing mail.

The next time you pick up your e-mail, you'll receive another reply from Internet For Dummies Central — our mail robot just can't leave a message unanswered!

Nice work! If you're like most people, you'll spend as much time replying to messages as you do writing new ones.

**heads up**

If you're replying to a message that's been sent to one or more people in addition to yourself and you want them all to see your response, press Ctrl+Shift+R or Shift+⌘R, or click the Reply button and click the Reply to Sender and All Recipients option. This has the same effect as the Reply⇨Reply to Sender command, except that it creates a message pre-addressed to *everyone* who received the original e-mail, not just the person who sent it to you.

## Forwarding a message

If you receive an interesting message or one that should really have been sent to someone else, you can easily forward it. Just select the message that you want to forward and click the Forward button on the Toolbar, choose

*(Handwritten margin note:)* include only relevant parts of original message in your reply

Message⇨Forward, or press Ctrl+L or Shift+⌘M. Netscape opens the Composition window. The message area appears blank, but the complete contents of the message you selected will appear when you send the message. The subject box contains *Fwd:* followed by the subject line from the original message. All you have to do is address the message and send it off.

Another way to forward a message is to choose Message⇨Forward Quoted from the menu bar. A Composition window appears with the contents of the original message in quoted format, and with a first line like *Bill says:* (with *Bill* being the name of the person who wrote the original message). By using this command, you can edit the message that you're forwarding, deleting the boring parts and inserting your own comments.

Try forwarding the message that you received from Internet For Dummies Central or any other message that you've received. You can forward the message to yourself (which doesn't make a lot of sense in real life, but it's a good way to practice).

**1  From the message list, click the message that you want to forward.**

Unless you have a better candidate, select the message that you received from us.

**2  Click the Forward button (the fourth button on the Toolbar).**

Or, if you'd prefer, choose Message⇨Forward, or press Ctrl+L or Shift+⌘M. The Composition window opens with a Subject line that says something like [Fwd: Re: Test Message]. The message area is currently empty, but the message you're forwarding will appear when the e-mail is sent.

**3  Address the message by typing your e-mail address on the To line.**

If you don't remember what your e-mail address is, look in the message that you received from us!

**4  Press Tab twice to move to the message area.**

You can type your own message to go along with the message you're forwarding.

**5  Type something like** Get a load of this!

What you type will appear at the top, followed by the contents of the message that you're forwarding.

**6  Click the Send button.**

Netscape transmits the message.

The original message is still sitting in your Inbox, in case you want to reply to it, forward it to someone else, or file it. (You learn how to file messages in other folders in Lesson 6-2.)

forward a selected message by clicking Forward button, choosing Message→Forward, or pressing Ctrl+L or Shift+⌘M

to print selected
message, click
Print button,
choose File→Print,
or press Ctrl+P
or ⌘P

# Printing a message

Sometimes you need to print a message to file in a manila folder, or to give to someone, or to carry around in your pocket. (Perhaps you just received a love letter by e-mail.) Printing your e-mail is easy — just click the Print button on the Messenger Toolbar, or choose File⇨Print, or press Ctrl+P or ⌘P.

Before you try to print, make sure that your printer is connected to your computer, turned on, has its on line light on, and is loaded with paper. Then you can begin.

**1  From the message list, click the message that you want to print.**

Check the message area to make sure that the message you selected is the one you want to get on paper.

**2  Click Print (the seventh button on the Toolbar).**

Alternatively, choose File⇨Print, or press Ctrl+P or ⌘P. A Print dialog box appears that gives you such standard options as choosing which pages to print and how many copies to print of each page.

**3  Click OK (on a PC) or Print (on a Mac) to print one copy of the entire message.**

Netscape displays a box telling you that the message is printing, and then voilà! Your message is on paper.

Netscape automatically prints a title at the beginning of the message containing incomprehensible gobbledygook about where the message is stored (as far as we can guess). At the bottom of each page it prints the page number and the date.

If you want to print only part of a long message, click the Pages option on the Print dialog box and fill in the range of pages that you want. Because you can't see on-screen where pages start and end, this option is useful mainly for printing just the beginning of a long message — for example, for printing only pages 1 through 1.

extra credit

## Avoiding gobbledygook when printing messages

If you're using Windows, you can tell Netscape to not include incomprehensible junk at the top of each e-mail message that you print. Choose File⇨Page Setup from the menu bar, click the Document Title and Document Location (URL) boxes to turn off those switches, and then click OK.

# Deleting a message

Having read a message, you may want to place it carefully in the circular file or in the Great Bit Bucket in the Sky. In Messenger, you place such important messages in the aptly-named Trash folder by first selecting the message from the message list and then clicking the Delete button on the Toolbar or pressing Delete. Messenger automatically creates a folder named Trash the first time that you delete a message.

**1  From the message list, click a message that you want to eliminate.**

You can delete the message from us or any other message that's sitting in your Inbox folder. When you select the message, its contents appear in the message area.

**2  Click the Delete button on the Toolbar (or press Delete).**

The message disappears from the Inbox folder. The message wasn't actually erased, though; it was just transferred to the Trash folder. If you suddenly decide that you want the deleted message back, you can undelete it.

**3  Switch to the Trash folder by clicking in the folder quick-access menu and clicking the Trash option.**

Wonder of wonders! Your deleted message is in the Trash folder, and it's not covered with old coffee grounds like when you throw something away in your off-screen trash.

**heads up**

You can read messages in your Trash folder by clicking them, just like messages in any other folder. You can also move a message from the Trash folder to a different folder by clicking the message to select it, clicking the File button (the fifth button on the Toolbar), and then clicking the folder you want from the list that appears.

Deleted messages lie around in your Trash folder until you take out the garbage by choosing File➪Empty Trash Folder from the menu bar. After you do that, your deleted messages are *really* deleted, freeing up space on your hard disk for new messages.

# Recess

You now know all the basics of e-mail. Take a quick breather and then come back to learn some rules of e-mail etiquette. After the next lesson, your messages will look like they're from an e-mail veteran.

to delete
selected message,
click Delete
button on Toolbar
or press Delete

the Messenger
Trash folder
contains messages
you've deleted

### ☑ Progress Check

If you can do the following, you've mastered this lesson:

❑ Reply to a message.

❑ Forward a message.

❑ Print a message.

❑ Delete a message.

## Lesson 5-5     # E-Mail E-tiquette

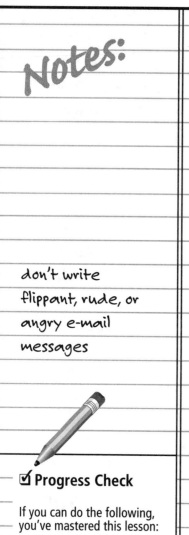

Notes:

don't write
flippant, rude, or
angry e-mail
messages

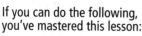

### ☑ Progress Check

If you can do the following, you've mastered this lesson:

❑ Respond to angry, unreasonable, and downright stupid messages by deleting them, or at least by waiting a day before replying.

❑ Respond to chain letters by pressing Delete.

❑ Use good e-mail etiquette when sending messages.

**heads up**

Something about e-mail makes people take offense easily and forget that they are corresponding with a living, breathing human being with feelings. Perhaps it's because you can't see the other person's face or hear a live voice, or perhaps it's a side effect of our pent-up hostility toward computers. Whatever the cause, ticking people off by e-mail is remarkably easy. This lesson doesn't have any steps, but don't skip over it because this stuff is really important.

So here are some words of advice about e-mail etiquette:

▶ **Use specific subjects.** Your subject appears in the listing of messages in the recipient's Inbox. Make it easy for your correspondent to decide what to read first by typing a very short summary of your message.

▶ **Don't use all capital letters in e-mail.** It looks like SHOUTING.

▶ **Avoid sarcasm.** In e-mail, it just sounds obnoxious. In an e-mail message, it can be hard to tell when someone is joking.

▶ **Check your spelling and punctuation before sending messages.** People who don't know you can only judge you on the content of your messages, so make them impressive!

▶ **Avoid writing anything in e-mail that would embarrass you if distributed widely.** You never know who may decide to forward your message to others.

**on the test**

▶ **If you get a truly offensive message and you're tempted to shoot off a truly offensive response, don't.** Take a walk instead and calm down. The person is probably just having a bad day. As Margy's mother used to say, "His feet probably hurt." If you feel that you need to respond, write the message and then delete it. Or send it to nobody@dummies.net, which gives your message the attention it deserves by automatically throwing your message away.

▶ **Don't flame.** An angry message is called a *flame.* Sending angry messages is called *flaming,* and an exchange of flames is called a *flame war.* Try to stay out of them — flame wars are bad for your blood pressure and for your reputation on the Net.

▶ **Don't get ticked off at someone for not responding to your e-mail.** The Internet eats e-mail from time to time, so you may want to send a follow-up message asking whether your correspondent got the first message.

▶ **Don't believe everything you read.** Just because you get e-mail from someone claiming to be a female 20-something aerobics instructor doesn't mean that you didn't actually just hear from a lonely 12-year-old boy looking for friends.

Here's another piece of advice: Never pass along chain letters by e-mail. A few well-known chain letters (that is, messages that tell you to pass the message along to lots of friends and coworkers) to avoid include messages announcing the Good News virus (the virus doesn't exist), get-rich-quick schemes (the most famous of which has the subject line *MAKE MONEY FAST*), messages about a nonexistent modem tax, and messages claiming that a dying boy in England wants to receive greeting cards. (He got well a decade ago.)

Just read chain letters and delete them. Optional: Skip reading them.

*never pass along chain letters*

# Unit 5 Quiz

For each of the following questions, circle the letter of the correct answer or answers. Remember, each question may have more than one right answer.

1. **An Internet e-mail address looks like this:**
   A. username@computername
   B. username@hostname
   C. yourname@myname
   D. vegetable@mineral
   E. ncomm101@dummies.net

2. **You can use the Netscape Messenger window to:**
   A. Read e-mail messages addressed to you.
   B. Send e-mail messages to anyone with an Internet account.
   C. Send e-mail messages to anyone with an account on America Online, CompuServe, or an Internet service provider, among others.
   D. Reply to e-mail messages you receive.
   E. Impress your friends.

3. **Clicking the New Msg button on the Messenger Toolbar:**
   A. Adds seasoning to your words.
   B. Opens a blank Composition window.
   C. Sends the current message to the president of the Internet.
   D. Lets you write an e-mail message.
   E. Makes your keyboard massage your fingers.

4.  **To send the same message to several people:**

    A.  Type the message over and over again, sending it to one person at a time.

    B.  On the To line of the message, type a list of the e-mail addresses to which you want to send the message, separated by commas.

    C.  Type each e-mail address on its own To line, using the Enter key to create each new line.

    D.  Send it to one person and ask that person to pass it along to the other people.

    E.  Type the message once, print it out, photocopy the printout, and mail the message to each person using envelopes and stamps.

5.  **When creating a message, you should avoid**

    A.  Writing in haste or anger.

    B.  TYPING IN ALL CAPS.

    C.  Saying something that you might regret later.

    D.  Not checking for proper spelling and punctuation.

    E.  Playing disco music in the background.

# Unit 5 Exercise

1.  Call a friend who has an Internet or online service e-mail account. Ask for your friend's e-mail address. Write it down very carefully, including the @ and all the dots (or type it right into a new message in Netscape). Don't worry about capitalization because it rarely matters in e-mail addresses.

2.  Fire up Netscape and create a new e-mail message. Address the message to your friend.

3.  In the text of the message, ask your friend to send back a reply.

4.  Send the message.

5.  Wait a day, or at least an hour or two, and check your incoming e-mail.

6.  Read your friend's message.

7.  Send your friend a reply.

# More Mail Moves

**Prerequisites**
▶ Opening the Netscape Messenger window (Lesson 5-1)
▶ Sending and receiving e-mail messages (Lessons 5-2, 5-3, and 5-4)

Objectives for This Unit

✓ Creating and using an e-mail address book

✓ Filing messages in e-mail folders manually

✓ Filing messages automatically using filters

✓ Sending files by e-mail

✓ Receiving attached files

**on the CD**   ▶ Leonardo.jpg

You've joined the world of online communications — you can send and receive e-mail. When your friends and colleagues exchange e-mail addresses, you can toss yours into the conversation. Why not put your e-mail address on your business cards and stationery?

Now that you know e-mail basics, it's time to learn some advanced features. In this unit, you'll create an e-mail address book, organize your messages using e-mail folders, and send data files (such as pictures, spreadsheets, and databases) along with your messages.

## Using Your Address Book

Typing e-mail addresses is painstaking and annoying work. One period or at sign (@) out of place and you're sunk. Luckily, you don't have to type any e-mail address more than once — just enter it right into your Netscape Address Book. Along with a person's e-mail address, you can enter his or her name, company, title, postal address, and telephone number. You can also supply a nickname of your choosing.

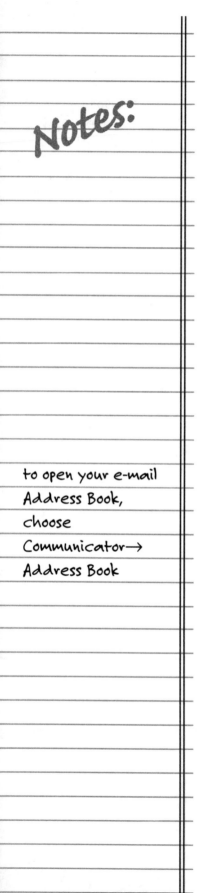

*Notes:*

to open your e-mail
Address Book,
choose
Communicator→
Address Book

on the test

In Netscape, a *nickname* is the name that you pick to stand for a person who will receive your e-mail. When you open the Composition window to compose a message, you can type the person's nickname on an address line (a line with a *To, Cc,* or *Bcc* header) rather than her e-mail address.

For example, for your mother, you might choose the nickname *Mom;* for your friend Herbert Pickleherring, you could assign the nickname *Herb;* and for a salesman you regularly deal with at Gizmos Corp., you could pick the nickname *Gizmo Sales.* A nickname can contain spaces and punctuation and can be as long as you want.

Nicknames are a big improvement over typing e-mail addresses, but Netscape doesn't stop there; it even types the nicknames for you! Specifically, when you type a first letter (say, the letter *D*) on a Composition window address line, Netscape automatically checks it against all the nicknames in your Address Book. If it finds one nickname that starts with the same letter (say, the nickname *Delilah*), it immediately inserts that nickname on the address line.

On the other hand, if Netscape finds two or more nicknames that start with the same letter (for example, *Delilah* and *Daisy*), it waits until you type enough to match just one nickname (say, *Da*), and then inserts that name on the address line (in this case, *Daisy*). Finally, if the nickname that Netscape suggests isn't what you want, no problem; just keep typing (for example, type *Dan*), and Netscape automatically deletes its suggestion and accepts what you type instead.

When you finish typing, press the Tab key as usual to move to the next header; if what you've typed (or let Netscape type) matches a nickname in your address book, the nickname instantly changes into the person's full name and e-mail address. Very cool!

You can open your Address Book by choosing <u>C</u>ommunicator⇨Address Book and create a new entry by clicking a New Card button on the window's Toolbar. In this lesson, you'll create an entry or two in your Address Book and then use a nickname to address a message.

## Adding names to your Address Book

The first person you should put in your Address Book is *you.* You can then use your nickname to easily send messages to yourself whenever you want to test your e-mail account. To add the entry, follow these steps:

**1** Launch Netscape (you don't have to connect to the Internet yet).

**2** Choose <u>C</u>ommunicator⇨<u>A</u>ddress Book from the menu bar.

You see the Address Book window in Figure 6-1. Unless someone else (such as the organization that supplied your copy of Netscape) has already entered data in it, your Address Book is initially empty.

Notice that the first button on this window's Toolbar is named New Card. This button allows you to add an entry to your Address Book (similar to the way you'd add a new card to a Rolodex).

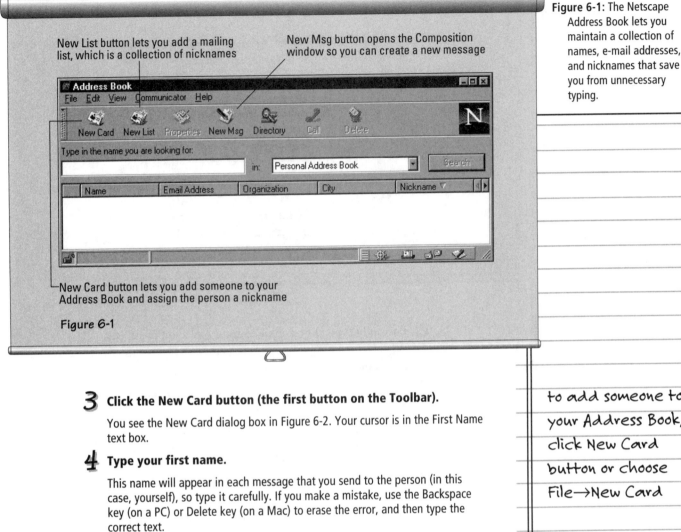

New List button lets you add a mailing
list, which is a collection of nicknames

New Msg button opens the Composition
window so you can create a new message

New Card button lets you add someone to your
Address Book and assign the person a nickname

Figure 6-1

Figure 6-1: The Netscape
Address Book lets you
maintain a collection of
names, e-mail addresses,
and nicknames that save
you from unnecessary
typing.

**3 Click the New Card button (the first button on the Toolbar).**

You see the New Card dialog box in Figure 6-2. Your cursor is in the First Name
text box.

**4 Type your first name.**

This name will appear in each message that you send to the person (in this
case, yourself), so type it carefully. If you make a mistake, use the Backspace
key (on a PC) or Delete key (on a Mac) to erase the error, and then type the
correct text.

**5 Press Tab.**

You move to the Last Name box. You can always move to the next text box by
pressing Tab and to the previous box by pressing Shift+Tab.

**6 Type your last name and then press Tab.**

Again, this name will appear in messages that you send to the person, so type it
carefully. After you press Tab, you move to the Organization box. (If you're on a
Mac, you move to the Email box instead; skip to Step 9.)

**7 Optionally, type the name of your company or organization (or just
leave this box blank), and then press Tab.**

The Organization box is primarily useful for identifying business associates; you
can skip it when adding a friend or relative to your Address Book. After you
press Tab, you move to the Title box.

**8 Optionally, type your professional title (or just leave this box blank)
and then press Tab.**

Again, if this box doesn't apply, skip it by just pressing Tab. You move to the
Email Address box.

to add someone to
your Address Book,
click New Card
button or choose
File→New Card

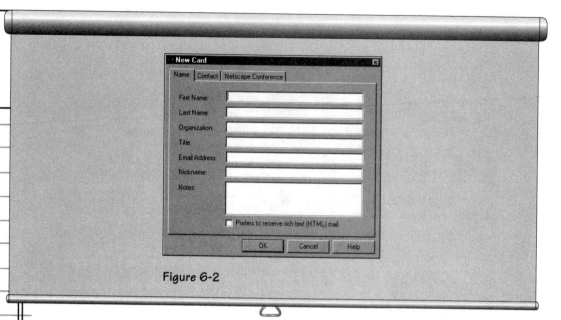

Figure 6-2

*Notes:*

**9** **Carefully type your e-mail address and then press Tab.**

This box is critical, so be sure to get all those pesky at signs (@) and periods right. After you're done, you move to the Nickname box.

**10** **Choose a nickname that will be easy to remember and type. When you're ready, carefully type the nickname.**

You can type your first name, or the word *me*, or some cute name that you've been called since childhood. This is the name that you'll use in place of an e-mail address in the Composition window.

**11** **If you want to add any information about this entry, press Tab and type the data in the Notes box.**

What you type doesn't appear anywhere except in this very window, so say whatever you like.

When you're done, notice that an option at the bottom lets you specify whether to send e-mail using the HTML format, which is a format that allows special effects such as colors and fonts. (For more information, see the "HTML and e-mail" sidebar in Lesson 5-4.) If you leave the option unchecked (which is the default), Netscape will send all messages to the person's e-mail address in plain text, or ASCII, format. Because you're entering data about yourself in this case and Netscape supports HTML, give HTML a green light.

**12** **Click the Prefers to receive rich text (HTML) mail option to turn it on.**

A check mark appears to the option's left. Keep in mind that many people still have e-mail programs that don't understand HTML, however, so always ask the person for which you're creating an entry whether he or she can handle HTML before turning this option on. (No risk is involved in leaving it turned off, because all programs understand the plain text format.)

You're now done with the Names entry form. This dialog box also has an optional Contact entry form. To access it, click its tab near the top.

**13** **Click the Contact tab near the top of the dialog box.**

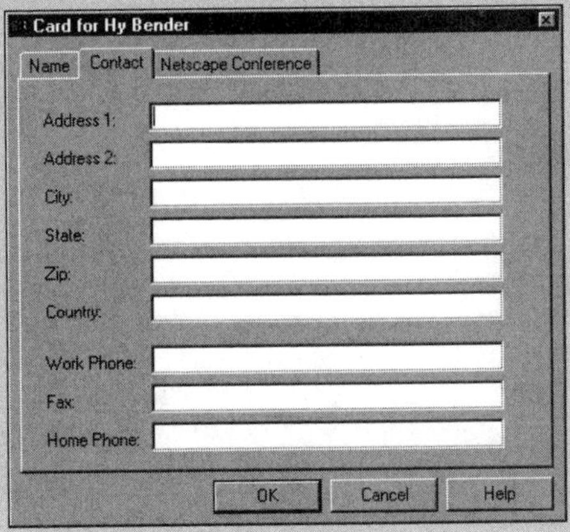


Figure 6-3

**Figure 6-3:** Use the Contact form to enter a person's postal address and telephone numbers into your Address Book.

You see the entry form in Figure 6-3, which lets you type a person's postal address and phone numbers.

**14 Type your postal address, work and home telephone numbers, and fax number into the Contact form, pressing Tab to move from text box to text box.**

This data won't help you send e-mail, but you may find it convenient to have all your contact information collected in the same Address Book. After you're done, briefly investigate the dialog box's third, and final, form.

**15 Click the Netscape Conference tab near the top of the dialog box.**

You see a form that asks for an electronic address that your company may have assigned you for using Netscape's Conference program, which lets business colleagues interact live over the Internet. Coverage of this program is beyond the scope of this book, but you can learn more about it later by choosing Help⇨Help Contents from any Netscape window and then clicking the Conference Help icon (which looks like a red telephone) from the window that appears.

You're now done entering contact information, so save your new Address Book entry.

**16 Click the dialog box's OK button.**

The information that you typed is saved to your hard disk, the dialog box goes away, and you see the Address Book window again. Notice that you now appear as the first entry in the window!

**17 If you already know people with e-mail addresses who you intend to trade messages with frequently, repeat Steps 3 through 16 for each person (substituting the person's information for your own, 'natch).**

After you're done entering each person's contact data, click the dialog box's OK button to save the information and see the entry appear in your Address Book window.

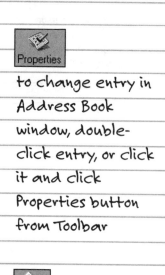

to change entry in Address Book window, double-click entry, or click it and click Properties button from Toolbar

to delete entry in Address Book window, first click entry to select it, then press Delete or click Delete button on Toolbar

**18** **After you're finished adding entries, choose File⇨Close or press Ctrl+W or ⌘W to close the Address Book.**

The Address Book window goes away. Your entries are preserved on your hard disk, however.

Great work! You now have a useful Address Book that will spare you lots of extra typing in the future.

If you later need to revise an Address Book entry, you can simply open the Address Book and double-click the entry (or click the entry to select it and click the Properties button from the Toolbar). The Card dialog box appears again, but this time is filled with the information that you supplied. Click in any text box that you want to change, edit the information appropriately, and click the OK button to save your changes.

You can also easily delete an Address Book entry that's become obsolete. To do so, click the entry from the Address Book window to select it, and then press Delete or click the Delete button (the last button on the Toolbar). If you change your mind, you can get your entry back by choosing Edit⇨Undo or by pressing Ctrl+Z or ⌘Z; but this trick works only right after you've made the deletion.

extra credit

# Don't retype e-mail addresses!

If you're reading a message from someone you want to add to your Address Book, choose Message⇨Add to Address Book⇨Sender from the Messenger menu bar. Netscape pops up a Card dialog box with the person's name and e-mail address already filled in! (Netscape copied the information from the Sender header of the message.) All you have left to do is supply a nickname, plus any other information that you care to provide.

Even if an e-mail address appears only in the contents of a message, you still don't have to retype it. Instead, highlight the e-mail address with your mouse, press Ctrl+C or ⌘C to copy the text; choose Communicator⇨Address Book to open your Address Book, click the New Card button to open a Card dialog box, click in the Email Address text box, and press Ctrl+V or ⌘V to paste the address into the box. You can then fill in the rest of the information as usual, knowing that the e-mail address is entered perfectly (assuming that your original source didn't commit any typos). Use copy-and-paste commands whenever possible so that you don't introduce errors while filling in those pesky e-mail addresses.

## Addressing messages using the Address Book

Now that you've created an entry for yourself in the Address Book, send a test message using your new nickname:

**Notes:**

**1** **Press Ctrl+M or ⌘M to open the Composition window.**

The Composition window pops up, ready to help you create a new message. Your cursor is on the To address line.

**2** **Start typing your nickname, slowly, until Netscape fills the rest of it in for you.**

When you've typed enough letters to uniquely identify your nickname (which, depending on the entries in your Address Book, may require only a first letter), Netscape supplies the remaining letters.

**3** **After your nickname appears, press the Tab key.**

Netscape automatically replaces your nickname with your real name and e-mail address! (Cool!) You move to the Subject box.

**4** **Type a subject for your message, such as *Nickname Test,* and press Tab.**

You move to the window's message area.

**5** **Type a short message, such as *Checking out the Nickname feature.***

Or whatever you want; you're the only one who will see this message.

**6** **If you aren't already connected to the Internet, dial in now. When you're ready, click the Send button (the first button on the Toolbar).**

After a few moments, Netscape sends your message (poof!), and the Composition window disappears.

Easy, no? As you've just seen, all you have to do to send someone e-mail is remember the first few letters of his or her nickname.

extra credit

## Creating mailing lists

Using your Address Book is convenient for sending e-mail to one person, but it's a virtual necessity when you need to repeatedly send e-mail to a group of people (for example, when it's part of your job to notify coworkers about upcoming meetings). To handle this chore, open your Address Book and click the New List button, which is the second button on the Toolbar. This opens a dialog box that lets you type an unlimited number of e-mail nicknames from your Address Book (pressing Enter after each name) and also lets you assign a nickname to represent the entire list! After you save the list by clicking OK, you can simply type the list's nickname on a Composition window address line; the Address Book will auto- matically insert all the e-mail addresses the list represents.

*Tip:* If you have a lot of people on your list, don't put the list's nickname on a To heading because it will force each recipient to wade through a bunch of e-mail addresses before getting to your message. Instead, type your own nickname on the first To header in the Composition window; press Enter to create a new header line; click the second To header and click the Bcc (Blind carbon copy) option from the menu that pops down; and type the list's nickname on the Bcc line. This ensures that each recipient sees only your name in the message's headers.

to display Address
Book from
Composition window,
click Address
button on Toolbar

*Notes:*

But what if you *can't* remember how a nickname starts? That's no problem, either, because you can always pop up the Address Book by clicking the Address button on the Composition window's Toolbar. Do that now to create a second test message:

**1** **Press Ctrl+M or ⌘M to open the Composition window again.**

The Composition window opens. Notice that the third button on its Toolbar is named Address.

**2** **Click the Address button.**

A Select Addresses dialog box like the one in Figure 6-4 appears. This dialog box lets you search through your Address Book for a particular name and then insert it on a Composition window address line.

**3** **Locate your name in the Address Book.**

If you have a lot of entries, scroll through them using the arrow keys or the vertical scroll bar. Alternatively, type part of the person's real first name in the text box in the upper-left corner; an outline appears around the name that you want. If you're on a Mac, click the Address Book's Close button, type the name on an address line, and skip to Step 6. Otherwise, continue to Step 4.

**4** **After you spot the name you're after, double-click it.**

The name that you've chosen is copied to the This message will be sent to box in the Select Addresses dialog box. The name is preceded by *To:*, which is the default address type. (To create a *Cc:* or *Bcc:* address instead, click a name and then click the appropriate button to the right.) You can repeat Steps 3 and 4 to insert as many e-mail addresses as you desire. In this case, however, you're done.

**5** **Click the OK button.**

The Address Book closes, and the e-mail address that you chose is copied to the Composition window.

**6** **Press the Tab key, type a subject for your message such as** *Address Book Test***, and press Tab again.**

You move to the window's message area.

**7** **Type a short message.**

Something like *You're terrific!* is always appropriate.

**8** **When you're ready, click the Send button on the Toolbar.**

After a few moments, Netscape sends your second message, and the Composition window exits. Finally, check to see whether your test messages were sent properly.

**9** **Wait about a minute and then click the Mailbox icon in the Component Bar to both open the Messenger window and check for new messages.**

Messenger opens and retrieves your e-mail, including (with any luck) the two messages you just sent. (If this doesn't happen, wait ten minutes and try again. If you still don't receive the messages you sent, make sure that your e-mail address is entered properly in the Address Book and then try creating and sending the test messages again.)

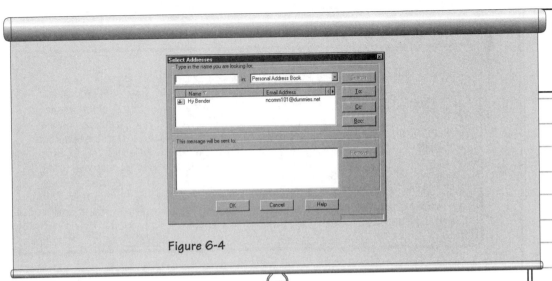

Figure 6-4

**Figure 6-4:** Use the Select Addresses dialog box to insert an address with a few mouse clicks.

**10** **Disconnect from the Internet.**

Pat yourself on the back; you're now an Address Book expert.

## Emoticons and e-mail abbreviations

E-mail messages contain lots of mysterious things, such as *emoticons*, which are pictures of faces drawn with punctuation.

To read an emoticon, tip your head to the left. Here are a few emoticons and widely used abbreviations:

| | |
|---|---|
| :-) | A happy face |
| :-( | A sad face |
| 8-) | A happy face with glasses |
| :-o | A shocked face |
| =\|;-) | A winking happy face wearing a top hat |
| <g> | Grin |
| BTW | By The Way |

| | |
|---|---|
| TIA | Thanks In Advance |
| IMO | In My Opinion |
| IMHO | In My Humble Opinion |
| IMNSHO | In My Not-So-Humble Opinion |
| RTFM | Read The, er, Fine Manual |
| YMMV | Your Mileage May Vary |

## Recess

Tilt your head and take another look at the "Emoticons and e-mail abbreviations" sidebar. Play around by typing a few. (You may even want to try creating a few of your own.) Emoticons and e-mail abbreviations aren't for everyone's tastes; but if you decide you like them, enjoy <g>.

### ☑ Progress Check

If you can do the following, you've mastered this lesson:

❑ Create Address Book entries for your relatives, friends, and coworkers.

❑ Address e-mail messages by using nicknames.

❑ Address e-mail messages by popping up the Address Book.

# What happens to dead letters?

If you type an e-mail address incorrectly, Netscape can't deliver the e-mail. An undeliverable message is usually returned to you with a large, scary-looking message from a Mail Delivery Subsystem (or some other official-sounding program). Read through the message until you find the part where it tells you what address your original message contained.

If you kept a copy of your original message in the Sent folder, you can quickly create a new message. To do so, copy the text from the old message (using Ctrl+C or ⌘C), paste the text to the new message (using Ctrl+V or ⌘V), type the correct e-mail address, and click the Send button. With any luck, the second time's the charm.

**Lesson 6-2**

# Filing Messages in Folders

When you receive important correspondence on paper, you file it in folders for safekeeping. (Yeah, right — who are we kidding? You probably just stack it on top of all those other important papers, like we do.) The same is true when you receive an important e-mail message — except that the folders are on your hard disk rather than in a filing cabinet. For example, the messages that you receive are normally stored in a folder named Inbox; copies of messages that you've sent are stored in a folder named Sent; and messages that you delete are temporarily stored in a folder named Trash (until you choose File▷ Empty Trash Folder to permanently eliminate the messages).

As you learned in Lesson 5-3, you can switch among these e-mail folders by opening the Messenger window, clicking in the folder quick-access menu (the big box directly below the Toolbar), and clicking the folder you want.

*create folders by project or for each person you correspond with*

But you aren't stuck with using only the handful of folders that Netscape creates. You can make as many folders as you want and use them to store messages based on such criteria as who sent the e-mail or the subject matter of the e-mail.

After you do, you can transfer messages from one folder to another manually, or you can tell Messenger to *automatically* direct incoming messages to appropriate folders!

In this lesson, you'll create e-mail folders, manually transfer messages between folders, and set Netscape to automatically sort your incoming messages into folders.

## Creating folders

Netscape normally throws all your incoming mail into the Inbox folder. If you get a lot of messages, however, it's more convenient to organize them into a number of different folders. You can create a folder for each project that you're working on (say, *Annual Budget,* or *Novel in Progress*). You can also make folders for people or groups with whom you correspond frequently (for example, *Shawna Epstein,* or *Gigantcorp Marketing*).

on the test

To make a new folder, choose File⇨New Folder from the Messenger menu bar. Type a name for the folder, choose whether you want to create a first-level folder or a subfolder of an existing folder, and click OK; the folder is instantly created.

Take a few moments now to pick a folder name. (If you have trouble deciding, just use *Personal,* which can serve to store e-mail from your friends.) When you're ready, go ahead and create the folder:

**1** **Fire up Netscape, if it's not already running.**

You don't have to connect to the Internet in this exercise; all the action takes place on your hard disk.

**2** **Choose Communicator⇨Messenger Mailbox to open the Messenger window.**

Netscape's e-mail window appears.

**3** **Click the File menu and click the New Folder option.**

You see the dialog box in Figure 6-5. Near its top is a Name text box, which lets you type the name of your folder. Below that is a Create as sub-folder of box, which lets you create either a first-level folder (that is, a folder on the same level as Inbox, Outbox, Sent, and so on) or a subfolder of an existing folder. The latter can be useful if you have lots of messages that are related but different — for example, within a Music folder, you might want to create subfolders named Classical, Rock, and Country & Western.

**4** **In the Name box, type the name you picked for your new folder (for example, type *Personal*); then press Tab.**

You move to the Create as sub-folder of box.

**5** **Press the Home key, or press the Up Arrow key repeatedly, until the top option Local Mail is displayed.**

By selecting Local Mail, you tell Netscape to create a first-level folder rather than a subfolder.

**6** **Press Enter or click OK.**

The dialog box closes . . . and your folder is created! To see it, use the folder quick-access menu.

**7** **Click anywhere inside the folder quick-access menu (the box in the upper-left portion of the Messenger window, directly below the Toolbar).**

Your new folder is listed, in alphabetical order, along with the other e-mail folders. Try switching to it.

**8** **Click the name of your folder.**

You move to your new folder, and its name is displayed in the folder quick-access menu.

*to create e-mail folder, choose File→New Folder from Messenger window*

*Notes:*

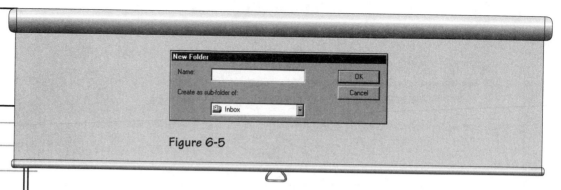

Figure 6-5

You don't see any messages in your folder right now because it starts off empty. You can fix that by transferring messages to it from other folders — which is exactly what you'll do in the next exercise.

*Tip:* If a folder stops being useful, you can delete it. To do so, choose Communicator➪Message Center from any Netscape menu bar to open a window that lists all your folders, click the folder that you want to eliminate, and press Delete. The folder is moved to the Trash folder. If you change your mind, press Ctrl+Z or ⌘Z immediately after the deletion to bring the folder back. Otherwise, the next time you empty the Trash folder, the folder that you deleted will be erased from your hard disk.

## Transferring messages to other folders

File

*to move message to another folder, click message, click File button, and click folder you want from drop-down list*

Moving a message from one folder to another requires only a few mouse clicks. Simply click the message from the Messenger window, click the File button (the fifth button on the Toolbar) to display a list of all your folders, and click the folder to which you want to move the message. Try it!

**1** **Click in the folder quick-access menu and then click the Inbox folder from the list that appears.**

You see a list of the messages in your Inbox.

**2** **Click a message that you want to move.**

The message is selected, and its contents appear in the lower portion of the window.

**3** **Click the File button (the fifth button on the Toolbar).**

A list of all your e-mail folders drops down.

**4** **Click the name of the folder you just created in the preceding exercise. (For example, if you created a folder named *Personal*, click Personal.)**

The message is moved to the folder that you clicked (as indicated by its contents disappearing from the lower portion of the window and replaced by the next message in your Inbox).

**5** **Click inside the folder quick-access menu and then click the name of the folder you created.**

You switch to your new folder and — lo and behold! — you see the message that you moved.

In other words, moving a message around is a snap. By creating folders and transferring messages, you can ensure that your e-mail stays well-organized.

*Tip:* You can also *copy* a message to another folder. To do so, select the message, choose Message⇨Copy Message from the menu bar, and click the appropriate folder from the list that appears. A copy of the message is placed in the folder you clicked, while the original message is unaffected.

## Filtering messages

If you receive e-mail only occasionally, manually transferring messages isn't much of a chore. However, if you start conducting a lot of business via e-mail, or if you begin subscribing to mailing lists (ongoing discussions conducted by e-mail; see Unit 7 and Unit CD-1 on your CD-ROM for more information), you can end up getting dozens of messages a day. Having to transfer so many messages to appropriate folders by hand can take up a lot of time and effort. In addition, when all those unrelated messages are dumped into the same Inbox folder, the clutter may cause you to accidentally overlook important and timely messages.

A better way to go is to take advantage of *Netscape's* terrific *message filtering* feature. Filtering sorts your messages automatically based on text you specify that appears in any portion of the message you choose. For example, you can tell Netscape to send all messages with *Gobbins* in the Sender header to a folder that you've created for your friend Bob Gobbins. As another example, you can direct all messages with the word *taxes* in the Subject header to a folder that you've created named *This Year's Taxes*. After you've set up your filters, download your mail as usual and then click in the folder quick-access menu; any folders containing new messages will be listed in boldface. You can switch to any boldfaced folder by simply clicking it and then read your new mail.

To set up an e-mail filter, first create the folder to which you'll be directing messages (if the folder doesn't already exist). Next, choose Edit⇨Mail Filters from the Messenger menu bar. From the dialog box that appears, click the New button, name the filter, define the filter's rules, and click OK. All your subsequent incoming e-mail is filtered through the rules that you've created. Those that match a rule are redirected to the appropriate folder, while the rest get dropped (as usual) into your Inbox.

To get a better sense of how filters work, create a folder for someone you'll be corresponding with and then direct that person's mail to the folder:

**1** **Choose File⇨New Folder from the Messenger menu bar.**

The New Folder dialog box appears.

**2** **In the Name box, type the name of a friend or colleague with whom you expect to chat frequently via e-mail; then press Tab.**

You move to the Create as sub-folder of box.

**3** **Press the Home key, or press the Up Arrow key repeatedly, until the Local Mail option is displayed; then press Enter.**

Your folder is created, and the dialog box goes away. You're now ready to create your filter.

*Notes:*

*Notes:*

**on the test**

**4** **Choose Edit⇨Mail Filters from the menu bar.**

A Mail Filters dialog box appears. To create a filter, click the New button in the upper-right section of the box.

**5** **Click the New button.**

You see the Filter Rules dialog box in Figure 6-6. Your cursor starts off in the Filter name text box (with the word *untitled* highlighted). Name this filter so you can identify it later from a list of your filters.

**6** **Type the name of your friend (again); then press Tab.**

You move to a box that lets you select which portion of messages you want to base your filtering on. The default is *sender,* which refers to the text in the Sender header. In this case, the default happens to be the setting that you need, but take a moment to look at your other options anyway.

**7** **Press the Down Arrow key repeatedly. Notice that each time you press Down Arrow, a different header is selected.**

(If you're using a Mac, click the sender option instead to display a drop-down list.) Among the message elements you see are *subject,* meaning the text in the Subject header; and *body,* meaning the contents of the message. These choices are appropriate when you're more interested in what a message is about than in who wrote it. For this exercise, though, return to the *sender* setting.

**8** **Press the Home key, or press the Up Arrow key repeatedly, to display the sender setting again; then press Tab.**

You move to a box that lets you choose which filtering rule to apply. The default is *contains,* which tells Netscape to look for text contained anywhere in the message element you selected. Other options include *doesn't contain,* which searches for messages that lack your specified text; *is,* which searches only for exact matches (as opposed to text contained within a larger section of text); and *begins with,* which searches only for text that starts a certain way. Stick with the *contains* setting, which is already selected.

**9** **Press Tab (or click in the box to the *right* of the *contains* setting).**

You move to a box that lets you type the text Netscape should search for. Use your person's last name as your search text.

**10** **Carefully type the last name of your friend or colleague; then press Tab three times to skip over the next two options.**

Your first Tab skips over a More button. This button lets you create additional rules for when you want to narrow your search criteria; but in this case the single rule that you've created is all you need.

You also skip over a box that lets you select what action should be taken when a message matches your filter. Options include *Change priority, Delete,* and *Mark read* (meaning mark the message as having already been read). Most of the time, though, you'll want to accept the default setting of *Move to folder,* and that's the case now as well.

You're currently in a box that lets you choose the folder to store your filtered messages. You can display available folders using either the arrow keys or your mouse.

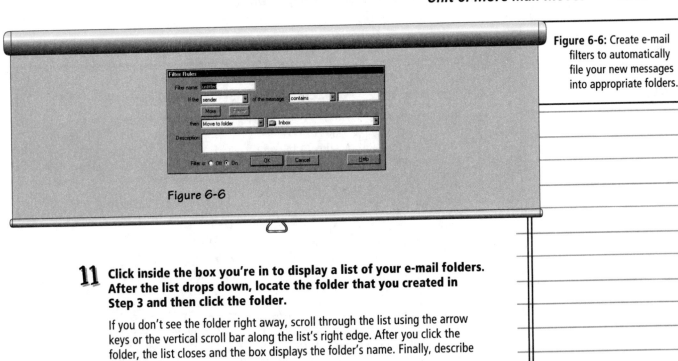

Figure 6-6

**11** **Click inside the box you're in to display a list of your e-mail folders. After the list drops down, locate the folder that you created in Step 3 and then click the folder.**

If you don't see the folder right away, scroll through the list using the arrow keys or the vertical scroll bar along the list's right edge. After you click the folder, the list closes and the box displays the folder's name. Finally, describe your filter.

**12** **Press Tab to move to the Description box and then type something like** *Direct to this folder all e-mail from Bob* **(or whatever your person's name is).**

You're almost done! The only other option that you should notice is a Filter on/off switch near the bottom of the Windows version of the dialog box. This option is useful if you ever want to temporarily disable the filter without having to delete it. Right now, though, the switch should be *on*.

**13** **Click the OK button (on a PC) or the dialog box's Close button (on a Mac).**

Your filter is saved and the Filter Rules dialog box exits, revealing the Mail Filters dialog box again. Notice that the box lists the filter you just created. You can edit this filter's contents at any time by double-clicking its name, and you can delete it by clicking its name and clicking the Delete button.

**14** **Click the OK button.**

The Mail Filters dialog box disappears. The next time that you receive e-mail from your friend, his or her messages will appear in the special folder you created rather than in the Inbox folder.

After you've set up your mail filters, follow these steps to find and read your incoming e-mail:

**1** **Pick up your mail as usual by clicking the Mailbox icon or Get Message button.**

Your messages are individually filed into appropriate folders rather than being deposited as one disorganized group into the Inbox folder.

*Notes:*

**extra credit**

# Creating a signature

Many e-mail users like to create a *signature* — that is, a few lines of text that Netscape automatically adds to the end of every message you send. Instead of typing your name and e-mail address at the end of every message, you can have Netscape do it for you.

Your signature should include your whole name, your e-mail address, and (optionally) a pithy saying or message that tells your correspondents something interesting about you (or your organization) and piques their interest. Don't include long sayings, quotes, or cute pictures created using characters (also known as *ASCII art*). They can be interesting the first time someone gets mail from you, but they get old fast after the second or third message. The entire signature should be no more than four lines long.

To create a signature for yourself, follow these steps:

1. **Create a *signature file* — that is, a plain text file that contains the lines you want in your signature.**

   You can use Notepad (the Windows built-in text editor) to create your signature file, or use any word processor that can save the signature file as ASCII (that is, text without special formatting).

2. **Save the file on your hard disk using the filename** Signature.txt.

Be sure to write down the name of the folder you used to store the file. Now set the Netscape option that adds the text in your signature file to each e-mail message you send.

3. **Choose Edit⇨Preferences from any Netscape menu bar.**

   You see the Preferences dialog box.

4. **Click the Identity category (under the Mail & Groups category).**

   Identity options appear in the right portion of the dialog box. Notice that one of the last options is Signature File and that a Choose button appears to its right.

5. **Click the Choose button to browse your hard disk; then find the signature file you just created, click the file's name, and click the Open button.**

   The hard disk location and name of your signature file appears in the Signature File box.

6. **Click OK.**

   Netscape saves the location and name of your signature file, and will use the file to insert your signature in all your subsequent messages. Whenever you want to change your signature, simply edit the contents of this file.

## ☑ Progress Check

If you can do the following, you've mastered this lesson:

❑ Create a new folder.

❑ Move a message into a folder.

❑ Create a message filter.

*2* **Click in the folder quick-access menu (the box directly below the Messenger Toolbar).**

A list of your e-mail folders drops down. Notice that some of the folders appear in boldface. The boldfacing means that these folders contain unread messages.

*3* **Click a folder whose messages you want to read.**

You're switched to the folder, and you see the unread messages in it boldfaced in the message list.

**4** **Click each boldfaced message from the message list until you've read all the new mail in the folder.**

After you've read all your new messages, the folder loses its boldfacing.

**5** **Repeat Steps 2 through 4 until you've read all your new messages.**

You'll know that you've gone through all your mail when none of your e-mail folders appear in boldface.

If you're in a hurry, though, just open the folders that are likely to contain important messages. If you've set up your mail filters effectively, you can skip examining the rest of your folders until you have more time because you know the messages in them can wait. You can also feel assured that you won't accidentally overlook critical messages that might otherwise have been buried amidst unimportant ones in the Inbox folder.

**heads up**

One other way you can check your mail is by choosing Communicator⇨ Collabra Discussion Groups, or by clicking the Discussions icon (which looks like two cartoon dialog balloons) from the Component Bar. After you do so, a Message Center window opens that lists all your e-mail folders and displays in boldface any folder containing unread mail. In addition, the right side of the window tells you the number of unread messages and the total number of messages in each folder. You can open any listed folder and explore its messages by simply double-clicking it.

Netscape's message filtering is a powerful feature that can revolutionize how you interact with your e-mail. We recommend that you play around with it and find creative uses for it tailored to your e-mail needs.

Even if you don't use filtering, though, try to file your important messages in e-mail folders rather than printing each message and filing it in a manila folder. Save a tree!

# Sending Files Along with Your Messages

**Lesson 6-3**

We love e-mail, and we use it for just about everything, including submitting the units in this book to our editor Kelly Ewing at IDG Books Worldwide. But e-mail messages are limited to just two formats, plain text and HTML (and, as mentioned in Lesson 6-1, not every e-mail program can even handle the latter). So to submit units with all the formatting that Kelly needs, we *attach* word processing documents to our e-mail messages. In fact, you can attach almost any file to a message — word processing documents, spreadsheets, data files, graphics files — you name it! The only qualifier is that some e-mail systems choke on large files, so if you encounter problems, call both your ISP and the ISP you're sending to and ask what their size limits are for e-mail.

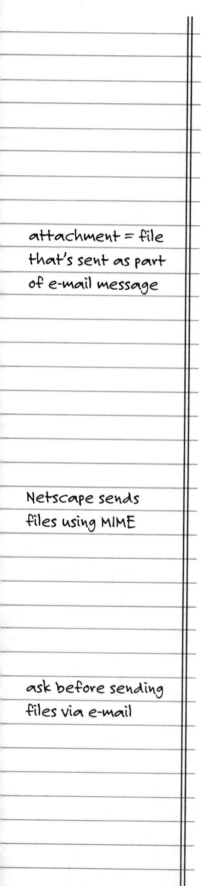

on the test

Why send a file by e-mail? Here are some common reasons:

▸ You want someone to know what you look like, so you want to send a graphics file containing a scanned picture of yourself.

▸ You need to get your company's sales figures to your business partner in an Excel spreadsheet file.

▸ You ran across a great public domain program for creating genealogy charts that you'd like to share with your sister.

▸ You've created an inventory of your jazz collection with a database program and now want to get it to a dealer who's interested in buying rare music albums.

To send a file by e-mail, you attach the file to an e-mail message. The file that you send is therefore called an *attachment*.

In this lesson, you'll learn how to send a message with a file attached to it. Lesson 6-4 will tell you what to do when you receive an attached file.

You have three ways to attach a file to a message: MIME, uuencoding, and BinHex. (Think of them as tape, staples, and glue.) All three methods work by converting your file into specially encoded text so that it can be sent by e-mail, and they all result in the same thing: your file arriving along with your e-mail message. The problem is that not all e-mail programs and online services can handle all three methods. For a file to arrive safely, both the sender and the receiver must be able to handle the same method. If the recipient's e-mail program can't convert the specially encoded text back into the original file, the file transfer doesn't work.

Netscape uses MIME (the most modern, up-to-date method) when sending attached files. Netscape can also handle incoming e-mail messages that use any of the three attachment methods. So you can receive attached files from anyone; but if you want to *send* an attached file, you should first find out whether your intended recipient uses a program that can handle the MIME format — or be prepared to find out by trial and error. (**Fair warning:** If you send a message with an attached file to folks whose e-mail programs can't deal with the attachment, the message appears as a long series of incomprehensible gibberish when they open it, and you may get some complaints.)

on the test

Which attachment method to use isn't the only consideration to keep in mind before you e-mail a file. Here are some others:

▸ **Make sure that your recipient can deal with the file that you want to send.** For example, if you plan to send a WordPerfect document or an Excel spreadsheet, first ask whether the person can read WordPerfect documents or Excel spreadsheets. You may need to save your file in a special format that he or she can handle. Most word processors, spreadsheet programs, and database programs can save files in a wide variety of formats.

▸ **Make sure that the addressee wants to receive it!** We get a lot of e-mail from people we don't know, and we find it annoying when people send us files, especially large ones. A large file can take several minutes

*attachment = file that's sent as part of e-mail message*

*Netscape sends files using MIME*

*ask before sending files via e-mail*

to download, tying up the phone line and making the recipient wait around to read his or her other incoming mail. If the recipient pays by the hour to connect to the Internet, this costs her money as well. Ask before you send!

▸ **Consider compressing the file before sending it.** Appendix B describes how to install and use WinZip for Windows and how to install Stuffit Expander for Macintosh, two extremely popular file compression programs that are on your *Dummies 101* CD-ROM. (But make sure that your recipient knows how to decompress the file!)

After you're certain that the person to whom you want to send a file both wants it and can deal with it, you're ready to e-mail the attachment. Follow these steps to send a file on the *Dummies 101* CD-ROM to yourself, just for practice:

**on the CD**

**1** **Insert the *Dummies 101* CD-ROM that came with this book into your CD-ROM drive.**

Be careful to touch only the sides of the CD-ROM and to insert the CD-ROM with its printed side up. If you're using Windows 3.1, you're set.

If you're using Windows 95, the CD-ROM's Installer program is set to run automatically, so after about a minute you probably see an initial Installer screen. In this case, however, all you want to do is copy a file from the CD-ROM, and Netscape can handle that task by itself. Therefore, follow the on-screen prompts until you see a Do Not Accept or Exit button, and then click the button to close the CD-ROM program.

If you're using a Mac, a window opens containing icons for the CD-ROM's various files and folders. Click the window's Close button to exit it.

**2** **Launch Netscape (if it isn't already running) and press Ctrl+M or ⌘M to start a new message.**

You see the Composition window.

**3** **On the To line, type your e-mail nickname (which you created in Lesson 6-1); then press Tab.**

Your nickname expands into your full name and e-mail address, and you move to the Subject box.

**4** **Type** Self-portrait by Leonardo da Vinci **and then press Tab.**

One of history's greatest artists drew himself late in his career. This image is stored in a file on your *Dummies 101* CD-ROM using a graphics format named JPEG. Electronic pictures are stored in a bewildering variety of formats with unpronounceable names. Happily, though, JPEG is a format that Netscape happens to understand.

**5** **In the message area, type** Leonardo da Vinci self-portrait, stored in graphics file Leonardo.jpg in JPEG format.

Always include information about the file that you're attaching, including what the file is about and what format the file is in. Otherwise, the recipient may not know what to do with it!

Attach

*to attach file,*
*click Attach*
*button and click*
*File option, or*
*choose*
*File→Attach→File*

**6** **Click the Attach button (the fourth button on the Toolbar) and then click the _File option from the menu that appears.**

If you prefer, you can choose File⇨Attach⇨File from the menu bar. Either way, an Enter file to Attach dialog box appears. This is a standard file dialog box, similar to what you see after choosing a File⇨Open or File⇨Save As command.

**7** **Select a file named Leonardo.jpg from your *Dummies 101* CD-ROM.**

- If you're using Windows, click in the File _name box and type **d:\Leonardo.jpg** (that is, the letter *d*, a colon, a backslash, and the filename Leonardo.jpg). If your CD-ROM drive isn't drive D, type the letter appropriate for your drive rather than D. When you're done, click the _Open button. The dialog box closes, and the location and filename of the Leonardo file are displayed in the Composition window.

- If you're using a Macintosh, use your mouse to browse the CD-ROM. When you locate a file named Leonardo.jpg, click it and then click the Open button.

**8** **Dial into the Internet. When you're connected, click the Send button.**

Netscape starts transmitting the message and displays a Sending Message box to show you what percentage of the transmission has been completed. Because the Leonardo.jpg file is of moderate size (about 100K), sending it should take a minute or two. When the transmission is completed, the Composition window closes.

Sending a file by e-mail is relatively easy: Compose a message, attach the file to the message, and send your message as usual. Receiving and viewing an attached file is just as easy — as you'll see shortly.

extra credit

## Attaching Web pages

In addition to attaching files, you can "send" someone who uses an HTML-capable e-mail program a Web page. The simplest way is to type the complete URL of the Web page (including the http:// prefix), surrounded by brackets; for example, `<http://www.hotbot.com>`. When your message is received, your URL text is underlined, and is colored blue or purple, just like a link. Further, the text functions like a link; specifically, if the recipient is connected to the Net and clicks the text, it activates the person's default browser program and makes it display the Web page.

Alternatively, you can click the Attach button from the Composition Toolbar and click the _Web Page option. This opens a dialog box that prompts you to type in a URL. After you do so and press Enter, the actual contents of the page (*except for* graphics) are copied into your message. As a result, when the recipient opens the message, she sees the Web page.

✓ **Progress Check**

If you can do the following, you've mastered this lesson:

❑ Attach a file to a message.

❑ Send the message.

# Receiving an Attached File                    Lesson 6-4

In the preceding lesson, you sent yourself an attached file. Now follow these steps to receive the file:

**1** **Run Netscape and connect to the Internet (if you aren't already connected).**

**2** **Click the Mailbox icon in the Component Bar.**

The Messenger window opens and retrieves your new messages. Among them should be the message you just sent to yourself. (If it didn't arrive yet, wait a few minutes and click the Get Msg button on the Toolbar to try again.)

**3** **After you receive your message, click it from the Inbox folder's message list.**

The text of the message appears in the lower portion of the Messenger window, along with an attachment box like the one in Figure 6-7. The right side of the box contains information about the attached file, such as its name and file format. The right side of the box contains blue underlined text, which is a link. Clicking this link lets you view and/or save the file.

In addition to the attachment box, you may see the name of the file at the bottom of your message. Double-clicking the filename will also let you view and/or save the file.

**4** **Click the link (that is, the blue underlined text) on the left side of the attachment box.**

After a moment, you're switched to a browser window, and . . . look at that! A self-portrait by one of the world's master illustrators! (See Figure 6-8.)

**5** **If you're using Windows, click the picture using your right (*not* left) mouse button. If you're using a Macintosh, click the picture and hold your mouse button down for several seconds.**

A menu pops up with a variety of options, including one named Save Image As. This option lets you save the picture in a separate file for use with other programs.

**6** **Click the Save Image As option.**

A standard Save As dialog box appears. Use it to save the file in an appropriate folder on your hard disk. The original name of the file is Leonardo.jpg. You can save your copy under a different name if you want, but be sure to retain the .jpg extension because that identifies the file's JPEG format.

Netscape doesn't know what to do with lots of file types — programs, word processing documents, sound files, video clips, and the like. When you receive such files as attachments, click the link in the left side of the attachment box. You'll see a dialog box that asks you what you want to do with the file. Accept the Save it to disk option (which is the default) and click OK. A standard Save As dialog box opens. Use this dialog box to save the attachment as a file.

**Notes:**

to save a picture file, right-click the picture (on a PC) or click it and hold down your mouse button (on a Mac), and then choose Save Image As option from menu that appears

to save attachment that Netscape can't display, click attachment link, click OK, and save data as file using the Save As dialog box

**Figure 6-7:** Click the link on the left side of the attachment box to view and/or save your attached file.

**Figure 6-8:** Netscape displays an attached picture in its browser window — cool!

Name: Leonardo.jpg
Type: JPEG Image (image/jpeg)
Encoding: Base64

Part 1.2

Figure 6-7

Figure 6-8

### ☑ Progress Check

If you can do the following, you've mastered this lesson:

❑ Receive a file with an attachment.

❑ Save an attached picture in a separate file.

❑ Save other types of attachments in separate files.

After you create the file, move to the folder it's in and double-click it. If the file is a program, your computer runs it. If it's a data file, your computer tries to recognize the format and run the appropriate program for viewing that type of file (assuming you have the program needed). If you get stuck, call the person who sent you the file and arrange to get it in a different format.

extra credit

## Practice safe computing

If someone sends you a program by e-mail, should you go ahead and run it? Depends on who sends it to you! If you don't know and trust the sender, don't run the program unless you run a virus-checker first. See Lesson 3-2 for information about checking programs for viruses.

# Unit 6 Quiz

For each of the following questions, circle the letter of the correct answer or answers. Remember, some questions may have more than one right answer.

1. **A nickname is**

    A. A computer term created by a guy named Nick.

    B. Something you type into Netscape's Address Book.

    C. A cute name that only your childhood friends can get away with calling you.

D. From the Middle English *eekname,* meaning "also name."

E. A name you can use when addressing e-mail messages in place of a person's actual e-mail address.

2. **To make an e-mail folder:**

   A. It takes a village.

   B. Open the Messenger window and click the File button from the Toolbar.

   C. Open the Messenger window and choose File⇨New Folder.

   D. Open the Composition window and click the New button.

   E. Buy the appropriate materials at a hardware store and start sawing.

3. **If you want to filter messages about making money into a Get Rich folder, you can tell Netscape to search for text in:**

   A. The sender header.

   B. The subject header.

   C. The message's body.

   D. The message's soul.

   E. The sender's bank account.

4. **Reasons to attach a file to an e-mail message include**

   A. Sending word processing documents to colleagues who are collaborating on a writing project.

   B. Sending pictures of your kids to your parents.

   C. Sending spreadsheets to your company's accounting department with your expense reports.

   D. Wanting to show off how much you know about the Internet.

   E. Sending a file full of vital top-secret information to yourself just before enemy agents break down your door so that you can delete the original file from your hard disk and claim that you don't know what file they are talking about.

5. **Before sending a file to someone, you should be sure that:**

   A. The person's e-mail program can handle MIME attachments, because Netscape attaches files by using MIME.

   B. The person has software that can read the type of file that you are sending; for example, the appropriate word processor, spreadsheet, or presentation program.

   C. The person feels like dealing with the whole subject of attached files.

   D. The person wants to receive the file.

   E. Your sun sign is compatible with the sign of the person receiving the file.

6.  In the children's classic *A Wrinkle in Time*, the main characters are helped by three beings (Mrs. Who, Mrs. Which, and Mrs. Whatsit) who used to be

    A.  Stars.

    B.  Planets.

    C.  Tesseracts.

    D.  Evil, but now they are good.

    E.  Tabloid journalists.

# Unit 6 Exercise

1.  Remember that friend with whom you exchanged messages in the exercise at the end of Unit 5? Get ahold of that person's e-mail address. You can find it by opening the message you sent to your friend, if the message is still in your Sent folder in the Messenger window.

    *Note:* If you skipped the Unit 5 exercise, call your friends until you find someone with an e-mail address. Write it down very carefully.

2.  In the Address Book, create an entry for your friend.

    *Extra credit:* Use the cut-and-paste commands to copy your friend's address from a message in your Sent folder to the Address Book entry.

3.  Create a new message and address it to your friend by using the Address Book.

4.  Type a message to your friend. Be sure to mention that you're reading this wonderful book about learning how to use Netscape Communicator.

    *Extra credit:* Find out whether your friend's mail program can handle MIME attachments and, if it can, attach the Leonardo.jpg file to your message.

5.  Send the message.

```
Unit 7
• • • • • • • • • •
```

# Joining Usenet Newsgroups

## Objectives for This Unit

- ✓ Understanding what Usenet newsgroups are all about
- ✓ Listing newsgroups
- ✓ Subscribing to newsgroups
- ✓ Reading newsgroup articles
- ✓ Finding newsgroups and newsgroup articles of interest
- ✓ Posting articles to newsgroups

Among the best resources of the Internet are its tens of thousands of ongoing discussion groups, which conduct lively conversations devoted to virtually every subject under the sun (and even a few beyond it).

Some of the most useful and interesting discussions take place via e-mail mailing lists. More information about this form of discussion group appears in Unit CD-1, "Joining Discussions by E-Mail," which is stored on the CD-ROM that came with this book in a file named Maillist.pdf. You can read and print this file by using the Acrobat Reader program, which is also stored on the CD-ROM. (For more information, see Appendix B.)

Another way to participate in online discussions is to join newsgroups. A *newsgroup* is a group devoted to an ongoing discussion of a particular topic that takes place via an area of the Internet called *Usenet*. More than 30,000 newsgroups exist, so you can find discussions on virtually any topic you can think of, ranging from baseball (rec.sports.baseball) to orthopedic surgery (sci.medicine.orthopedic), and from pantyhose (alt.pantyhose) to the afterlife (alt.life.afterlife). More than 50,000 new messages — or, as they're referred to on Usenet, *articles* — pour into newsgroups every day, making these collective talkfests a rich resource for both learning and fun.

**Prerequisites**

- ▶ Running Netscape (Lesson 1-2)
- ▶ Entering a URL to go to a Web page (Lesson 2-3)
- ▶ Setting up Netscape to handle e-mail and newsgroups (Lesson 5-1)
- ▶ Reading, sending, and replying to e-mail messages (Lessons 5-2, 5-3, and 5-4)
- ▶ E-mail etiquette (Lesson 5-5)

▶ Maillist.pdf

on the CD

---

newsgroup =
ongoing discussion
or series of
announcements

Usenet = system of
thousands of
newsgroups

article = message
that's distributed
by a Usenet
newsgroup

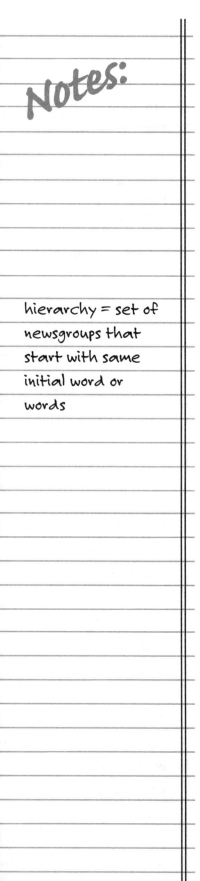

*hierarchy = set of newsgroups that start with same initial word or words*

Each newsgroup has a name consisting of a bunch of words (or parts of words) strung together by dots.

The first word in a newsgroup name tells you the general category that the newsgroup falls under (for example, rec for recreational or sci for scientific). The following word or words in the name further define the newsgroup's topic. Depending on how specific the newsgroup is and how many similar newsgroups exist, the name may have several words or only two. For example, precisely one U.S. newsgroup discusses the joy of flying kites, so the name of the newsgroup is rec.kites. Lots of newsgroups talk about pets, however, so the name of the cats newsgroup is rec.pets.cats.

on the test

All the newsgroups that start with the same initial word or words collectively form what is called a *hierarchy*. The following are the seven major hierarchies; that is, the seven types of newsgroups that are the most widely distributed:

- ♦ **rec:** Recreational topics, such as sports, games, collecting, music, and art

- ♦ **soc:** Both social issues (such as politics, religion, and human rights) and socializing (such as singles and pen-pal newsgroups)

- ♦ **talk:** Impassioned debate about topical and controversial issues (though often more heat than light is shed here)

- ♦ **sci:** Scientific topics, such as physics, chemistry, biology, and medicine

- ♦ **comp:** Computer-related topics, including discussions of PC software and hardware

- ♦ **news:** Topics concerning Usenet and newsgroups themselves

- ♦ **misc:** Miscellaneous topics that don't fit neatly under the other six hierarchies, such as health and fitness, screenwriting, jobhunting, and for-sale notices

Many newer or more narrow hierarchies aren't as "official" but are of great interest anyway. The most notable of these by far is alt (short for alternative), which contains more than 4,000 wildly diverse newsgroups. These range from the benign (alt.sewing, alt.algebra.help, alt.comedy.slapstick. 3-stooges) to the serious (alt.adoption, alt.alcohol, alt.censorship, alt.save.the.earth) to the off-the-wall (alt.alien.visitors, alt.fan.lemur, alt.barney.dinosaur. die.die.die).

Other newsgroup hierarchies include those devoted to a particular company (for example, microsoft for Microsoft or netscape for Netscape Communications) or region (for example, ca for topics related to California or fr for topics related to France *and* that are discussed in French).

Because keeping up-to-date on all these newsgroups consumes a huge amount of an Internet provider's computer resources, some providers choose to not carry hierarchies outside the seven long-established ones listed earlier.

Netscape includes a program for reading newsgroups named *Collabra* (short for *collaborate* because it allows a group of people to join a discussion). In this unit, you'll use the Collabra program to list newsgroups, join newsgroups, read newsgroup articles, find newsgroups and newsgroup articles devoted to topics that interest you, and post your own newsgroup articles.

extra credit

## What's the difference between newsgroups and mailing lists?

If you've read Unit CD-1, "Joining Discussions by E-Mail," you may wonder how getting involved in newsgroups differs from joining mailing lists.

Newsgroups are similar to mailing lists in that they let you read and participate in focused discussions along with other nice people on the Internet. Also, like mailing lists, newsgroups can be announcement only (just one person posts articles to the newsgroup), moderated (one person acts as a censor, approving articles before making them public), or open discussion (anyone can post articles).

However, a mailing list is managed at one computer, by one person or program, and sends each of its messages directly from the list manager to the subscriber. In contrast, newsgroup articles aren't sent directly to subscribers but are passed along all over the Internet by various computers (called *news servers*) that are especially assigned to receive them, with no central management. This means that you can reach out and grab articles from any newsgroup at any time, without providing any notification to the people who run the newsgroup. In fact, when you subscribe to a newsgroup, that action affects only the behavior of your copy of Netscape, not other computers. (Specifically, your subscribing to a newsgroup makes Netscape list the newsgroup along with your e-mail folders, allowing you to switch to the newsgroup and read its articles in the same way that you switch to and read your e-mail messages. Subscribing to a newsgroup also allows Netscape to keep track of your unread articles in the newsgroup.)

The bottom line, however, is that both mailing lists and newsgroups let you share information with millions of other knowledgeable people around the world. What you should concentrate on isn't picking which message distribution system you prefer (there's no reason to not use both), but discovering which discussions taking place on the Internet are the most likely to help you out or make you happy.

Collabra =
Netscape program
that lets you read
newsgroups

**Lesson 7-1**

# Listing and Subscribing to Newsgroups

*Notes:*

to open Message
Center window,
click Discussions
icon from
Component Bar or
choose
Communicator→
Collabra Discussion
Groups

Discussions icon

To show you the names of available newsgroups, Netscape must connect to a *news server* (or *news host*), a computer that provides newsgroup articles. If you followed the instructions in Lesson 5-1, you've already told Netscape the name of your Internet provider's news server (or discovered that Netscape already knew it). If you skipped Lesson 5-1, work through it now and then return here.

To access the newsgroups list, first open the Netscape Message Center window by choosing Communicator⇨Collabra Discussion Groups from any Netscape menu bar. Alternatively, open the window by clicking the Discussions icon (also called the Discussion Groups icon), which looks like two cartoon dialog balloons. Discussions is the third icon in the Component Bar, which is typically located in any Netscape window's lower-right corner. When you see your ISP's news server at the bottom of the Message Center window, click the server to select it and then click the window's Subscribe button (on a PC) or Join Groups button (on a Mac). A dialog box that you can use to list the thousands of newsgroups on the server opens.

*Note:* You can actually read messages from a number of different servers. For example, the company that publishes Netscape has its own news server that you can employ to read special newsgroups run for Netscape users. For more information, see the "Subscribing to Netscape Newsgroups" sidebar that appears later in this unit.

In this lesson, you'll open the Message Center window, select your Internet provider's news server, explore the newsgroups on the server, and subscribe to a few newsgroups.

## Listing newsgroups

To see a list of the newsgroups that you can join through your ISP, follow these steps:

**1** **Connect to your Internet and launch Netscape.**

**2** **Click the Component Bar's Discussions icon (the third icon in the lower-right corner of your window).**

Alternatively, choose Communicator⇨Collabra Discussion Groups. Either way, you see a Message Center window like the one in Figure 7-1. This window displays all your e-mail folders, and it also displays your ISP's news server at the bottom. After you join a few newsgroups, you'll see them listed in this window below the server name.

**3** **Click the Subscribe button on the window's Toolbar.**

Alternatively, choose File⇨Subscribe to Discussion Groups from the menu bar. You see a Subscribe to Discussion Groups dialog box similar to the one in Figure 7-2. Notice that the name of your news server appears at the bottom of the dialog box to indicate that Netscape is connected to it.

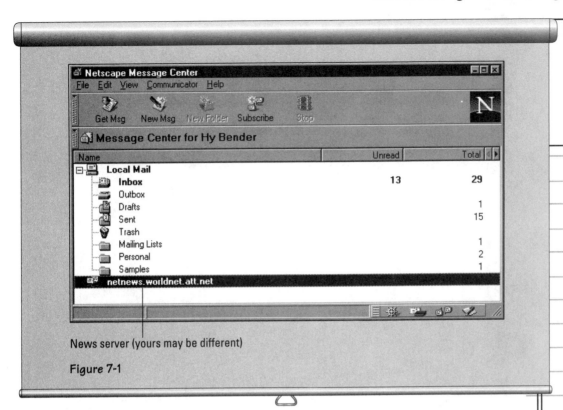

**Figure 7-1:** The Netscape
Message Center window
lists all your e-mail
folders, your news
servers, and the
newsgroups to which
you've subscribed.

News server (yours may be different)

Figure 7-1

Also notice the big white box in the middle of the dialog box. Your newsgroups
list normally appears in this box. Because you haven't accessed your ISP's news
server before, however, Netscape first must spend about 10 or 15 minutes
downloading newsgroup information. Netscape may have already started doing
this automatically, as indicated by a status bar in the left corner of the bottom
message bar telling you what percentage of the transmission has been
completed (see Figure 7-2). Otherwise, start the ball rolling by clicking the Get
Groups button.

**4** **If Netscape isn't automatically transferring your newsgroup data,
click the Get Groups button on the right side of the dialog box.**

If you find that the button is grayed out, that means Netscape is already
getting the information, so you don't have to do anything else with Netscape
for a while.

Go make yourself a cup of coffee, or perhaps some nice herbal tea, and return
to your computer in 10 or 15 minutes. You should see a list of newsgroups
similar to the one in Figure 7-2. (**Note:** If you don't see a list, click the Stop
button on the right side of the dialog box and then try again by clicking the Get
Groups button.)

**5** **Scroll through the newsgroups list.**

You can use the PgDn and PgUp keys or click the vertical scroll bar along the
right edge of the list. If your ISP's server is typical, you see hundreds of names.

Nice going! You now have a solid collection of newsgroups to work with.

to list newsgroups,
click a news
server to select it
and then either
click Subscribe
button on Message
Center Toolbar
or choose
File→Subscribe
to Discussion
Groups

**Figure 7-2:** Use the
Subscribe to Discussion
Groups dialog box to
list the newsgroups on a
news server.

*Notes:*

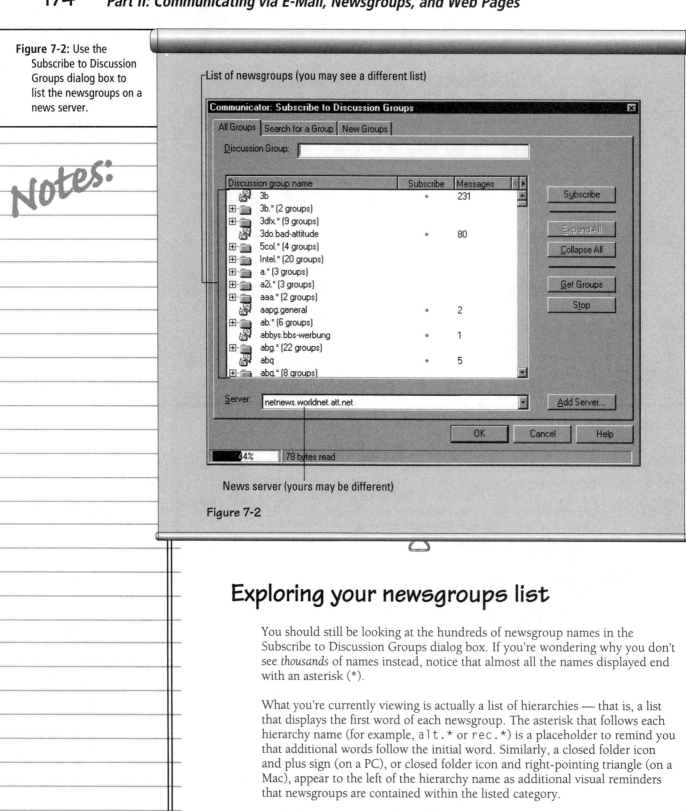

List of newsgroups (you may see a different list)

News server (yours may be different)

Figure 7-2

# Exploring your newsgroups list

You should still be looking at the hundreds of newsgroup names in the
Subscribe to Discussion Groups dialog box. If you're wondering why you don't
see *thousands* of names instead, notice that almost all the names displayed end
with an asterisk (*).

What you're currently viewing is actually a list of hierarchies — that is, a list
that displays the first word of each newsgroup. The asterisk that follows each
hierarchy name (for example, alt.* or rec.*) is a placeholder to remind you
that additional words follow the initial word. Similarly, a closed folder icon
and plus sign (on a PC), or closed folder icon and right-pointing triangle (on a
Mac), appear to the left of the hierarchy name as additional visual reminders
that newsgroups are contained within the listed category.

To the right of each hierarchy name is a number in parentheses that tells you
how many newsgroups start with that word. For example, at the time we write

this, rec (short for *recreation*) has 675 groups, and the popular alt category (short for *alternative* and a catch-all for any topic that falls outside the other hierarchies) has 4,225 newsgroups!

To display the newsgroups within a hierarchy, you can simply click the plus sign or right-pointing triangle to its left. After you do so, the plus sign becomes a minus sign (on a PC) or the triangle turns to point downward (on a Mac). In addition, the closed folder icon changes to an open folder icon, and the newsgroups within the hierarchy are listed directly below the hierarchy name.

Try expanding some hierarchies now to further explore your newsgroups list:

**1 Press PgDn or click the vertical scroll bar until you see the** rec.* **hierarchy.**

Alternatively, double-click in the text box at the top and type **rec**. After you do so, the list jumps to select the rec.* category.

**2 Click the plus sign (on a PC) or right-pointing triangle (on a Mac) to the left of the** rec.* **hierarchy.**

Netscape retrieves the data that you requested and, after a few moments, displays the names of scores of newsgroups in the rec hierarchy (such as rec.antiques, rec.birds, and rec.skydiving), as shown in Figure 7-3. In addition, it displays the names of many second-level hierarchies, such as rec.arts.* and rec.music.*. To dig deeper into the rec category, open one of these lower-level hierarchies.

**3 Locate the** rec.arts.* **hierarchy and click the plus sign or triangle to its left.**

You see additional newsgroups within this narrower category (such as rec.arts.dance and rec.arts.poems). You also see third-level hierarchies, such as rec.arts.books.*, rec.arts.movies.*, and, of course, the wildly popular rec.arts.startrek.*. To see the newsgroups within a third-level hierarchy — or any other hierarchy — you again click the plus sign or right-pointing triangle by the hierarchy name.

Of course, you also can go in the other direction and contract hierarchies rather than expand them. Doing so prevents your newsgroup list from displaying a lot of items you're not regularly interested in. To contract an open hierarchy, simply click the minus sign or down-pointing triangle to its left. Give it a shot!

**4 Click the minus sign or triangle to the left of the** rec.arts.* **hierarchy.**

The arts newsgroups list disappears and the open folder icon changes back to a closed icon. Also, the minus sign reverts to a plus sign (on a PC), or the triangle turns to the right again (on a Mac).

You can explore your entire newsgroup list in a similar fashion, clicking to the left of every hierarchy that sounds interesting to display the newsgroups one level below it. Sometimes, however, you want to immediately expand not only your selected hierarchy but also *all* the hierarchies within it. You can do so by using the Expand All button on the right side of the dialog box. Similarly, you can collapse all hierarchies using the Contract All button.

*to display hierarchy's newsgroups, click its plus sign (on PC) or right-pointing triangle (on Mac)*

*to expand hierarchy and all hierarchies within it, click it to select it and click Expand All button*

**Figure 7-3:** When you expand the `rec.*` entry, Netscape displays the newsgroups and second-level hierarchies within this hierarchy.

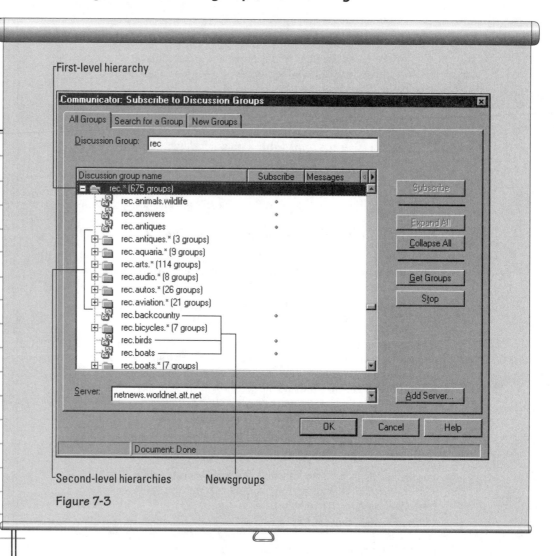

Figure 7-3

Try expanding and contracting every subhierarchy within the `rec.*` hierarchy:

### 1 Locate and click the `rec.*` hierarchy.

The hierarchy is highlighted to show that it's selected.

### 2 Click the Expand All button (on the right side of the dialog box).

As in the preceding exercise, `rec.*` expands to show the newsgroups and hierarchies directly beneath it. This time, however, all the hierarchies that it contains are also expanded.

### 3 Scroll through the expanded `rec.*` list.

Notice that this expanded list offers the convenience of not making you have to guess at which newsgroups are contained within any hierarchy. At the same time, though, the expanded list forces you to wade through the clutter of many newsgroups that you're not interested in, which can ultimately make finding the newsgroups that you want more difficult. Whether you click a plus sign or triangle or click the Expand All button to open a hierarchy therefore depends on both your research needs and your personal taste. For now, close the `rec.*` hierarchy.

*Notes:*

**4** **Click** `rec.*` **(if it isn't already selected) and click the Contract All button.**

All the hierarchies within `rec.*` close and then `rec.*` itself closes.

As you've just seen, an enormous number of diverse newsgroups is available. Some of them are relatively quiet, receiving only a few messages a week; but some of the more popular ones can draw scores of messages a day. You can tell how many messages are in a particular newsgroup by looking at the number to its right under the Messages column.

Take some time to explore the newsgroups list on your own and write down the name of any newsgroup that interests you. When you're ready, push on to the next exercise, in which you subscribe to a few newsgroups.

## Subscribing and unsubscribing to newsgroups

If you want to read a newsgroup, you *subscribe* to it. This makes Netscape list the newsgroup along with your e-mail folders in both the Message Center window and in the Messenger window's folder quick-access menu (see Lesson 5-3). You can then select the newsgroup and read its articles as easily as you can switch to an e-mail folder and read its messages. Also, your subscribing allows Netscape to keep track of which articles you've read in the newsgroup, sparing you from accidentally reading an article twice.

You should still be displaying your newsgroup list. To subscribe to a few helpful newsgroups, follow these steps:

**1** **Double-click inside the text box named Discussion Group (on a PC) or Group (on a Mac), which is located at the top of the Subscribe to Discussion Groups dialog box.**

Any text inside the box is highlighted and will disappear when you type your new text.

**2** **Type** news.announce.newusers **very carefully.**

Be sure to include both dots in the newsgroup name. As you type, the list jumps to match your text with an appropriate newsgroup. After you're done typing, the `news.announce.newusers` newsgroup should be selected. (If it isn't, select it manually by scrolling through the list to locate it and then clicking it.) This newsgroup is devoted to providing basic information and guidelines to Usenet novices.

on the test

**3** **Click the Subscribe button in the upper-right section of the dialog box.**

A check mark appears to the right of the newsgroup (under the Subscribe heading near the top of the dialog box) to show that you've joined the newsgroup. Also, the name of the button that you just clicked changes to Unsubscribe, giving you the opportunity to change your mind.

subscribe = join newsgroup

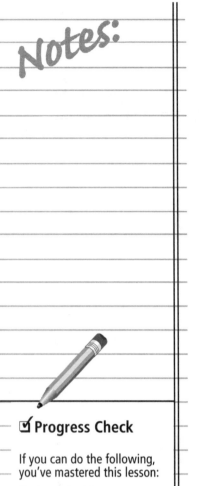

**Notes:**

☑ **Progress Check**

If you can do the following, you've mastered this lesson:

❑ Open the Message Center window.

❑ Open the Subscribe to Discussion Groups dialog box.

❑ List all top-level newsgroup hierarchies on your ISP's news server.

❑ Expand or contract a hierarchy by one level.

❑ Expand or contract a hierarchy and also all the hierarchies within it.

❑ Subscribe and unsubscribe to newsgroups.

**4** **Click the Unsubscribe button.**

The check mark to the right of the newsgroup disappears, canceling your subscribe command, and the button returns to saying *Subscribe*. You can quit a newsgroup that you've joined at any time by simply selecting it and then clicking the Unsubscribe button.

**5** **Click the Subscribe button again.**

The check mark reappears to show that you've rejoined the newsgroup.

**6** **Double-click inside the top text box again, type** news.newusers. questions **very carefully, and click the Subscribe button.**

A check mark appears to the right of the news.newusers.questions newsgroup, which is devoted to taking the questions of new Internet users and providing answers.

**7** **Double-click inside the top text box again, type** news.answers **very carefully, and click the Subscribe button.**

A check mark appears to the right of the news.answers newsgroup, which is devoted to carrying the *FAQs* (that is, *F*requently *A*sked *Q*uestions lists) of other newsgroups. (For more information, see the sidebar "Just the FAQs, ma'am," later in this unit.)

**8** **Optionally, repeat Step 7 to subscribe to a few newsgroups you're personally interested in.**

Restrict yourself to two or three additional newsgroups for now. (Life is too short to be reading newsgroups all day!)

**9** **Click the dialog box's OK button.**

Netscape saves your subscription choices and closes the dialog box.

You can now see the Message Center window again. The window contains some additions since you last viewed it, though — under your ISP's server are the names of all the newsgroups to which you just subscribed. (See Figure 7-4.) You'll read articles from these newsgroups in the next lesson.

**on the test**

*Tip #1:* If you already know the name of a newsgroup that you want to join, click in the Location box of the Netscape browser window, type **news:** followed by the newsgroup's name, and press Enter. If the newsgroup is on your ISP's news server, Netscape immediately subscribes you to it and switches you to its articles via the Messenger window.

*Tip #2:* You can unsubscribe from a newsgroup right from the Message Center window. To do so, simply click the newsgroup to select it, choose Edit⇨ Delete Discussion Group, and click OK. (We'll go through these steps again in the next lesson.)

## Recess

Now that you know how to list and subscribe to newsgroups, you're ready for more advanced instruction. But first, take a stretch. Be sure to disconnect from your Internet provider so that you don't tie up your phone line. Then, focus on something far away — out the window, if possible. Focusing on something close up for hours at a time is bad for your eyes!

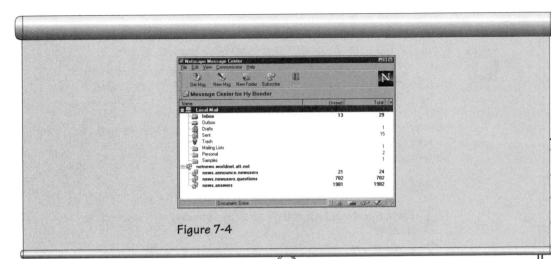

Figure 7-4

## Subscribing to Netscape newsgroups

Netscape Communications maintains its own newsgroups by using its own news server. The Netscape newsgroups are, not surprisingly, in the `netscape.*` hierarchy. Your ISP's news server probably doesn't carry the `netscape.*` newsgroups; instead, you have to connect to Netscape's own news server at `secnews.netscape.com`. To do so, follow these steps:

1. Run Netscape and connect to the Internet.

2. Click in the browser window's Location box, type **snews:// secnews.netscape.com/ netscape**, and press Enter. That's *snews* (for "secure news"), a colon, two slashes, the news server name, and the name of a generic

newsgroup on the service. Don't type any spaces. When you press Enter, Netscape opens the Message Center window and adds the `secnews.netscape.com` (`secure`) news server to your list of news servers. (The newsgroup is marked *secure* because it uses Netscape security features.)

Subscribe to any Netscape newsgroup that looks promising; Netscape technical support folks can answer your questions about the program.

If you later want to delete the server, click it from the Message Center window to select it, choose Edit➪Delete Discussion Group Server, and click the OK button to confirm.

# Reading Newsgroup Articles

## Lesson 7-2

As we indicated earlier in this unit, reading the articles of a newsgroup is very similar to reading the messages in an e-mail folder.

on the test

All the newsgroups to which you've subscribed are listed with your e-mail folders in the Message Center window and you can switch to any of them by double-clicking. Alternatively, you can switch to a subscribed newsgroup by clicking in Messenger's folder quick-access menu and then clicking the newsgroup from the list that appears. After you perform either action, the newsgroup's articles are listed in the upper portion of the Messenger window. To read any article, just click it; the article's contents appear in the lower portion of the Messenger window.

To read a few newsgroup articles, follow these steps:

**1 Launch Netscape (if it isn't already running) and connect to the Internet.**

**2 Open the Messenger window by choosing Communicator⇨ Messenger Mailbox; then maximize the window.**

You want to have plenty of room for listing and reading your newsgroup articles.

**3 Click in the folder quick-access menu (the box directly below the Toolbar).**

As usual, a list appears that displays your e-mail folders. This time, however, the list also displays the newsgroups to which you subscribed in the preceding exercise.

**4 Click the** news.announce.newusers **newsgroup to switch to it.**

A Download Headers dialog box like the one in Figure 7-5 appears. The dialog box tells you how many unread articles are currently in the newsgroup and lets you choose how many article headers you want to download at a time. It also gives you the option of marking most of the articles as having been read in case you don't want to deal with older articles.

**5 Double-click inside the Download Header's text box, type** 50, **and click the Download button.**

After a few moments, the headings of the first 50 articles in news.announce. newusers are transmitted. You can see the first few listed in the upper portion of the window.

**6 Click an article that looks interesting.**

The text of the article appears in the lower portion of the Messenger window, allowing you to read it. Click the text and then scroll through it with the PgDn key or your mouse to read the article.

**7 Click another article that looks interesting.**

Notice that each time you select an article, its header loses its boldfacing to indicate that it's been read. Also, the Unread messages counter in the upper-right side of the window decreases by one.

**8 If you haven't already done so, locate and click an article called** *Answers to Frequently Asked Questions about Usenet* **(you may see only the first part of the title).**

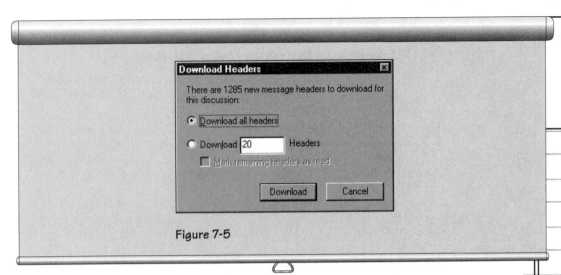

Figure 7-5

**Figure 7-5:** When you select a newsgroup with a lot of articles, Netscape allows you to choose how many article headers to receive at a time.

*Notes:*

This article is the *FAQ* (*F*requently *A*sked *Q*uestions list) about Usenet newsgroups. The article lists 50 questions at its top and then repeats each question followed by an answer. First read through the list of questions to identify the ones that interest you and then scroll down the article to read the pertinent answers. For more information about FAQs, see the "Just the FAQs, ma'am" sidebar, later in this unit.

In addition to clicking articles, you can select them by pressing certain keys. For example, try pressing the N key.

**9** **Press** N **a few times.**

Every time you press N, you move to the *n*ext unread message.

You can also select messages by pressing the T key, which moves you to the next unread *t*hread. A *thread* is an article that begins a discussion, followed by responses to that article, followed by responses to the responses, and so forth. In the list of articles in the upper portion of the window, Messenger displays the title of the thread (the subject line of the original article) with responses to the original article indented below. Responses to responses are indented further under the articles to which they respond; it's like a family tree.

Sometimes the first article in a thread is no longer present because news servers typically don't keep articles for more than about three days. If the first articles in the thread are older than that, they vanish, leaving behind the later articles in the thread. You can usually figure out what the earlier articles said, though, because responses frequently quote parts of the original article.

**10** **Press** T **a few times.**

Every time you press the T key, you move to the next thread — that is, the next set of unread articles with a different subject heading.

Messenger automatically orders all your articles by thread, which is usually convenient because it allows you to easily follow a conversation about a particular topic. If you want to organize your articles differently, however, you can do so by choosing <u>V</u>iew⇨S<u>o</u>rt and then clicking the ordering criteria that you desire.

thread = series of
articles responding
to initial article

**11** **Continue looking through the articles in the newsgroup.**

If you run out of your initial batch of messages, you can get more by choosing either File⇨Get Messages⇨New or File⇨Get Messages⇨Next 50. When you've had enough of this newsgroup, move on to another one.

**12** **Repeat Steps 3 through 6 to look through articles in the other newsgroups to which you've subscribed.**

That's about all there is to reading newsgroups!

As you just saw, you can read any article in a newsgroup to which you've subscribed with just a few mouse clicks. New messages in your newsgroups arrive automatically, so the only hard part is figuring out which articles you want to take the time to read — and that's a skill you'll develop with practice.

If you decide that you're enjoying your current newsgroups, simply stay subscribed to them. If you get bored with a newsgroup, however, you can quit it quickly by doing the following:

**1** **Click the Discussions icon in the Component Bar.**

The Message Center window opens.

**2** **Click the newsgroup that you want to quit.**

The newsgroup is highlighted to show that it's selected.

**3** **Choose Edit⇨Delete Discussion Group.**

You're asked whether you're sure that you want to unsubscribe to the newsgroup.

**4** **Click the OK button.**

The newsgroup disappears from the Message Center window. If you later change your mind, however, you can subscribe to it again at any time.

**☑ Progress Check**

If you can do the following, you've mastered this lesson:

❑ Switch to a newsgroup in the Messenger window.

❑ Download the newsgroup's article headers.

❑ Read the newsgroup's articles.

**extra credit**

## Just the FAQs, ma'am

A *FAQ* is a list of frequently asked questions and their answers. Many newsgroups create FAQs that include the questions that come up over and over and that folks on the newsgroup are sick of answering. If you pose one of these questions, you're likely to get responses that say, *Read the $%#(\* FAQ!*

How do you read the FAQ for a newsgroup? If the FAQ appears on the list of articles for the newsgroup, read it like any other article. If you don't see the FAQ among the articles in the newsgroup, go to the news.answers newsgroup. This newsgroup contains the FAQs for many newsgroups that have FAQs, listed in no particular order. Many FAQs are really long and have been divided into several parts. Long FAQs appear as a series of articles, with titles like *alt. backyard.chickens FAQ, Part 2 of 5.*

# Searching for Newsgroups of Interest

You can find interesting newsgroups by wading through the hierarchy list, but you can miss a lot of interesting ones, too. Isn't there a better way to find the newsgroup you're looking for? There is, and the route, as usual, is the Web! This lesson, therefore, shows you how to use a Web page to search for newsgroups devoted to your favorite subjects.

The Deja News Web site can match you with the right newsgroups and it also can find newsgroup articles of interest. Follow these steps:

**1 Launch Netscape (if it's not already running) and connect to your Internet provider.**

**2 Click in the browser window's Location box, type** dejanews.com**, and press Enter.**

You see the Deja News Quick Search page shown in Figure 7-6.

**3 Click the Find Newsgroups option.**

Otherwise, Deja News will search for any newsgroup article mentioning your topic, which can be handy but isn't quite what you're after right now.

**4 Click in the Quick Search For box, type a word or phrase (such as** cooking **or** baseball **or** xfiles**), and press Enter.**

You see a page listing newsgroups that discuss your topic (as in Figure 7-7). Each newsgroup name is blue and underlined, which means that it's a link.

**5 Click a newsgroup that looks promising.**

You see a page listing articles from the newsgroup that include the word or phrase that you typed. For each article, you see the date it was posted, the article's title, the newsgroup to which the article was posted, and the e-mail address of the author of the article. Both the title of each article and the e-mail address of its author are links. If more matches are found than can fit on the page, you can click a *next* link near the bottom of the page to see additional matches.

**6 Click the title of an article that looks interesting.**

Deja News displays the article in your browser window. The Newsgroups heading of the article tells you which newsgroup the article comes from.

**7 Press Netscape's Back button to return to the list of articles.**

Continue clicking articles to get a feel for the newsgroup. If what you see convinces you that you'd enjoy reading the newsgroup regularly, subscribe to the newsgroup. Otherwise, use Netscape's Back button to return to the original list of newsgroups, and repeat Steps 5 through 7 until you find a newsgroup that satisfies you.

Pretty cool! If you ever want to return to Deja News to do article searching, you can find a bookmark for the page under the Web Search Programs category of the *Dummies 101* bookmarks that you installed in Lesson 2-1.

*Notes:*

**Figure 7-6:** Type a search phrase in the Deja News text box to find newsgroup articles containing the phrase.

**Figure 7-7:** Deja News lists newsgroups that contain the search phrase you entered.

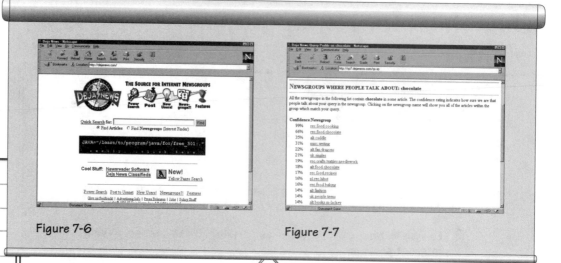

Figure 7-6                                      Figure 7-7

### ☑ Progress Check

If you can do the following, you've mastered this lesson:

❑ Find newsgroups devoted to your favorite subjects using the Deja News Web site.

❑ Find newsgroup articles covering a particular topic using the Deja News Web site.

❑ Read the articles that Deja News finds.

extra credit

# Other ways to find newsgroup articles

Here are two other Web pages that help you search for newsgroups and newsgroup articles:

▶ **The AltaVista page that you used in Lesson 2-5 to search for Web pages:** Near the top of its home page (at `altavista. digital.com`), AltaVista says something like `Search the Web and Display the Results in Standard Form`, and the phrase `the Web` appears in a box. Click in the box and choose the Usenet option from the little menu that appears; this sets AltaVista to search through newsgroup articles instead of Web pages. Next, click in the Search text box, type a word or phrase, and press Enter. When you see a list of articles, click the subject line to read the article; AltaVista displays the text right in your browser window. If you want to read other articles in the newsgroup, subscribe to the newsgroup by locating its name in the article header, clicking in the Location box, typing **news:** followed by the name of the newsgroup, and pressing Enter.

▶ **The Liszt of Newsgroups page:** Go to `www.liszt.com/news`, type a word or phrase in the Search box on the page, and press Enter. Liszt searches only in the names and descriptions of newsgroups, not in the text of articles. When you see a list of the newsgroups that Liszt found, you can click the newsgroup name to read its articles in the Messenger window. (**Note:** Liszt is also a wonderful resource for finding electronic mailing lists. For more information, see Unit CD-1 in the file Maillist.pdf on your *Dummies 101* CD-ROM.)

# Replying to Newsgroup Articles          Lesson 7-4

After you read the articles in a newsgroup for a while, you may be ready to chime in. You have two ways to respond to an article that you read in a newsgroup:

▶ **By e-mail:** If your response is of interest only to the person who posted the original article, if your response is a bit personal and you don't want to share it with the whole newsgroup, or if the original article requested replies by e-mail, respond with an e-mail message directly to the person who wrote the article.

▶ **With your own article:** If your response is of interest to lots of people who read the newsgroup, you are sure of your facts, and you have time to write a clear, concise response, then respond by posting your own article to the newsgroup. Remember, thousands of people around the world will read your article, so make sure that you really have something to say!

You also can post an article that doesn't respond to another article. If you want to bring up a new topic, you can post a new article.

In this lesson, you'll create an article using the Composition window. You'll then send your article to the misc.test newsgroup, which is designed precisely for the purpose of letting new folks try out their posting skills. You'll also respond to your test article by e-mail.

## Posting a test article

Here's how to post an article on a newsgroup, just to make sure that you know how:

**1 Run Netscape and connect to the Internet.**

Use the browser window to quickly subscribe to misc.test, which is a newsgroup that allows beginners to post test messages.

**2 Click in the Location box, type news:misc.test (that is, news, a colon, and misc.test, with no spaces), and press Enter.**

The misc.test newsgroup appears in the Messenger window, and a Download Headers dialog box asks you how many article headers you want to receive. Because this newsgroup is provided exclusively for the purpose of letting new users test their skills at posting articles, none of the messages in misc.test is really worth reading. To make ignoring the newsgroup's articles easy, use a little trick: mark all the existing messages as read. This will make finding your own article after you post it much easier.

*Notes:*

**3** **Double-click inside the text box, type 1, click the <u>M</u>ark remaining headers as read option, and click the Download button.**

The other articles in `misc.test` are marked as read, as indicated by the number to the right of the Unread messages counter. Now start creating your test article.

***Tip:*** You can also mark all messages as read at any time by choosing <u>M</u>essage➪<u>M</u>ark➪<u>A</u>ll Read or, if you're using Windows, by pressing Shift+C.

**4** **Click the New Msg button on the Toolbar to open the Composition window.**

The same Composition window that you use for writing e-mail appears. The name of the current newsgroup, `misc.test`, has been automatically inserted on the first address line, which is labeled *Group* to remind you that you aren't writing to an individual or a handful of people but to a large audience. Your cursor is in the Subject text box.

**5** **For your subject, type** Test: Please ignore **(or something like that).**

The article that you're about to post won't be of interest to anyone but you (and maybe your mother).

**6** **Click anywhere inside the message box to select it and then type** This is a test posting from Netscape **(or something like that).**

Type whatever you'd like to see when you read the article later.

**7** **When the article looks satisfactory, click the Send button (or choose <u>F</u>ile➪<u>S</u>end Now or press Ctrl+Enter or ⌘Enter).**

Netscape posts the article to the `misc.test` newsgroup.

Your article is winging its way to newsgroup readers all over the world!

If you start composing an article and then think better of it, you can close the Composition window by clicking its Close button. When Netscape asks whether you're sure that you want to discard your changes, click the Yes button.

to post an article you've composed, click Send button, choose File→ Send Now, or press Ctrl+Enter or ⌘Enter

## Reading the article that you posted

In a few minutes, the article that you just posted should appear in the `misc.test` newsgroup. You should still be in Messenger with `misc.test` selected. Here's how to see whether your article was sent successfully:

**1** **Press Ctrl+T or ⌘T to get new messages from your selected newsgroup (in this case, `misc.test`).**

Alternatively, choose <u>F</u>ile➪Get Messages➪<u>N</u>ew. Netscape retrieves the latest articles, including yours. If your article doesn't appear, wait a few more minutes and try again. (If your article doesn't appear within a half hour, call your Internet provider to find out what's amiss.)

**2** **Click your article.**

The text of your article appears in the lower portion of the Messenger window.

heads up

## Rules and regulations for posting articles

All the rules of e-mail netiquette that you learned in Lesson 5-5 apply to newsgroup articles, too. Follow the rules in the sidebar "Mailing list do's and don'ts" in Unit CD-1 as well, because mailing lists and newsgroups have a lot in common. In addition, follow these rules to avoid getting flamed by angry newsgroupies:

▶ Read a newsgroup for at least a week before posting anything, to be sure that your posting is appropriate for the newsgroup.

▶ Read the newsgroup's FAQ before posting anything. (See the sidebar "Just the FAQs, ma'am," earlier in this unit.)

▶ Don't post ads! If you have a product that relates directly to the subject of the newsgroup, you can post a brief article about it *once*, but you'll have better luck if the article is short and informational rather than salesy and vague. Be sure to include an e-mail address to which people can write for more information.

▶ Never post an article to a newsgroup that you don't read regularly.

▶ Don't post the same article to lots of newsgroups. (This is called *crossposting,* and it's frowned upon.) Sometimes an article is of interest to two or three newsgroups, but think long and hard before you crosspost.

Cool! You posted an article to a newsgroup! When you next have something reasonably interesting and wise to say, consider following the same procedure to post articles to newsgroups that you read regularly.

If you read an article and want to reply to it with an article (because your response is of interest to everyone in the newsgroup), post an article in response by clicking the Reply button on the Messenger Toolbar and then clicking the Reply to Group option. (Alternatively, click the Reply button and choose Reply to Sender and Group, which both posts your article and e-mails a copy to the original author.) Netscape displays a Composition window for posting a reply to the newsgroup.

If your response isn't of interest to most of the group, however, reply to an article privately by clicking the Reply button and clicking the Reply to Sender option, which brings up a Composition window addressed only to the article's author. Always use e-mail when replying to an annoying, clueless, or downright stupid article — there's no point embarrassing people in the public arena of a newsgroup.

## Forwarding, printing, and saving articles

Here are a few other things you can do with newsgroup articles:

▶ **Forward an article by e-mail:** If you see an article that would interest a friend, send her a copy by clicking the article to select it and then clicking the Forward button on the Toolbar.

▶ **Print an article:** Click the article to select it, click the Print button on the Toolbar to display the Print dialog box, make sure that your printer is on and has paper in it, and click OK.

▶ **Save the article in a text file:** Click the article to select it, choose File⇨Save As, and use the Save As dialog box to save the article in a plain text file.

**extra credit**

## Other newsreader programs

Netscape's Collabra isn't the only tool available for reading and participating in newsgroups. Two other excellent news-readers, Free Agent (a free Windows program) and InterNews (a shareware Macintosh program) are on the *Dummies 101* CD-ROM that came with this book. If you're interested in trying out an alternative approach to handling newsgroups, you won't go wrong with either of these acclaimed programs. For installation information, see Appendix B.

### ☑ Progress Check

If you can do the following, you've mastered this lesson:

❏ Post a test article.

❏ Receive and read your test article.

## Recess

Congratulations! You now know how to read articles in newsgroups, find articles by topic, and post your own articles to newsgroups. You are an amazing person, and we're pleased to know you! Don't get a swelled head, though; you still have to face the Unit 7 quiz.

# Unit 7 Quiz

For each of the following questions, circle the letter of the correct answer or answers. Remember, each question may have more than one right answer.

## Multiple Choice

1.  **A newsgroup:**

    A. Is the staff at a newspaper or radio station.

    B. Is an ongoing discussion devoted to a particular topic that takes place on the Internet.

    C. Provides the daily headlines and sports scores with your morning coffee.

    D. Has a name consisting of words, or parts of words, separated by dots.

    E. Consists of articles posted by Internet users around the world.

2. **The seven major newsgroup hierarchies include**

   A. `news` and `comp`

   B. `rec` and `misc`

   C. `Doc` and `Sneezy`

   D. `soc` and `sci`

   E. Star Trek and Star Wars

3. **To subscribe to a newsgroup:**

   A. Double-click its FAQ.

   B. Double-click its name or folder.

   C. Click the newspaper icon to its left.

   D. Click the <u>S</u>ubscribe button in the upper-right of the Subscribe to Discussion Groups dialog box.

   E. Choose <u>F</u>ile⇨A<u>d</u>d Newsgroup, enter the newsgroup's name in the dialog box that appears, and click OK.

4. **To read a newsgroup's articles, you can**

   A. Subscribe to it.

   B. Double-click the newsgroup from the Message Center window.

   C. Click in the Messenger folder quick-access menu and then click the newsgroup.

   D. Type **news:** followed by a newsgroup's name in the Location box of the browser window.

   E. All of the above.

5. **Curious George lives with:**

   A. Dumbo the Elephant.

   B. The man with the yellow hat.

   C. Curious Georgina.

   D. His parents.

   E. All the animals at the zoo.

# Unit 7 Exercise

1. Run Netscape and display the Deja News Web page.

2. Search for something you're interested in, such as *chocolate* or *lizards* or *antiques*. Make careful note of the newsgroup.

3. Subscribe to the newsgroup you found.

4. Read the newsgroup's articles for a week or so.

5. Look in the `news.answers` newsgroup for the FAQ on the newsgroup that you joined, and read the FAQ.

6. When you have a question to ask or want to contribute an answer or comment, post an article to the newsgroup. (But make sure that the question isn't answered in the FAQ!)

7. Continue reading the newsgroup to see how your article looks and what reaction it causes.

# Creating Your Own Web Pages

## Objectives for This Unit

✓ Opening the Netscape Composer window

✓ Creating a Web page

✓ Entering and formatting Web page text

✓ Saving a Web page

✓ Retrieving an existing Web page

✓ Creating links and bulleted lists in a Web page

✓ Adding pictures to a Web page

✓ Getting your Web pages up on the Internet

**Prerequisites**

▶ Browsing the Web (Units 1, 2, 3, and 4)

on the CD

▶ Mounts.gif (picture of mountains)

▶ Fern.gif (picture of a fern)

▶ Rainbow.gif (picture of a rainbow)

As you've worked through this book, you've probably seen and enjoyed hundreds of interesting Web pages. Cruising the Net is a terrifically rewarding skill, and you may be perfectly happy with using the Web just as an information and entertainment resource (similar to the way you use magazines, radio, and television).

Cruising isn't the only way you can interact with the Web, though; you can also publish your *own* Web pages. Doing so allows you to reach out and communicate with the tens of millions of other people on the Net.

To construct your Web pages, you can use Netscape's *Composer*. This program lets you create a Web page from scratch, edit the page to your heart's content, and then transmit the page to the Web.

To get your Web pages online, you need to obtain disk space on a computer that constantly communicates with the Web. This type of computer is called a *Web server,* and many Internet providers offer disk space on a Web server as

*Composer = Netscape's Web page editor*

*Notes:*

part of their service to their subscribers. Alternatively, you may be able to obtain disk space on a Web server through a company you're affiliated with or through a nonprofit organization. (See Lesson 8-4 for details.) When you're ready to unveil your pages to the public, you can use Composer to copy them from your PC to the Web server you've selected. You also can use Composer to edit and recopy your files at any time, which means that you can update your Web pages as often as you want.

If the prospect of publishing your own material on the Web sounds appealing — and if you're willing to learn a bit of technical stuff involving how Web pages are put together — then this unit is for you.

## Lesson 8-1          Creating a Web Page

Creating a Web page is not hard, but you should understand a few things about how pages are constructed before you get started.

A Web page actually consists of several files. The foundation of the page is its text file, which contains (as you may have guessed) the page's text. In addition, this file holds the names of other files to be incorporated into the page (such as picture and sound files) and special codes that direct how the text and other elements should be formatted and arranged on the page.

**on the test**

The formatting codes are called *tags,* and they come from a computer language called *HTML* (short for *Hypertext Markup Language*). In fact, the main job of all Web browsers — including Netscape's Navigator program — is to correctly interpret HTML tags and use them to display each Web page precisely as its designer intended it to look. Browsers perform this "page construction" on the fly every time you access a new Web page; they simply do it so quickly that you're normally not aware that it's happening.

HTML = Hypertext
Markup Language,
the language
Web pages are
written in

This structure means that you can create a Web page by typing text and appropriate HTML codes into any word processor that saves documents in a *plain text* (also known as *ASCII*) format. Some people simply use a text editor such as the Windows Notepad program to create their Web pages (naming each text file with the extension .htm to identify it as an HTML document). Taking this approach requires a strong understanding of HTML codes, however — such as knowing that you have to enclose a word in `<B>` and `</B>` tags to boldface it, and knowing that to place a link on a page, you have to use the format `<A HREF="http://www.yoururl.com"></A>`.

Learning HTML inside-out is useful if you need to create fancy effects or exercise super-precise control over your Web pages. For most people, though, life is too short to memorize a bunch of HTML codes. Fortunately, Netscape provides an alternative; by using its Composer program, you can format Web pages with menu commands and Toolbar buttons. Composer then automatically (and invisibly) converts all your instructions into HTML tags for you so that you never have to deal with the programming language directly.

You can begin creating a Web page with Composer in several ways. One method is to choose File➪New from any Netscape menu. This command offers you three choices:

- ◆ **Blank Page:** Lets you create a Web page from scratch.

- ◆ **Page From Template:** Opens a dialog box with a Netscape Templates button. If you're connected to the Net, clicking the button takes you to a Web page on the Netscape Communications site that contains a bunch of sample Web pages (or *templates*) that you can use as jumping-off points. After you download a sample Web page, you can edit it to display your own information and revise its look to your tastes, which can sometimes be faster and easier than starting from a blank page.

- ◆ **Page From Wizard:** If you're connected to the Net, takes you to an interactive program on the Netscape Communications site that steps you through the process of creating a very simple Web page.

Alternatively, you can choose Communicator➪Page Composer from any Netscape menu, or you can click the last icon in the Component Bar (that is, the bar that typically resides in the lower-right corner of any Netscape window). Performing either action has the same effect as choosing File➪New➪ Blank Page.

In this lesson, you'll open Composer using a blank Web page. You'll then type the information that you want to appear on your page, edit how your text is formatted, and save your page to your hard disk. We won't step you through using the Page From Template and Page From Wizard options, but after you master the basic skills that are covered in this unit, you can try out those options on your own.

*Note:* Before you start composing Web pages, you should create a folder devoted to storing your Web files:

- ▶ If you're using Windows 95, double-click the My Computer desktop icon, double-click the icon representing your hard drive, choose File➪New➪Folder from the menu, type the name of the new folder (for example, WebPages), and click anywhere outside the folder to save the folder name.

- ▶ If you're using Windows 3.1, run File Manager, choose File➪ Create Directory from the menu, type the name of the new folder (for example, WebPages), and press Enter to save the folder name.

- ▶ If you're using a Macintosh, click the Desktop, choose File➪ New Folder, type the name of the new folder (for example, WebPages), and click anywhere outside the folder to save the folder name.

## Opening a Netscape Composer window

Here's how to get started making a Web page:

**1 Run Netscape, but don't bother to connect to the Internet.**

You don't have to be connected to the Internet to create a Web page. Initially, you can simply store the page on your computer's hard disk.

*Margin notes:*

to open blank Web page, choose File→New Document→Blank Page, or choose Communicator→Page Composer, or click Composer icon from Component Bar

store your Web pages in separate folder

**Figure 8-1:** Netscape's
Composer window lets
you create and revise
Web pages.

*Notes:*

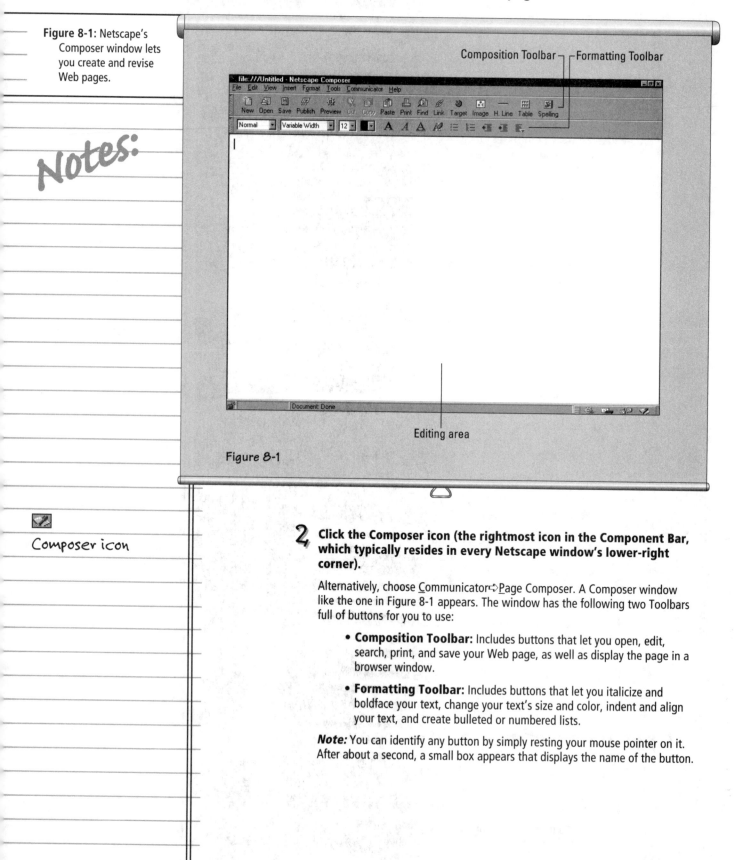

Figure 8-1

Composer icon

2. **Click the Composer icon (the rightmost icon in the Component Bar,
which typically resides in every Netscape window's lower-right
corner).**

Alternatively, choose Communicator⇨Page Composer. A Composer window
like the one in Figure 8-1 appears. The window has the following two Toolbars
full of buttons for you to use:

- **Composition Toolbar:** Includes buttons that let you open, edit,
  search, print, and save your Web page, as well as display the page in a
  browser window.

- **Formatting Toolbar:** Includes buttons that let you italicize and
  boldface your text, change your text's size and color, indent and align
  your text, and create bulleted or numbered lists.

***Note:*** You can identify any button by simply resting your mouse pointer on it.
After about a second, a small box appears that displays the name of the button.

**3** **Click the <u>V</u>iew menu to ensure that both Toolbars are displayed.**

You should see two options at the top named Hide Composition Toolbar and Hide Formatting Toolbar. If you see an option named Show Composition Toolbar or Show Formatting Toolbar instead, click the option to display the Toolbar that's currently hidden. Otherwise, simply click anywhere outside the View menu to close it.

Alternatively, click the tabs in the window's upper-left corner. If a Toolbar is hidden, clicking its tab displays it; if the Toolbar is displayed, clicking its tab hides it, providing more room for the display of your Web page.

Your browser window remains open while you're using the Composer window. As a result, if you want inspiration while creating a Web page, or if you need to search the Web for information associated with your page, you can always connect to the Internet, click the browser window, and cruise the Net!

*Tip:* You'll be working with a single Composer window in this unit, but you can activate as many Composer windows as you want. Opening multiple Composer windows is useful when you need to create or revise several related Web pages at the same time.

## Composing text for your Web page

The Composer window works like a word processor, letting you enter, edit, and format text and graphics. Rather than create a document to be printed on paper, however, Composer's design makes it turn your information into a Web page that can be displayed by Netscape and other browser programs.

Follow these steps to type some text into Composer:

**1** **Click in the editing area — that is, the big blank box below the two Toolbars.**

A blinking cursor appears in the upper-left corner of the editing area, waiting for you to type something. As in a word processor, the cursor shows where your typing will appear in your document.

**2** **Type a few words that you want to use as the title of your Web page.**

You may want to call it John Smith's Home Page, or The John Smith Page, or All About John Smith. (You may even prefer to use your own name!)

If you make a typo or change your mind about what you've typed, you can use your mouse to reposition the cursor and then correct your error. If you're using Windows, you can also use the keys listed in Table 8-1 to move around your document and fix your mistakes.

---

*Margin notes:*

use View menu or click Toolbar tabs to hide or display Toolbars

type in editing area to add text to your Web page

*Notes:*

| Table 8-1 | Keystroke Shortcuts for Editing Web Page Text |
|---|---|
| **PC Keystroke** | **What It Does** |
| Home | Moves your cursor to the beginning of the current line |
| End | Moves to the end of the current line |
| Ctrl+Home | Moves to the beginning of the Web page |
| Ctrl+End | Moves to the end of the Web page |
| Backspace | Deletes the character to the left of the cursor; on a blank line, deletes the blank line |
| Delete | Deletes the character to the right of the cursor; on a blank line, deletes the blank line |
| Ctrl+Z | Undoes your last editing change |
| Ctrl+C | Copies your selected text to the Windows Clipboard |
| Ctrl+X | Copies your selected text to the Windows Clipboard and removes the text from your document |
| Ctrl+V | Pastes the contents of the Windows Clipboard into your document, starting at the cursor position |
| Ctrl+B | Boldfaces your selected text; if the text is already boldfaced, removes boldfacing (or you can click the Bold button on the Formatting Toolbar to perform the same action) |
| Ctrl+I | Italicizes your selected text; if the text is already italicized, removes italics (or you can click the Italic button on the Formatting Toolbar to perform the same action) |
| Ctrl+K | Removes all formatting (such as boldface, italics, and underlining) from your selected text |

**A**

Bold button

*A*

Italic button

press Enter only at
end of each
paragraph

**3  Press Enter to end your page heading.**

You move to a new paragraph. Notice that Composer leaves a little extra space between paragraphs.

**4  Type a paragraph describing yourself, pressing Enter only when you get to the end of the paragraph.**

**heads up**

*Don't* press Enter at the end of every line. Like all word processors, Composer *word wraps,* which means that when a line of text goes past the right margin, Composer automatically wraps the text down to the beginning of the next line.

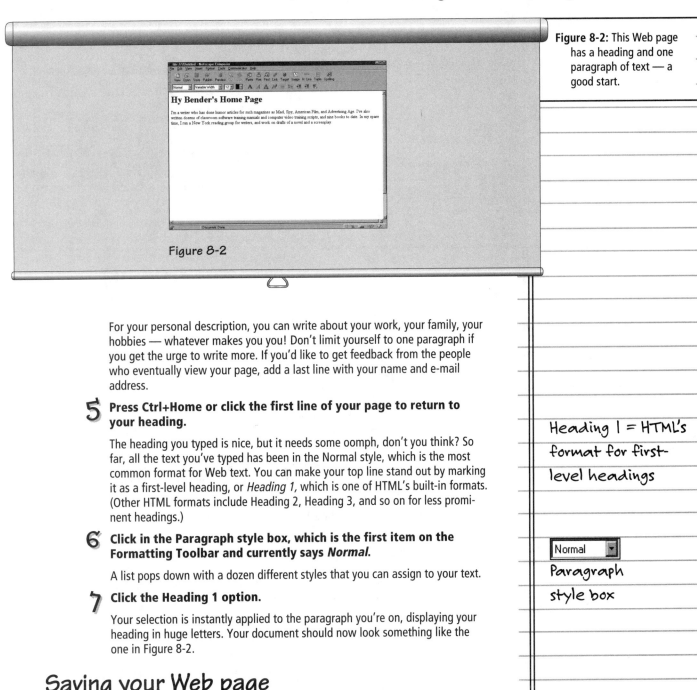

Figure 8-2

**Figure 8-2:** This Web page has a heading and one paragraph of text — a good start.

For your personal description, you can write about your work, your family, your hobbies — whatever makes you you! Don't limit yourself to one paragraph if you get the urge to write more. If you'd like to get feedback from the people who eventually view your page, add a last line with your name and e-mail address.

**5** **Press Ctrl+Home or click the first line of your page to return to your heading.**

The heading you typed is nice, but it needs some oomph, don't you think? So far, all the text you've typed has been in the Normal style, which is the most common format for Web text. You can make your top line stand out by marking it as a first-level heading, or *Heading 1,* which is one of HTML's built-in formats. (Other HTML formats include Heading 2, Heading 3, and so on for less prominent headings.)

> Heading 1 = HTML's format for first-level headings

**6** **Click in the Paragraph style box, which is the first item on the Formatting Toolbar and currently says *Normal*.**

A list pops down with a dozen different styles that you can assign to your text.

**7** **Click the Heading 1 option.**

Your selection is instantly applied to the paragraph you're on, displaying your heading in huge letters. Your document should now look something like the one in Figure 8-2.

> Normal
>
> Paragraph style box

## Saving your Web page

You should always save your documents frequently so that if your keyboard suddenly freezes up or your cat pulls out the power plug, you don't lose more than a few minutes of work. Saving is so important that Composer will nag you periodically to save your Web page (though you can make it stop by clicking a Cancel button). We recommend that you develop the habit of saving your work so that you don't even need to be nagged.

**Figure 8-3:** Where do you want to store your Web page and what do you want to name it?

**Figure 8-4:** What do you want to title your Web page?

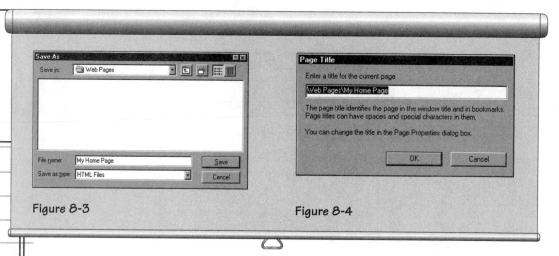

Figure 8-3                                          Figure 8-4

Save

*to save your Web page, click Save button, press Ctrl+S or ⌘S, or choose File→Save*

To save your current Web page as an HTML file on your hard disk, follow these steps:

**1  Choose File⇨Save, press Ctrl+S or ⌘S, or click the Save button (the Composition Toolbar's third button, which looks like a floppy disk).**

The Save As dialog box appears and prompts you to supply a name for your Web page (see Figure 8-3).

**2  Click in the text box near the bottom (which is labeled File name under Windows and Save as on a Mac) and type the appropriate drive letter, folder name, and filename for your Web page.**

For example, if you placed your folder for storing Web pages on drive C and named it Web Pages, and you wanted to name your current file My Home Page, you'd type C:\Web Pages\My Home Page.

**3  Press Enter or click the Save button.**

If you're using Windows, a Page Title dialog box appears that prompts you to supply a title for your Web page (see Figure 8-4). The text that you select will appear in the title bar running across the top of the window. It will also be the name that represents your page when someone locates your site using a Web search program and/or when someone creates a bookmark to point to it.

If you're using a Mac, your file is saved. To continue this exercise, choose Format⇨Page Properties to bring up a dialog box and then click in the Title box.

**4  Type a title that accurately and concisely represents your Web page.**

Most people use the same text for both a Web page's heading and the page's title, so we suggest that you just type your heading again. It's your page, though, so it's your call. (***Note:*** Don't worry about being stuck with your title; you can always revise it later by choosing Format⇨ Page Colors and Properties on a PC or by choosing Format⇨Page Properties again on a Mac.)

**5  Press Enter or click OK.**

Your file is saved under the name that you typed and the extension .htm (on a PC) or .html (on a Mac). For example, if you named your file My Home Page under Windows 95, it was saved under the filename My Home Page.htm.

Now that you've both named and titled your Web page, you can save it rapidly.

**6** **Add another sentence or two to your Web page and then click the Save button.**

Your revised page is saved in seconds to your hard disk. Now that your work is secure, exit Composer.

**7** **Choose File⇨Close (or press Ctrl+W or ⌘W).**

The Composer window closes, leaving Netscape running with whatever other Netscape windows you happen to have open.

Congratulations! You created your first Web page.

extra credit

---

## Ideas for Web pages

In this lesson, you created a personal home page with a little information about yourself, which is fun for your friends and family to see. But what about making Web pages that will interest a broader audience? Here are ideas for other types of Web pages:

▶ **Charitable organizations:** If your church, synagogue, school, club, or other nonprofit organization needs publicity, a Web site is a good way to supply it. Be sure to include information that is of interest to outsiders, such as who the organization is open to, when meetings take place, who to contact for more information, and so on. You can include mission statements, text from a recent newsletter, pictures of buildings and people — you name it. (You'll learn how to place pictures on Web pages later in this unit.)

▶ **Family tree:** Make a Web page for each person in your extended family, with links to spouses, parents, siblings, and children. (You'll learn how to insert links in Web pages in the next lesson.) Each person's page can contain a photo, vital statistics (birthdate, birthplace, current address), interests, hobbies, and reminiscences.

▶ **Show off your expertise:** Is there something that you know a lot about, like antique beer cans or comic books or independent telephone companies? If so, consider creating a Web page about the subject. Include your personal knowledge, relevant pictures, references to appropriate books and magazines, and links to other Web sites on the topic (which you can find by using search programs such as Yahoo! and HotBot).

## Recess

After all that typing, you probably need to limber up. Go lie in the sun and stretch your arms, flex your fingers, wiggle your toes, and relax. When you're sufficiently loose, set your sights on the next lesson, which tells you how to liven up your page with pictures.

---

**Notes:**

to close Composer window, choose File→Close or press Ctrl+W or ⌘W

☑ **Progress Check**

If you can do the following, you've mastered this lesson:

❑ Open Netscape's Composer window.

❑ Create a new Web page.

❑ Type text in your Web page.

❑ Format a paragraph as a heading.

❑ Save your Web page.

❑ Close the Composer window.

## Lesson 8-2 Editing Your Web Page

*Notes:*

to reopen Web
page, choose
File→Open Page or
press Ctrl+O (on PC)
or choose File→
Open→Page in
Composer or press
Shift+⌘O (on Mac)

You've already made a good start on your Web page. In this lesson, you'll spiff it up with links to other nifty pages (which is a standard courtesy provided by virtually all Web pages) and with a bulleted list (which is a great format for spotlighting important information).

## Retrieving a Web page

As you learned in the preceding lesson, you can start a Web page from scratch by choosing File⇨New⇨Blank Page from the Netscape browser window. After you create a Web page, however (or when you want to edit a Web page that's been created by someone else), you reopen it by choosing File⇨Open Page and using a dialog box (on a PC) or by choosing File⇨Open⇨Page in Composer (on a Mac). Alternatively, you can press Ctrl+O or Shift+⌘O. After you select the file you want and press Enter, you can revise the page's contents.

Follow these steps to retrieve the Web page that you created in the preceding exercise:

**1** **Run Netscape (if it isn't already running), but don't bother to connect to the Internet.**

You're going to continue working on the Web page that you created in the preceding lesson.

**2** **If you're using Windows, choose File⇨Open Page from any Netscape menu bar (or press Ctrl+O).**

If you're using a Macintosh, choose File⇨Open⇨Page in Composer instead and then skip to Step 4.

On a PC, you see the Open Page dialog box shown in Figure 8-5. Notice that the option toward the bottom of this dialog box lets you select whether to open the Web page in a Navigator (that is, browser) window or a Composer window.

**3** **Click the Composer option to indicate that you want to *edit* the Web page, not merely view it.**

A bullet appears next to the Composer option to show that it's selected. Now notice the long text box above the Composer option. This text box lets you type the name and location of your Web page file. Also, to the right of this box is a Choose File button that lets you select the file using your mouse.

**4** **Click in the text box and type the drive letter, folder name, and filename of the Web page that you saved in the preceding lesson.**

For example, if you placed your folder for storing Web pages on drive C and named it Web Pages, and you named your HTML file My Home Page, you'd type C:\WebPages\HomePage.htm. (Remember to include the .htm extension.)

Alternatively, click the Choose File button to pop up an Open dialog box, or use the Open dialog box on your Macintosh, to select the file using your mouse.

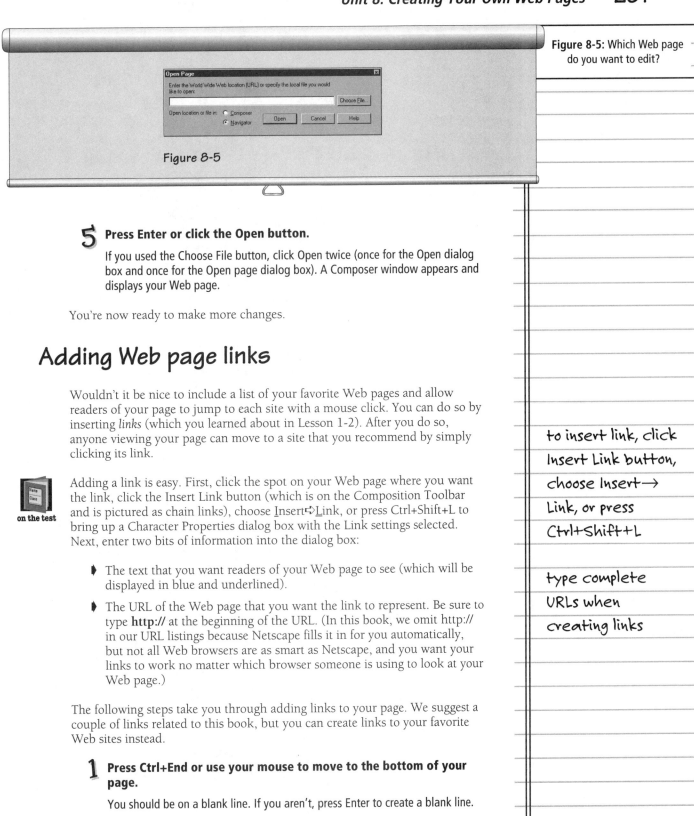

**Figure 8-5:** Which Web page do you want to edit?

Figure 8-5

**5 Press Enter or click the Open button.**

If you used the Choose File button, click Open twice (once for the Open dialog box and once for the Open page dialog box). A Composer window appears and displays your Web page.

You're now ready to make more changes.

## Adding Web page links

Wouldn't it be nice to include a list of your favorite Web pages and allow readers of your page to jump to each site with a mouse click. You can do so by inserting *links* (which you learned about in Lesson 1-2). After you do so, anyone viewing your page can move to a site that you recommend by simply clicking its link.

**on the test**

Adding a link is easy. First, click the spot on your Web page where you want the link, click the Insert Link button (which is on the Composition Toolbar and is pictured as chain links), choose Insert⇨Link, or press Ctrl+Shift+L to bring up a Character Properties dialog box with the Link settings selected. Next, enter two bits of information into the dialog box:

▶ The text that you want readers of your Web page to see (which will be displayed in blue and underlined).

▶ The URL of the Web page that you want the link to represent. Be sure to type **http://** at the beginning of the URL. (In this book, we omit http:// in our URL listings because Netscape fills it in for you automatically, but not all Web browsers are as smart as Netscape, and you want your links to work no matter which browser someone is using to look at your Web page.)

The following steps take you through adding links to your page. We suggest a couple of links related to this book, but you can create links to your favorite Web sites instead.

**1 Press Ctrl+End or use your mouse to move to the bottom of your page.**

You should be on a blank line. If you aren't, press Enter to create a blank line.

*to insert link, click Insert Link button, choose Insert→ Link, or press Ctrl+Shift+L*

*type complete URLs when creating links*

**Figure 8-6:** To create a link, fill in the Link source box (which sets the link's displayed text) and the Link to box (which sets the URL that the link represents).

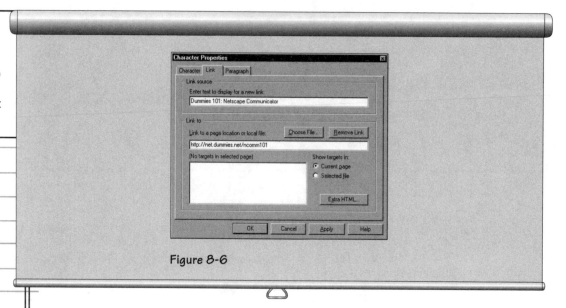

Figure 8-6

Insert Link button

**2** **Type** My Favorite Web Pages **(but don't press Enter).**

This line is the heading for your list of Web sites. Because it's a subtopic under your main heading, make it a level 2 heading.

**3** **Click in the Paragraph style box again (the first item on the Formatting Toolbar, with the word *Normal* in it) and click the Heading 2 option from the list that drops down.**

Now your line is boldfaced and large, though not as large as the heading at the top of the page. Looks good!

**4** **Press Enter to start a new line.**

You're automatically switched back to the Normal paragraph style for the new line, as you can tell by looking at the Paragraph style box. Composer figures that you want to type normal text after a heading — good guess!

You're now ready to add a link to a Web page. How about this book's home page at net.dummies.net/ncomm101?

**5** **Click the Insert Link button (the button on the Composition Toolbar that looks like chain links) or choose Insert⇨Link.**

A Character Properties dialog box appears (as shown in Figure 8-6). This box has tabs along the top that enable you to format characters, adjust paragraphs, and insert links — which is the current selection. Your cursor starts off in a Link source box, which establishes the name of the link that people see when they view your Web page.

**6** **Type** *Dummies 101:* Netscape Communicator 4 **(the name of the Web site that you visited in Units 2 and 3) as the name for your link; then press Tab to move to the next text box.**

The cursor jumps to the Link to box. This box lets you enter the URL of the Web page that your link represents.

**7**  **Type** http://net.dummies.net/ncomm101 **very carefully.**

That is, type **http**, a colon, two slashes, **net.dummies.net**, another slash, and **ncomm101** (with no spaces in any part of the URL).

That's all Composer needs to know to create the link!

**8**  **Press Enter or click OK.**

Your Dummies 101: Netscape Communicator 4 link appears on your Web page. Cool!

**9**  **Place your mouse pointer anywhere on the link you've just created.**

The message bar at the bottom of the window displays the URL you set for the link, confirming that you created the link successfully.

**10**  **Press Enter to move to a new line.**

Now create a second link, this time to the Internet For Dummies Central home page.

**11**  **Click the Insert Link button again, type** Internet For Dummies Central, **and press Tab.**

You move to the Link to box.

**12**  **Type** http://net.dummies.net **very carefully.**

That is, type **http**, a colon, two slashes, and **net.dummies.net** (with no spaces in any part of the URL).

**13**  **Press Enter or click OK.**

The link Internet For Dummies Central is displayed on your Web page. As before, if you point to the link, the URL that you assigned it appears in the message bar.

**14**  **Repeat Steps 10 through 13 to add additional links for Web pages you like.**

If you don't remember the exact names or URLs of certain Web pages, connect to the Internet and use the Netscape browser window to cruise to those pages for the information you need. Be creative and have fun! And see the sidebar "Dragging links from the browser" for ways to make links with no typing.

**15**  **When you're done, click the Save button to save your page to your hard disk.**

As we noted previously, saving frequently ensures that you don't lose more than a few minutes of work if a software problem or power outage occurs.

Your page is starting to look really professional!

*Note:* You can edit the text of the link by just clicking the text and typing. If you need to change the URL of a link, click the link anywhere and then click the Insert Link button. Alternatively, right-click the link (click with your *right* mouse button) and choose Link Properties from the menu that appears (under Windows), or click the link, hold down your mouse button for a few seconds, and click Insert Link from the menu that appears (on a Mac).

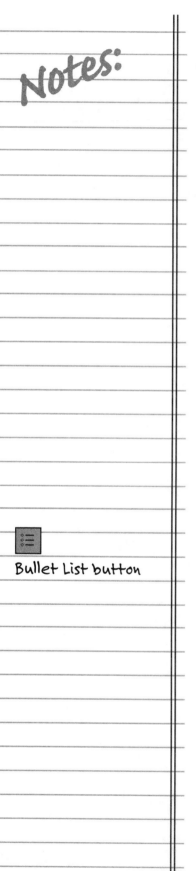

Notes:

**extra credit**

## Dragging links from the browser

If you keep the Netscape browser and Composer windows open side by side, you can add links to your Web page by using your mouse. To do so, first set the browser window to display the Web page for which you want to create a link. Next, click the Page Proxy icon to the left of the Location box and, while holding down your mouse button, drag your mouse pointer to the spot in the Composer window where you want to insert the link. Finally, release your mouse button. A link that points to the Web page in the browser window is added to your Web page.

Making a link to a Web page that you've added to your bookmarks is also easy: Press Ctrl+B or ⌘B to open the Bookmarks window, select a bookmark, and drag the bookmark onto the Web page. Composer creates a link to the bookmarked Web page — quick and easy, with no typing!

## Making a bulleted list

**on the test**

Your list of Web pages is already attractive. However, it would look even better if each entry was indented with a little bullet to its left. Follow these steps to create just such a bulleted list:

**1** **Select all your links.**

Specifically, click in front of your first link, hold down your mouse button, and (while keeping the button pressed) drag down until you reach the end of your last link. When all your links are highlighted, release the mouse button.

You're now ready to choose a new format, which will be applied to all your selected text.

**2** **Click the Bullet List button, which is the fifth from last button on the Formatting Toolbar and looks like three little bulleted lines.**

Your selected paragraphs — in this case, your links — are instantly reformatted as items in a bulleted list. We feel that the bullets are an improvement, but if you don't care for them, simply click the Bullet List button again to return the links to their previous format.

**3** **Click anywhere outside of your selected text to make the highlighting go away.**

The links are no longer selected.

**4** **Save your work by pressing Ctrl+S.**

Your page is saved to your hard disk.

Bullet List button

You can follow similar steps to apply any other kind of formatting to a section of your text. For example, try highlighting your links again and clicking other buttons on the Formatting Toolbar, such as the Numbered List, Increase Indent, and Alignment buttons. (Remember, if you aren't sure what a particular button does, you can simply rest your mouse pointer on the button for about a second to display its name.)

## Other ways to spruce up your Web pages

Here are some other formatting tricks that you can use when editing a Web page:

▶ To center a line of text, move your cursor anywhere on the line, click the Alignment button (the last button on the Formatting Toolbar), and click the middle option from the drop-down list. The line is centered between the page's left and right margins.

▶ To insert a horizontal line, move the cursor to the beginning of the line over which you want the horizontal line to appear and then click the Insert Horiz. Line button (the third-from-last button on the Composition Toolbar).

▶ To make your words appear in a different color, highlight the text that you want to affect and then click the Font Color box (the box directly to the left of the first letter *A* on the Formatting Toolbar). A Color dialog box pops down. Click the color that you want and then click OK to apply the color to your selected text. (This option doesn't work with links, only standard text.)

▶ To reverse a change you've just made, choose Edit⇨Undo or press Ctrl+Z or ⌘Z.

### ☑ Progress Check

If you can do the following, you've mastered this lesson:

❑ Open an existing Web page.

❑ Add links to a Web page.

❑ Format Web page text as a bulleted list.

# Adding Pictures to Your Web Page

Lesson 8-3

Formatting text is fine, but to *really* dress up your Web pages, you should insert a few colorful pictures (which, as the saying goes, are worth a thousand bulleted lists). On the Net, such electronic pictures are also referred to as *graphics files* or *clip art*.

In this lesson, you learn how to obtain such pictures, pick out the best ones for use on a Web page, revise unsuitable pictures to make them usable, and then add the pictures that you select to Web pages.

## Getting electronic pictures

You can obtain graphics files in many ways. For example, you can find thousands of public domain images on the Internet by using search programs such as Yahoo!, HotBot, and AltaVista (see Lessons 2-5 and 3-2). You can also get a list of top Web sites that offer such graphics files by going to this book's home page at net.dummies.net/ncomm101 and clicking the link named Clip Art on the Web.

*Notes:*

When you find a picture that you want from a Web graphics library, you can download it following the instructions in Lesson 3-2. Alternatively, you can download *any* image displayed on a Web page by doing the following:

▶ If you're using Windows, click the picture with your right (*not* left) mouse button, choose the Save Image As option from the menu that appears, type the folder name and filename under which you want to store the picture, and click Save to copy the picture file to your hard disk.

▶ If you're using a Macintosh, click the picture, hold your mouse button down for a few seconds, click the Save this Image as option from the menu that appears, use your mouse to select the folder in which you want to store the picture, type a filename, and click Save to copy the picture file to your hard disk.

In fact, you can even just *drag* a picture from a Netscape browser window to a Composer window; for details, see the sidebar at the end of this lesson.

On the other hand, if you have images that you'd like to use but that happen to be on paper, you can feed them into a PC device called a *scanner* that can copy them to disk as electronic pictures. If you don't want to buy a scanner, you may be able to rent one by the hour at a local photocopying shop or computer store.

Another possibility is to take photographs and then get them in disk form at the same time as they're being developed. Some photo shops now offer this option along with their standard service of providing negatives and prints.

Finally, if you have artistic talent and a lot of patience, you can try drawing your own electronic pictures. A fine program that you can use for this purpose is Paint Shop Pro, which is included on the CD-ROM in the back of this book. (For more information about Paint Shop Pro, see the sidebar "Painting pictures with Paint Shop Pro.")

**extra credit**

# Painting pictures with Paint Shop Pro

If you want to create, edit, convert, or just look at pictures for your Web page, consider the excellent Windows shareware program Paint Shop Pro. If you've got more artistic abilities than we do, you can use Paint Shop Pro to create pictures from scratch. You can also use it to convert graphics files from one format to another. For example, if you have a picture in PCX format (a common format, but one not often used on the Web), you can save it in a GIF or JPEG format (the usual Web picture formats). In addition, Paint Shop Pro lets you crop pictures (cutting off unwanted edges), resize pictures, or reduce the number of colors of a picture, which are all great ways to reduce the size of graphics files.

Alternatively, if you're on a Macintosh, you can use the shareware program GraphicConverter to convert pictures from one format to another. GraphicConverter also lets you crop and edit pictures.

Both Paint Shop Pro and GraphicConverter are stored on your *Dummies 101* CD-ROM. To install either program, see Appendix B.

# Choosing and preparing your pictures

In addition to finding electronic images, you need to decide which ones you should use. Your decision should be based mostly on whether you like particular pictures and feel that they work well with the other elements of your Web pages. However, you should also keep in mind some technical issues.

For example, you must be legally entitled to use the images. If you created the pictures yourself, if the pictures are from a collection of public domain clip art, or if you paid for permission to use the pictures, then you're set. Otherwise, you should make sure that using the graphics you want for your Web page doesn't violate anyone's copyright ownership of those graphics — that is, use only art that you created, that isn't copyrighted, or for which you have written permission from the copyright holder.

**on the test**

You should also verify that the pictures are in the appropriate file format. Electronic pictures come in dozens of different formats, but only two formats are capable of being displayed by virtually all Web browsers: GIF (short for *Graphics Interchange Format*) and JPEG (short for *Joint Photographic Experts Group*). You can recognize these files by their three-letter filename extensions, which are, respectively, .gif and .jpg. If you have a picture in a different file format, you don't have to give up on it, though; you can try turning it into a GIF or JPEG file by using a format conversion feature that's built into the Paint Shop Pro program.

*use graphics files with .gif or .jpg extensions*

Lastly, you need to keep your picture files relatively small. That's because all graphics take a long time to be transferred over the Web, but large graphics seem to take *forever*. If you want people to visit your page, be sensitive to how long it takes them to view it. There are always exceptions, but as a rule of thumb we recommend that you stick to pictures that are about 50K or less in file size. (You can check a file's size by listing it in a My Computer or Windows Explorer window, in the Windows 3.1 File Manager, or in a Macintosh folder.)

If you have a huge picture file that you really like, however, you can try reducing it by using a graphics editor such as Paint Shop Pro. For example, you can crop out less important parts of the image, and/or you can reduce the number of colors used in the image. In many cases, putting a graphic through such a "quick-loss diet" doesn't seriously hurt the quality of the picture.

# Placing a picture on your Web page

**on the test**

After you pick out and (if necessary) revise the graphics that you want to use, you're ready to put them on your Web page. To add a picture, you simply click the spot on your page where you want the image to be displayed, click the Insert Image button or choose Insert⇨Image, type the name of the graphics file in the dialog box that appears, and press Enter.

*to add picture, click Insert Image button or choose Insert →Image*

Try it out by using the following steps to place a restful picture of distant mountains from this book's CD-ROM onto your Web page:

**Figure 8-7:** What's the name of the graphics file that you want to place on your Web page?

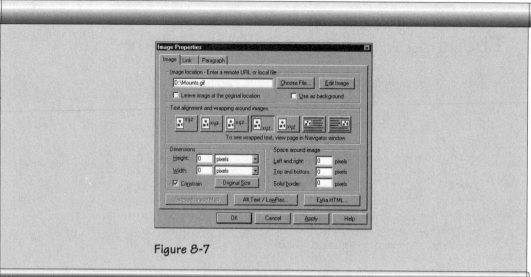

Figure 8-7

on the CD

**1**  **Insert the *Dummies 101* CD-ROM that came with this book into your CD-ROM drive.**

Be careful to touch only the sides of the CD-ROM and to insert the CD-ROM with its printed side up. If you're using Windows 3.1, you're set.

If you're using Windows 95, the CD-ROM's Installer program is set to run automatically, so after about a minute, you probably see an initial Installer screen. All you want to do right now is copy some pictures from the CD-ROM, though, and Netscape can handle that task by itself. Therefore, follow the on-screen prompts until you see a Do Not Accept or Exit button and then click the button to close the CD-ROM program.

If you're using a Mac, a window will open containing icons for the CD-ROM's various files and folders. Click the window's Close button to exit it.

**2**  **If the Web page that you worked on in the preceding lesson isn't still open, open it now.**

You should be in a Composer window with your Web page displayed.

**3**  **Place your cursor in the spot on your Web page where you want the picture to appear.**

For example, if you want to place the image at the bottom of your page, press Ctrl+End or use your mouse to move to the bottom and then press Enter to create a blank line.

**4**  **Click the Insert Image button (the fourth-from-last button on the Composition Toolbar) or choose Insert⇨Image.**

An Image Properties dialog box appears with the Image location box selected, as shown in Figure 8-7. You're now ready to specify the graphics file, which in this case is Mounts.gif.

Insert Image
button

**5** **Select file Mounts.gif from your *Dummies 101* CD-ROM.**

- If you're using Windows, type **d:\Mounts.gif** — that is, the letter *d,* a colon, a backslash, and the filename Mounts.gif. If your CD-ROM drive isn't drive D, type the letter appropriate for your drive.

- If you're using a Macintosh, click the Choose File button and then use your mouse to browse the CD-ROM. When you locate a file named Mounts.gif, double-click that file to select it.

**6** **Press Enter or click the OK button.**

The dialog box goes away and the picture that you specified appears on your Web page. To spiff up your page up a bit more, center the picture.

**7** **Click the Alignment button (the last button on the Formatting Toolbar) and then click the middle option (which looks like centered lines) from the drop-down list.**

The picture is centered on the page. You can perform a number of formatting tricks with images by using the buttons on the Formatting Toolbar. Covering them all is beyond the scope of this book, but we recommend that you experiment with the buttons on your own.

**8** **Double-click the picture (that is, click it twice in rapid succession).**

Or right-click the image and choose Image Properties from the menu that appears. Either way, the Image Properties dialog box appears again. This box offers several options for fine-tuning the appearance of your picture, including adjusting its size, the amount of space around it, and the width of the border around it. Again, discussing these options is beyond the scope of this book, but you can play with them on your own.

**9** **Click Cancel to close the dialog box and click the Save button to save your revised page.**

The Image Properties dialog box disappears, and your page — which now includes the mountain image — is saved to disk.

If you'd like to continue practicing with pictures, you can repeat Steps 3 through 6 using two other files on the CD-ROM named Ferns.gif and Rainbow.gif. If you decide that you don't like a picture, you can delete it at any time simply by clicking it and pressing Delete.

When you're done using Netscape Communicator, choose File⇨Exit from the menu and click the Yes button on the dialog box that appears. All Netscape windows close, and the program exits.

*Notes:*

Preview in
Navigator button

☑ **Progress Check**

If you can do the following,
you've mastered this lesson:

❑ Understand how to
locate, select, and
prepare pictures for a
Web page.

❑ Add a picture to a Web
page.

extra credit

# Taking a different view

The Composer window doesn't always accurately show exactly where a picture will appear on your Web page. To be certain of what your page looks like in a browser window, click the Preview in Navigator button (the fifth button on the Composition Toolbar) or choose File⇨ Browse Page. A new Netscape browser window opens that displays your Web page precisely as it will appear to your fellow cruisers on the Web.

Another way to view your page is to peek at the HTML code that Composer generates from your menu options and Toolbar button selections. If you ever get curious about these program tags, choose View⇨View Page Source from the menu. (You can also choose this command from the browser window, allowing you to examine the HTML code of *any* Web page that you encounter.) You typically see text mixed together with a jumble of angle brackets (< and >) and somewhat obtuse program instructions — for example, the picture of mountains that you inserted in the last exercise is represented by the code `<IMG SRC="mounts.gif" HEIGHT=92 WIDTH=237>`. After you're done ogling HTML codes, you can close the window by clicking its Close button.

extra credit

# Dragging pictures from the browser

If you keep the Netscape browser and Composer windows open side by side, you can add pictures to your Web page by using your mouse. To do so, first set the browser window to display an image that you want to copy. Next, click the picture and, while keeping your mouse button held down, drag your mouse pointer to the spot in the Composer window where you want to insert the image. Finally, release your mouse button. A copy of the picture is added to your Web page.

You can also drag graphics files from a folder window (for example, a Windows Explorer or File Manager window). Drag only GIF or JPEG files, which Netscape and most other browsers can display. When you drag a graphics file to the Composer window, the picture appears in your Web page.

Lesson 8-4    # Publishing Your Web Page

Well, you've made a lovely Web page. You can continue to expand it and spiff it up by using the Composer window. But unless you share files with other people on a local area network, you're probably the only person who can look at it right now. What if you want to go public?

## What's a Web server?

To make a Web page available to the rest of the world, you must store the file that contains the page's text and HTML tags, as well as store all related files (such as the picture files that appear on the page), on a *Web server,* which is a computer that communicates with Web browsers over the Internet and sends out the Web pages that they request.

For example, we store the Web pages for this book on a Web server named `net.dummies.net`. When your Netscape browser asks for the Web page at `net.dummies.net/ncomm101` (the URL of this book's home page), the server sends back the file containing the text and HTML codes that make up the page, along with the graphics files that contain the pictures on the page. (The picture of the cover of this book is stored in one graphics file; the little blue lines that run down the left margin of the page are stored in another graphics file; and the cute little arrow buttons at the very bottom of the page are stored in a third graphics file.) After your browser receives all these files, it can display them on your screen.

So to make your Web page public, you need a Web server to serve it up to the world.

## Getting your Web pages onto a Web server

Here are ways to find a Web server that can play host to your Web pages:

- Ask your Internet provider or online service whether it provides disk space for Web pages to its subscribers; many do so at no extra charge.

- If you use America Online, go to keyword **Personal Publisher** to find out how you can create personal Web pages on this service.

- If you use CompuServe, go to **HPWIZ** to learn about CompuServe's Home Page Wizard, which gives you Web server space.

- If you use Prodigy, jump to keyword **PWP** or **Personal Web Pages** to discover how to take advantage of the Web space that comes with your Prodigy account.

- If you're affiliated with a company or university that's hooked up to the Net, check whether you can get space on its Web server for your Web pages.

- Look for some outside group to host your Web pages, especially if your pages are related to a nonprofit organization. To find such groups, go to the Yahoo! search page at `www.yahoo.com` and poke around. We found a list by choosing Business and Economy, then Companies, then Computers, then Internet, then Free Services, and then Web Services.

When you find a Web server that can house your Web pages, you need the organization that runs it to tell you the user name and password you must type to access the server, and the URL of the area on the Web server that's assigned to storing your files. The latter typically begins with `ftp://` or `http://` and is followed by the name of the Web server and the name of your file area on the server. (For example, the URL for your Web pages section on

*Notes:*

Notes:

Publish button

publicize your Web
page at www.
submit-it.com

☑ **Progress Check**

If you can do the following,
you've mastered this lesson:

❏ Find a Web server to play
host to your Web pages.

❏ Gather the information
you need to upload your
Web page files to the
Web server.

❏ Upload your Web page
files to the Web server.

❏ Jump on the Web to
check out your cool new
pages.

America Online might be `ftp://ftp.aol.com/docs/yourname/index.html`, whereas the URL for your Web pages section on a server using the HTTP standard might be `http://servername.com/docs/yourname/index.html`.) In addition, you should find out the URL that the general public needs to use to access your Web pages. (For example, in contrast to the URL for an America Online file storage area, the public URL for personal Web pages on America Online is in the format `http://home.aol.com/yourscreenname`.)

After you have all the necessary information, you're ready for the big step: copying your files to the server so that the rest of the world can see your Web pages.

## Copying your Web pages to a Web server

After you're set up with a Web server, you can copy, or *upload,* your Web page files to it by using Composer's Publish command.

To begin, open one of your Web pages in a Composer window and either click the Publish button (the fourth button on the Composition Toolbar) or choose File➪Publish. A Publish dialog box appears that lets you type the URL of the Web server, your user name, and your password. (To learn more about these and other options in the dialog box, click the box's Help button.)

When you're done entering your information, click the box's OK button (on a PC) or Publish button (on a Mac). Composer uploads all the files associated with your page to the Web server.

When Composer finishes the copying, switch to Netscape's browser window, click in the Location box, type the public URL for your Web page, and press Enter. You should see the page that you created up on the Web and available to the millions of people on the Net. Totally cool!

If you later decide to make changes to your Web page, simply revise the page in a Composer window and then use the Publish button to upload the changed files.

Finally, if your Web pages are of general interest, don't hesitate to publicize them! You can do so by going to the Submit It! Web site at `www.submit-it.com` and following the instructions to get listed on Yahoo!, HotBot, AltaVista, Excite, and lots of other Web directories. All this work may not make you rich, but if you create a popular Web site, it *may* make you moderately famous!

extra credit

## Uploading files via FTP

You can typically use the Publish button in Composer to upload your Web files. In some cases, however, the Web server you're dealing with may require you to use special *File Transfer Protocol,* or *FTP,* software. If this occurs, you can turn to either WS_FTP LE, which is a Windows program that's free for noncommercial use; or Anarchie, which is a Macintosh shareware program. Both of these programs are on your *Dummies 101* CD-ROM. To install them, see the instructions in Appendix B.

extra credit

## Other Web page editors

Netscape's Composer is a fine Web page editor, but if you're not entirely satisfied with it for some reason, or if you'd simply like to see another approach to creating Web pages, you can try using a different program. If you're on a Macintosh, we recommend the shareware program BBEdit Lite, which is on your *Dummies 101* CD-ROM. (For installation instructions, see Appendix B.)

If you're running Windows, we suggest trying the popular HotDog shareware program from Sausage Software at www.sausage.com.au. Alternatively, visit the excellent Tucows software library at www.tucows.com and pick a program from one of the HTML Editor categories at this site. For instructions on how to download files from the Web, see Lesson 3-2.

# Unit 8 Quiz

For each of the following questions, circle the letter of the correct answer or answers. Remember, each question may have more than one right answer.

1. **Web pages are written in:**

   A. The Netscape Composer window.

   B. A language called HTML (Hypertext Markup Language).

   C. Japanese rice paper.

   D. Netscape-ese.

   E. Haste.

2. **To add a link to your Web page, you can**

   A. Type the text of the link and then use Composer's formatting features to underline it and color it blue.

   B. Click the chain-like Insert Link button on the Composition Toolbar.

   C. Click the Glue Pages button.

   D. Choose Insert⇨Link from the menu.

   E. Drag the Page Proxy icon from a browser window to your Composer window.

3. **To create a bulleted list:**

   A. Type an asterisk (*) at the beginning of each paragraph.

   B. Select the paragraphs that make up the list and click the Bullet List button.

   C. Click the Bullet List button and then type the paragraphs that make up the list. (Try it!)

D. Type **bullet:** at the beginning of each paragraph.

E. Shoot the beginning of each paragraph with your Smith & Wesson .45.

4. **In *101 Dalmatians*, the two dog heroes are named**

A. Spot and Blackie.

B. Pongo and Perdita.

C. Click and Clack.

D. To and Fro.

E. Rush and Newt.

5. **Pictures for Web pages are stored in:**

A. HTML files. (**Hint:** This is wrong!)

B. Graphics files.

C. Air-conditioned vaults.

B. GIF or JPEG files.

E. Battered shoe boxes.

6. **Ways to get graphics files for you to put on your Web pages include**

A. Drawing pictures by using Paint Shop Pro or another graphics program.

B. Downloading graphics files from Web sites.

C. Turning paper images into electronic ones by using a scanner.

D. Taking photographs and having them developed as electronic pictures.

E. Always keeping an eye out for good-looking images and, whenever you spot one, offering it candy to follow you to your home page.

# Unit 8 Exercise

1. Make a Web page for each member of your immediate family. Store each Web page in a separate file.

2. If you have a way to scan in pictures, add a picture of each person to that person's page.

3. Create links from each person's page to the person's mother, father, siblings, children, and other relations. Make the link point to the page for that relative.

4. Show off your pages to your family and friends.

   *Extra Credit:* If you have access to a Web server, upload the pages to the Web server. Send the URLs of the resulting pages to all your friends who have e-mail addresses.

# Part II Review

## Unit 5 Summary

▶ **Setting up Netscape to handle your e-mail:** Choose Edit⇨Preferences to open the Preferences dialog box and click any plus sign (+) or right-pointing triangle by the Mail & Groups category to display its Identity, Mail Server, and Groups Server subcategories. Click the Identity category and fill in your name and e-mail address; click the Mail Server category and fill in your user name, the name of your ISP's SMTP server, and the name of your ISP's POP server; and click the Groups Server category and fill in the name of your ISP's NNTP server. Finally, click the OK button to save your settings.

▶ **Opening the Messenger e-mail window:** Choose Communicator⇨Messenger Mailbox from any Netscape menu bar or click the Mailbox icon from the Component Bar (which typically resides in the lower-right corner of every Netscape window) to both open the Messenger window and make Messenger pick up your e-mail.

▶ **Opening the Composition window:** Click the New Msg button from the Messenger Toolbar or press Ctrl+M or ⌘M from any Netscape window to open a window for creating and sending e-mail messages.

▶ **Addressing an e-mail message:** Open the Composition window and type the e-mail address of each recipient on the To line near the top, separated by commas. Alternatively, press Enter to create new To lines and then type e-mail addresses on separate lines. Optionally, click the word *To* on any address line to drop down a menu with alternative addressing, such as *Cc* (carbon copy) or *Bcc* (blind carbon copy), and then click the type of addressing that you want to select it.

▶ **Completing and sending an addressed message:** Click in the Subject box and type a brief heading; click in the message area and type your message; and click the Send button or press Ctrl+Enter or ⌘Enter to transmit your message over the Net.

▶ **Sending e-mail later:** If you want to stop working on a message but return to it later, choose File⇨Save Draft; the message is saved in Messenger's Drafts folder, where you can reopen it at any time by switching to the folder and double-clicking the message. Alternatively, if you've completed your message but don't want to send it right away (for example, if you want to create a number of messages offline and then send them all simultaneously), choose File⇨ Send Later to save your message in the Outbox folder. When you're ready to send all the messages in the Outbox, choose File⇨ Send Unsent Messages from the Messenger menu bar.

▶ **Getting your mail:** Click the Mailbox icon from the Component Bar to both open the Messenger window and pick up your new messages. If you're already in the Messenger window, click the Get Msg button on the Toolbar or press Ctrl+T or ⌘T to download your new e-mail. New messages are normally stored in Messenger's Inbox folder.

▶ **Switching to a different e-mail folder:** Click in the folder quick-access menu (the box in the upper-left corner of the Messenger window) and click the name of the folder you want.

▶ **Reading messages:** Switch to a folder that contains messages you want to read and click a message you're interested in from the message list in the upper portion of the Messenger window. (Unread messages are displayed in

# Part II Review

boldface.) After you do so, the contents of the message appear in the lower portion of the window. Continue clicking the message list to read additional messages.

▶ **Replying to a message:** Click the message to select it, click the Reply button on the Messenger Toolbar, and click either Reply to Sender (to respond exclusively to the message's author) or Reply to Sender and All Recipients (to respond to everyone who received the message). A Composition window appears with both the address line(s) and subject filled in and with the original message quoted (see next item). Type your response in the message area and then click the Send button.

▶ **Quoting messages:** Remind your correspondent of what he or she said by including parts of the original message in your reply. Quoted material appears with each line preceded by a > or, in e-mail programs like Messenger that support HTML, a vertical blue line. Include only the relevant parts of the message and delete the rest.

▶ **Forwarding messages:** Click the message to select it and then click the Forward button on the Messenger Toolbar. A Composition window appears with the subject already filled in. Address the message, add your comments at the top of the message area, and click the Send button.

▶ **Printing messages:** Click the message to select it, click the Print button on the Messenger Toolbar or press Ctrl+P or ⌘P, make any necessary adjustments to the Print dialog box's settings, make sure that your printer is on and has paper in it, and click the OK or Print button.

▶ **Deleting messages:** Click the message to select it and then click the Delete button on the Messenger Toolbar or click the Delete key to move the message to Messenger's Trash folder. The next time you choose File⇨Empty Trash Folder, the message will be erased from your hard disk.

▶ **Following Netiquette:** *Don't* send unnecessarily angry messages, *don't* distribute chain letters, and *don't* believe everything you read! *Do* check your spelling and *do* think of your correspondents as real people with feelings and foibles.

# Part II Review

## Unit 6 Summary

- **Opening the Address Book:** Choose Communicator➪Address Book to open a window that lets you enter contact information.

- **Adding someone to the Address Book:** Click the New Card button on the Address Book Toolbar and enter the person's name, e-mail address, physical address, and phone numbers in the dialog box that appears. Also enter a nickname to stand in for the person's e-mail address. After you're done, click the OK button to save your entry.

- **Creating a mailing list:** Click the New List button on the Address Book Toolbar and enter the nicknames or e-mail addresses of people you've previously added to the Address Book. After you're done, click the OK button to save your list.

- **Editing an Address Book entry:** Double-click the entry to pop up a dialog box with the entry's information. Make any necessary revisions and then click OK to save your changes.

- **Deleting an Address Book entry:** Click the entry to select it and then click the Delete button from the Address Book Toolbar or press the Delete key. If you change your mind, press Ctrl+Z or ⌘Z immediately after the deletion to restore the entry.

- **Using the Address Book to address a message:** Open the Composition window, click an address line, and type a person's nickname (or let Netscape type it for you based on the first few letters you enter). After you move off the address line, the nickname is replaced by the person's full e-mail address. Alternatively, click the Address button on the Composition window's Toolbar to pop up a dialog box that lets you select Address Book entries with your mouse.

- **Creating e-mail folders:** Messenger automatically creates Inbox, Outbox, Sent, Drafts, and Trash folders to hold, respectively, your incoming, outgoing, previously sent, partially written, and deleted messages. To create an e-mail folder yourself, choose File➪New Folder from the Messenger menu bar to pop up a New Folder dialog box, type the name for your new folder in the Name box, click in the Create as subfolder of box to select a parent folder (for example, click Local Mail to create a first-level folder), and click the OK button. Repeat these steps to create additional folders.

- **Moving a message to another e-mail folder:** Click the message to select it, click the File button from the Messenger Toolbar, and click the name of the folder from the list that drops down. The message is immediately moved to the folder you selected.

- **Copying a message to another e-mail folder:** Click the message to select it, choose Message➪Copy Message from the Messenger menu bar, and click the name of the folder from the list that pops down. A copy of the message is placed in the folder that you selected, but the original message is unaffected.

- **Deleting an e-mail folder:** Choose Communicator➪Message Center from any Netscape menu bar, click the folder that you want to eliminate, and press Delete to move the folder to Messenger's Trash folder. The next time you choose File➪Empty Trash Folder, the folder will be erased from your hard disk.

- **Creating a message filter:** Choose Edit➪Mail Filters from the Messenger menu bar to pop up a Mail Filters dialog box, click the New button in the upper-right section to open a Filter Rules dialog box, name your filter, set the rules for your filter, and click OK twice to save your filter.

# Part II Review

## Unit 7 Summary

▶ **Checking for new messages after setting up message filters:** Click in the folder quick-access menu and look for folders listed in boldface, which indicates that they contain new messages. Click a boldfaced folder to switch to it and then read the new messages it contains (which are also listed in boldface). Repeat these steps until you've read all your new messages.

▶ **Creating an e-mail signature:** Create a short text file that you want to appear at the end of every e-mail message, choose Edit⇨Preferences from any Netscape menu bar to pop up the Preferences dialog box, click the Identity category (under the Mail & Groups category), identify the folder and name of your text file in the Signature File box, and click the OK button.

▶ **Attaching a file:** Open the Composition window, click the Attach button on the Toolbar, click the File option from the menu that appears, use the Enter file to attach dialog box that appears to select the file, and click the Open button to attach the file. Address and fill in your message as usual and then click the Send button to transmit both your message and the file.

▶ **Receiving and saving an attached file:** Receive the e-mail message as usual, select it from the Messenger window, locate a box in the message with a link in its left side, and click the link. If the file isn't a GIF or JPEG picture, a Save As dialog box appears that you can use to save the file. If the file *is* a GIF or JPEG picture, then the image is displayed in a Netscape browser window. To save the picture, click it with your right mouse button (on a PC) or click it and hold your mouse button down for a few seconds (on a Mac) and click the Save Image As option from the menu that appears to bring up a Save As dialog box. Use the dialog box to save the picture as a file on your hard disk.

▶ **Usenet newsgroups:** Usenet is a system that includes more than 30,000 ongoing discussions (newsgroups) on the Internet. You can read and participate in these discussions by using the Netscape Collabra program. Messages distributed via newsgroups are called *articles*. Sending a message to a newsgroup is called *posting an article*.

▶ **Hierarchies:** Groups of newsgroups whose names start with the same word. The seven major hierarchies are rec, soc, talk, sci, comp, news, and misc. The major unofficial hierarchy is alt. Other hierarchies include discussions dedicated to companies, schools, or countries.

▶ **Open the Message Center window:** Click the Discussions icon from the Component Bar, which typically resides in the lower-right corner of every Netscape window; or choose Communicator⇨Collabra Discussion Groups from any Netscape menu bar; or click in the folder quick-access menu and click the Local Mail option at the top of the list that appears.

▶ **Listing newsgroups:** Click the name of the news server that you want from the Message Center and then click the Toolbar's Subscribe button (on a PC) or Join Groups button (on a Mac). A Subscribe to Discussion Groups dialog box appears that lists the newsgroups on the server. To refresh the list, click the Get Groups button.

▶ **Expanding and contracting a newsgroup hierarchy:** To display the newsgroups directly below a hierarchy, click the plus sign (+) or right-pointing triangle to its left. To hide the newsgroups directly below a hierarchy, click the minus sign (-) or down-pointing triangle to its left. To display or hide *all* the newsgroups in hierarchy, click the hierarchy to select it and then click the Expand All or Contract All button.

# Part II Review

▶ **Listing a newsgroup by typing its name:** Click in the <u>D</u>iscussion Group text box at the top of the Subscribe to Discussion Groups dialog box. As you type the newsgroup's name, the list below displays the newsgroup names that most closely match what you're typing.

▶ **Subscribing and unsubscribing to a newsgroup:** Subscribe to a newsgroup by opening the Subscribe to Discussion Groups dialog box, clicking the newsgroup's name to select it, and then clicking the S<u>u</u>bscribe button to make a check mark appear to the newsgroup's right. To unsubscribe, click the newsgroup's name again and click the button again (which is now labeled <u>U</u>nsubscribe) to make the check mark to the right disappear.

▶ **Reading subscribed newsgroups:** Open the Message Center window and double-click the newsgroup's name; or open the Messenger window, click in the folder quick-access menu, and click the newsgroup's name. Either way, the articles in the newsgroup are listed in the upper portion of the Messenger window. Click any listed article you're interested in to read its contents in the lower portion of the window.

▶ **Searching for newsgroups:** Use the Liszt Web page at `www.liszt.com` to search for newsgroups whose names contain a specified word.

▶ **Searching for newsgroup articles:** Use the Deja News Web site at `dejanews.com` or the AltaVista Web site at `altavista.digital.com` to search for articles that contain specified words or phrases.

▶ **Posting an original newsgroup article:** After you've read a newsgroup for at least a week and have something wise, witty, and wonderful to say, you can post a new article by switching to the newsgroup in the Messenger window, clicking the New Msg button on the Toolbar to open a preaddressed Composition window, typing a subject heading in the <u>S</u>ubject box, and

pressing Tab to move to the big message area. Carefully write and edit your message, being sure to check your spelling, grammar, and tone. When you're ready to post your article, click the Send button.

▶ **Responding privately to a newsgroup article:** If what you have to say is of interest primarily to the person who wrote the article or is private, reply to the author via e-mail by clicking the article to select it, clicking the Reply button from the Messenger Toolbar and clicking the <u>R</u>eply to Sender option, typing your message, and clicking the Send button.

▶ **Responding publicly to a newsgroup article:** If what you have to say will be of general interest to newsgroup readers, respond publicly in the newsgroup by first clicking the article to select it, clicking the Reply button from the Messenger Toolbar, and clicking the Reply to <u>G</u>roup option (or, if you want to be sure that the author sees your response, clicking the Reply to Sender and Gro<u>u</u>p option, which sends a copy of the message to the author's electronic mailbox in addition to posting it to the newsgroup). Write your response in the Composition window, carefully checking your spelling, grammar, and tone, and then click the Send button.

# Unit 8 Summary

▶ **Deciding where to store Web pages:** You can create and store Web pages on your own hard disk. To make your pages visible on the Web, however, you must copy them to a *Web server,* which is a computer that's in constant communication with the Internet and that sends Web pages in response to requests from other people's Web browsers.

# Part II Review

▶ **Understanding the anatomy of a Web page:** Web pages are text files that consist of HTML (Hypertext Markup Language) codes. The pictures on Web pages are stored in separate GIF or JPEG graphics files. A Web page editor such as Netscape Composer lets you design your pages using Toolbar buttons and menu commands and then generates the necessary text files with HTML codes for you automatically.

▶ **Opening the Composer window to a blank Web page:** Click the Composer icon, the fourth icon in the Component Bar (which typically resides in the lower-right corner of every Netscape window), or choose either Communicator⇨Page Composer or File⇨ New Document⇨Blank Page from any Netscape menu bar.

▶ **Opening an existing Web page:** Choose File⇨Open Page or press Ctrl+O (on a PC), or choose File⇨Open⇨Page in Composer or press Shift+⌘O (on a Mac), to pop up an Open Page dialog box. Select the file you want using the dialog box and then click the Open button. The Composer window opens and displays the Web page that you selected, allowing you to revise it.

▶ **Saving your Web page:** Choose File⇨Save, press Ctrl+S or ⌘S, or click the Save button (the Composition Toolbar's third button, which looks like a floppy disk). When Netscape saves a Web page, it typically uses the filename extension .htm (on a PC) or .html (on a Mac). Save your page frequently to ensure that if your keyboard freezes up or some other accident occurs, you lose no more than a few minutes of work.

▶ **Using the Composer window's Toolbars:** The Composer window has two Toolbars, Composition and Formatting. The Composition Toolbar includes buttons that let you open, edit, search, print, and save your Web page and display the page in a browser window. The Formatting Toolbar includes buttons that let you italicize and boldface your text, change your text's size and color, indent and align your text, and create bulleted or numbered lists.

▶ **Identifying a Toolbar button's full name:** Rest your mouse pointer on any Toolbar button. After about a second, a small box appears that displays the name of the button.

▶ **Adding text to your Web page:** Just type!

▶ **Creating headings on your Web page:** Click anywhere on a line that you want to turn into a heading, click in the Paragraph style box (the first item on the Formatting Toolbar), and click the heading style you want from the list that drops down. Composer immediately applies the text style you selected to the line you're on.

▶ **Creating a bulleted list on your Web page:** Click and drag your mouse to highlight all the paragraphs that you want to make into a bulleted list and then click the Bullet List button (which is the fifth from last button on the Formatting Toolbar and looks like three little bulleted lines). Composer immediately turns the text that you selected into a bulleted list. Click anywhere outside the text to remove the highlighting.

▶ **Adding links to your Web page manually:** Click the spot on your Web page where you want the link to appear and then click the Insert Link button (the button on the Composition Toolbar that looks like chain links) or choose Insert⇨Link to pop up the Character Properties dialog box. Click in the Link source text box and type the text that you want readers of the Web page to see, click in the Link to text box and type the full URL (including the http:// prefix) of the Web page that the link represents, and click the OK button. The dialog box closes, and the link appears on your Web page at the spot you clicked.

# Part II Review

▶ **Adding links to your Web page by clicking and dragging:** Resize the Netscape browser and Composer windows so that they're side by side, set the browser window to display the Web page you're interested in, and click and drag the Page Proxy icon (which appears to the left of the Location box) to the spot in the Composer window where you want to insert the link. After you release your mouse button, a link that points to the browser's Web page is inserted in your own Web page. Similarly, you can click and drag any bookmark in the Bookmarks window to the Composer window to add a link that points to the same page as the bookmark.

▶ **Editing a link:** Click anywhere on the link and click the Insert Link button. Alternatively, right-click the link and choose Link Properties from the menu that appears (under Windows); or click the link, hold down your mouse button for a few seconds, and click Insert Link from the menu that appears (on a Mac). Revise the text in the dialog box that appears and then click the OK button to save your changes.

▶ **Finding pictures for your Web page:** Locate GIF or JPEG graphics files in various clip art collections — for example, try the links at this book's Web site at `net.dummies.net/netscape101/clipart.htm`. Don't use copyrighted artwork in your Web pages unless you have permission from the copyright owner.

▶ **Adding pictures to your Web page manually:** Click the spot on your Web page where you want the picture to appear, and then click the Insert Image button (the fourth-from-last button on the Composition Toolbar) or choose Insert⇨ Image to pop up the Image Properties dialog box. Select the picture file that you want to use and click the OK button. The dialog box closes, and the picture appears on your Web page at the spot you clicked.

▶ **Adding pictures to your Web page by clicking and dragging:** Resize the Netscape browser and Composer windows so that they're side by side; set the browser window to display an image that you want to copy; and click and drag the picture to the spot in the Composer window where you want to insert the image. After you release your mouse button, the picture from the browser is added to your own Web page. Similarly, you can click and drag any picture file from a folder window, but you should do so only for files in the GIF or JPEG graphics format.

▶ **Setting up storage for your public Web pages:** To make your Web page visible to the rest of the Internet, you store the files that make up your Web page on a Web server. Your Internet provider or online service may let you use its Web server, or you can sign up with a commercial Web service. You need to know the URL to use when transferring Web page files from your computer to the Web server, and the URL to use when you or other people want to look at your Web pages.

▶ **Publishing your Web page:** To transmit the files that make up your Web pages to a Web server, click the Publish button (the fourth button on the Composition Toolbar) or choose File⇨Publish. A Publish dialog box appears that lets you type the URL of the Web server, your user name, and your password. After you type in all the necessary information, click the dialog box's OK button (on a PC) or Publish button (on a Mac); Composer uploads all the files associated with your page to the Web server. Finally, switch to Netscape's browser window, click in the Location box, type the public URL for your Web page, and press Enter to view the page. When your Web site is ready for prime time, publicize it by going to the Submit-It Web page at `www.submit-it.com`.

# Part II Test

The questions on this test cover all the material presented in Part II, Units 5-8.

## True  False

T  F  1. E-mail is like paper mail because it's written and can be kept for future reference.

T  F  2. E-mail is like the telephone because it's quick, easy, and informal.

T  F  3. `thisbook101@idgbooks.com@dummies.net` is a valid e-mail address.

T  F  4. If you're angry about something, you should take advantage of e-mail's speed and convenience by writing a message quickly and sending it off before you have a chance to calm down.

T  F  5. You can attach picture files to messages, but you can't attach other files such as word-processing documents or spreadsheets.

T  F  6. You read Usenet newsgroup articles from the Netscape Newsgroup window.

T  F  7. To test posting an article, you can send it to the `misc.test` newsgroup.

T  F  8. To create a great Web page, you must first learn HTML, the language in which Web pages are encoded.

T  F  9. All the information on a Web page is stored in one file.

T  F  10. Even if you create a Web page and store it on a Web server, it's still not an *official* Web page because it hasn't been approved by the people who own the Internet.

## Multiple Choice

For each of the following questions, circle the correct answer or answers. Remember, each question may have more than one right answer.

**11.  When addressing an e-mail message, you can**

A. Type multiple addresses on one address line, separated by commas.

B. Create additional address lines using the Enter key and then type each address on its own line.

C. Click the word *To* to change an address line to *Cc* or *Bcc*.

D. Pop up your Address Book by clicking the Address button from the Composition window's Toolbar.

E. Use zip-plus-four codes to speed up delivery.

**12.  The nickname feature of Netscape's Address Book:**

A. Calls you mean names when you're not looking.

B. Makes you sound tough in your messages.

C. Lets you pick an easy-to-remember word to represent an e-mail address.

D. Spares you from having to constantly type difficult e-mail addresses.

E. Works only with e-mail programs that support HTML.

# Part II Test

13. **To file an e-mail message in a folder, you can**

    A. Print the message, label a new manila folder, stick the printed message in the manila folder, and shove the whole thing into your filing cabinet.

    B. Select the message, click the File button, and click the folder.

    C. Repeat "Message, move!" three times.

    D. Select the message, choose Message⇨Copy Message, and click the folder.

    E. Set up mail filters to file the message automatically as soon as it arrives.

14. **To list a newsgroup in the Subscribe to Discussion Groups dialog box, you can**

    A. Click the plus sign or right-pointing triangle to the left of its hierarchy.

    B. Click the multiplication sign or inverted polygon to the right of its hierarchy.

    C. Click its hierarchy and click the Expand All button.

    D. Send in a subscription card and wait six to eight weeks.

    E. Type its name in the text box near the top of the dialog box.

15. **The following newsgroups are excellent choices for learning about Usenet:**

    A. `news.newusers.questions`

    B. `news.announce.newusers`

    C. `talk.bizarre`

    D. `alt.barney.die.die.die`

    E. `news.answers`

16. **HTML stands for:**

    A. Happy Times Means Love.

    B. Hot Tea Mixed Lightly.

    C. Highly Tethered Microsoft Language.

    D. Hypertext Modeling Language.

    E. Hypertext Markup Language.

17. **Reasons to create and publish your own Web pages include**

    A. You want to create a place that your family and friends can easily visit to find out what you've been up to lately.

    B. You want to create a public advertisement for yourself that will impress potential employers (or potential dates).

    C. You have ideas or information that you want to get across to a large number of people.

    D. You crave fame and riches. (Well, fame, anyway.)

    E. It's fun.

18. **To make your Web page accessible to anyone on the Internet:**

    A. Click the Publish button on the Composition Toolbar.

    B. Submit your Web page to Internet Galactic Central.

    C. Store the files that make up the Web page on a Web server.

    D. Buy your own Web server computer, install it in your attic, install a special high-speed dedicated phone line attached to the Web server, install Web server software, sign up for a dedicated-line Internet account, leave your Web server computer up and running 24 hours a day, seven days a week, and store the files that make up your Web page on the Web server's hard disk.

    E. Send e-mail to everyone on the Internet telling them about your Web page and telling anyone interested in seeing the Web that you can e-mail the files in which the Web page is stored.

# Part II Test

## Matching

19. **Match the following Messenger Toolbar buttons with the corresponding descriptions:**

    A. Reply
    1. Compose a new message.

    B. Forward
    2. Reply to the selected message.

    C. Get Msg
    3. Move the selected message to a different folder.

    D. File
    4. Retrieve your new e-mail messages.

    E. New Msg
    5. Forward the selected message to someone else who you feel would like to see it.

20. **Match the following Composition window and Address Book Toolbar buttons with the corresponding commands:**

    A. Attach
    1. Add someone's contact information to your Address Book.

    B. Address
    2. Attach a file that will be transmitted with your e-mail message.

    C. Send
    3. Add an e-mail mailing list to your Address Book.

    D. New Card
    4. Pop up the Address Book so you can address a message using your mouse.

    E. New List
    5. Transmit your message over the Internet to its intended recipient.

21. **Match the following newsgroup terms with their corresponding descriptions:**

    A. Usenet
    1. Message distributed to a newsgroup.

    B. Article
    2. Send angry or inflammatory message.

    C. Post
    3. Decentralized organization that administers newsgroups.

    D. Flame
    4. Series of messages in which each message is a response to a previous message.

    E. Thread
    5. Transmit an article for distribution to a newsgroup.

22. **Match the following great communicators with their birthdates:**

    A. Winston Churchill    1. February 12, 1809

    B. Martin Luther King Jr.    2. 1995

    C. William Shakespeare    3. January 15, 1929

    D. Abraham Lincoln    4. November 30, 1874

    E. Babe    5. April 23, 1564

# Part II Lab Assignment

## Step 1: Run Netscape, connect to your Internet provider, and open the Subscribe to Discussion Groups dialog box.

Get ready to do some news-reading!

## Step 2: Find and subscribe to an interesting-looking newsgroup.

You can find a newsgroup by looking through the newsgroup names in the various newsgroup hierarchies or by using the Deja News or Liszt Web pages.

## Step 3: Find an interesting article.

This step shouldn't take long!

## Step 4: Forward a copy of the article to yourself for future reference.

If you know other people who would be interested, forward the article to them, too.

## Step 5: (optional) Send an e-mail message to the author of the article, thanking her.

Press Ctrl+R or ⌘R to respond to the article via e-mail. If you have information to add concerning the topic of the article, do so.

## Step 6: (optional) If you like the newsgroup, give it a plug on your Web page.

That is, if you have a Web page. If you don't, consider creating one!

# Answers

## Part I Test Answers

| Question | Answer | If You Missed It, Try This |
|---|---|---|
| 1. | True | Review Lessons 1-1 and 4-2. |
| 2. | False | Review Lesson 1-1. |
| 3. | True | Review Lesson 1-2. |
| 4. | False | Review Lesson 1-2. |
| 5. | True | Review Lesson 1-3. |
| 6. | True | Review Lesson 2-1. |
| 7. | True | Review Lesson 2-5. |
| 8. | True | Review Lesson 4-1. |
| 9. | False | Review Lesson 4-1. |
| 10. | True | Review Lesson 4-2. |
| 11. | E | Review Lesson 1-1. |
| 12. | D, E | Review Lesson 1-2. |
| 13. | B, D | Review Lessons 1-2 and 1-3. |
| 14. | E | Review Lesson 2-5. |
| 15. | A, B, C | Review Lesson 3-1. |
| 16. | A, B, C, D | Review Lesson 3-2. |
| 17. | D | Review Lesson 4-2. |
| 18. | E | It's a wonderful world we live in. |
| 19. | A, 4 | Review Lessons 1-3, 2-5, 3-1, 3-2, and 4-1. |
|  | B, 3 |  |
|  | C, 2 |  |
|  | D, 5 |  |
|  | E, 1 |  |

| 20. | A, 3 | Review Lessons 1-3, 4-1, and 4-2. |
|-----|------|-----------------------------------|
|     | B, 4 |                                   |
|     | C, 5 |                                   |
|     | D, 1 |                                   |
|     | E, 2 |                                   |
| 21. | A, 3 | Review Lessons 1-3, 2-1, and 3-1. |
|     | B, 5 |                                   |
|     | C, 4 |                                   |
|     | D, 2 |                                   |
|     | E, 1 |                                   |
| 22. | A, 4 | Review your grade-school geography notes. |
|     | B, 3 |                                   |
|     | C, 5 |                                   |
|     | D, 2 |                                   |
|     | E, 1 |                                   |

# Part II Test Answers

| Question | Answer | If You Missed It, Try This |
|----------|--------|----------------------------|
| 1. | True | Review Lesson 5-2 for how to create e-mail and Lesson 6-2 for how to file a message for future reference. |
| 2. | True | Review Lesson 5-2 for how to send e-mail and Lesson 5-5 for rules of e-mail etiquette. |
| 3. | False | Review Lesson 5-2. An e-mail address contains only one at sign (@), which appears between the user name and the computer name. |
| 4. | False | Don't *ever* do this! Review Lesson 5-5. |
| 5. | False | Review Lesson 6-3. |
| 6. | False | Review Lesson 7-2. |
| 7. | True | Review Lesson 7-4. Never post test messages to other newsgroups, because you'll just make people mad! |
| 8. | False | Review Lesson 8-1. |
| 9. | False | Review Lesson 8-1. |
| 10. | False | Review Lessons 1-1 and 8-4. No one owns the Internet and the Web is for everyone, so as soon as you get your Web page up and running, you can consider it an "official" Web page. |

| 11. | A, B, C, D | Review Lessons 5-2 and 6-1. |
|-----|------------|------------------------------|
| 12. | C, D | Review Lesson 6-1. |
| 13. | A, B, D, E | Review Lessons 5-4 and 6-2. |
| 14. | A, C, E | Review Lesson 7-1. |
| 15. | A, B, E | Review Lesson 7-1. The other newsgroups might be educational if you're interested in the sociology and psychology of eccentric newsgroups! |
| 16. | A, B, C, D, E | Review Lesson 8-1. |
| 17. | E | Review Lesson 8-1. |
| 18. | A, C, D | Review Lesson 8-4. Note, however, that answer D is a big pain in the neck (not to mention expensive) and is not recommended for the faint of heart. |

| 19. | A, 2 | Review Lessons 5-2, 5-3, 5-4, and 6-2. |
|-----|------|-----------------------------------------|
|     | B, 5 | |
|     | C, 4 | |
|     | D, 3 | |
|     | E, 1 | |

| 20. | A, 2 | Review Lessons 5-2, 6-1, and 6-3. |
|-----|------|------------------------------------|
|     | B, 4 | |
|     | C, 5 | |
|     | D, 1 | |
|     | E, 3 | |

| 21. | A, 3 | Review Lessons 7-1, 7-2, and 7-4. |
|-----|------|------------------------------------|
|     | B, 1 | |
|     | C, 5 | |
|     | D, 2 | |
|     | E, 4 | |

| 22. | A, 4 | Review your grade-school history notes. (And movie ticket stubs.) |
|-----|------|-------------------------------------------------------------------|
|     | B, 3 | |
|     | C, 5 | |
|     | D, 1 | |
|     | E, 2 | |

# Using the CD-ROM

This appendix tells you about the programs and other files on your *Dummies 101* CD-ROM. The appendix first provides a brief description of each program and exercise file on the disc. It then explains how to install programs from the CD-ROM to your hard disk. Finally, it provides further details about each program, such as installation tips and pointers on where to obtain more information.

## Programs on the CD-ROM

Here is a summary of the programs on the CD-ROM, organized into two groups: one for Windows 95 and Windows 3.1 software, and one for Macintosh software.

The CD-ROM's Windows programs are as follows:

- **Acrobat Reader:** A free program that lets you view and print Portable Document Format, or *PDF,* files. There are a number of such document files on the CD-ROM, including four bonus units for this book: one that teaches you how to join e-mail mailing lists, another that covers how to use Netscape plug-ins, and two that provide step-by-step instructions on how to install AT&T WorldNet Service software for Windows (see the next entry).

- **AT&T WorldNet Service:** Software that helps you sign up for an Internet account with AT&T WorldNet Service and that includes a free copy of Netscape Navigator 3.0.

- **Eudora Light:** An excellent free electronic mail program that lets you send and receive e-mail messages over the Internet.

- **Formula One/NET plug-in:** A free Netscape plug-in that lets you view and interact with spreadsheets on Web pages.

- **Free Agent:** An excellent free newsgroup reader (or *newsreader*) program that lets you participate in thousands of online discussions over the Internet.

*Notes:*

- **ichat plug-in:** A free Netscape plug-in that lets you interact live with groups of people on the Internet via your keyboard using Web page chat rooms or Internet Relay Chat (IRC).

- **mIRC:** A shareware program that lets you interact live with groups of people on the Internet via your keyboard using Internet Relay Chat (IRC).

- **Netopia Virtual Office plug-in:** A Netscape plug-in that lets you quickly create an electronic office on a Web page. This version is a demo that expires after 30 days if you don't register it by paying a fee to its publisher, Farallon Communications.

- **Paint Shop Pro:** A versatile shareware graphics program that lets you view virtually any image you're likely to encounter on the Web. Paint Shop Pro also enables you to create and edit images and convert them into different file formats, which is useful if you want to make your own Web pages.

- **Quick View Plus plug-in:** A Netscape plug-in that lets you display and print virtually any file on your hard disk using the Netscape browser window. This version is a demo that expires after 30 days if you don't register it by paying a fee to its publisher, Inso Corporation.

- **Shockwave Director plug-in:** A free and essential Netscape plug-in that lets you play movies, animations, and sound on multimedia Web pages.

- **Shockwave Flash plug-in:** A free Netscape plug-in that, like Shockwave Director, lets you play the movies, animations, and sound on multimedia Web pages.

- **ThunderBYTE Anti-Virus plug-in:** A shareware virus detection tool that helps you safeguard your data from destructive programs.

- **Trumpet WinSock:** A shareware TCP/IP program that provides the foundation a Windows 3.1 PC needs to get connected to the Internet. (Windows 95 has TCP/IP software built in.)

- **VDOLive plug-in:** A free Netscape plug-in that lets you play video clips from Web pages without having to wait for a clip to fully download, using *streaming video* technology.

- **WinZip:** An invaluable shareware decompression utility that you can employ to make compressed files useable again.

- **WS_FTP LE:** A free (for noncommercial use) File Transfer Protocol, or *FTP,* program that you can use to copy files between your PC and a computer on the Internet.

The CD-ROM's Macintosh programs are as follows:

- **Acrobat Reader:** A free program that lets you view and print Portable Document Format, or *PDF,* files. There are a number of such document files on the CD-ROM, including three bonus units for this book: one that teaches you how to join e-mail mailing lists, another that covers how to use Netscape plug-ins, and a third that provides step-by-step instructions on how to install AT&T WorldNet Service software for the Macintosh (see the third entry).

- **Anarchie:** A File Transfer Protocol, or *FTP,* shareware program that you can use to copy files between your Macintosh and a computer on the Internet.

- **AT&T WorldNet Service:** Software that helps you sign up for an Internet account with AT&T WorldNet Service and that includes a free copy of Netscape Navigator 2.02.

- **BBEdit Lite:** A shareware program that allows you to create your own World Wide Web pages without requiring you to be an HTML programming whiz.

- **Disinfectant:** A shareware virus detection tool that helps you safeguard your data from destructive programs.

- **Eudora Light:** An excellent free electronic mail program that lets you send and receive e-mail messages over the Internet.

- **FreePPP:** A shareware TCP/IP program that provides the foundation software a Macintosh needs to get connected to the Internet.

- **GraphicConverter:** A shareware graphics program that you can use to view virtually any image you're likely to encounter on the Web. GraphicConverter also lets you transform images from one file format to another, which is useful if you want to make your own Web pages.

- **ichat plug-in:** A free Netscape plug-in that lets you interact live with groups of people on the Internet via your keyboard using Web page chat rooms or Internet Relay Chat (IRC).

- **InterNews:** A shareware newsgroup reader (or *newsreader*) program that lets you participate in thousands of online discussions over the Internet.

- **Ircle:** A shareware program that lets you interact live with groups of people on the Internet via your keyboard using Internet Relay Chat (IRC).

- **Shockwave Director plug-in:** A free and essential Netscape plug-in that lets you play the movies, animations, and sound on multimedia Web pages.

- **Shockwave Flash plug-in:** A free Netscape plug-in that, like Shockwave Director, lets you play the movies, animations, and sound on multimedia Web pages.

- **StuffIt Expander and DropStuff with Expander Enhancer:** Invaluable shareware decompression utilities that you can employ to make compressed files useable again.

**A few words about shareware:** Shareware programs are available to you for an evaluation period (typically, anywhere from 30 to 90 days). If you decide that you like a shareware program and want to keep using it, you're expected to send a registration fee to its author or publisher, which entitles you to technical support and notifications about new versions. (It also makes you feel good.)

Most shareware operates on an honor system, so the programs continue working even if you don't register them. However, it's a good idea to support the shareware concept and encourage the continued production of quality low-cost software by sending in your payment for the programs you use.

# Document and Exercise Files on the CD-ROM

*Notes:*

In addition to programs, the *Dummies 101* CD-ROM contains several document and exercise files that we believe you'll find extremely useful. Here's what else is on the CD-ROM:

- **Maillist.pdf:** Bonus unit for this book (Unit CD-1, "Joining Discussions by E-Mail") that teaches you how to join and participate in the tens of thousands of ongoing discussions that take place via electronic mailing lists — which are even more numerous than Usenet newsgroups! Read this document using the Acrobat Reader program described later in this appendix.

- **Plugins.pdf:** Bonus unit for this book (Unit CD-5, "Extending Netscape's Capabilities with Plug-Ins") that teaches you how to enhance Netscape's already-impressive abilities by adding mini-programs to it called *plug-ins* that make the Web a multimedia experience. This unit covers how to install and use plug-ins on your *Dummies 101* CD-ROM that let you play recorded words, music, or video clips from a Web page; stroll through 3-D virtual reality; browse all types of files on your hard disk; chat live with other Net users; and more! Read this document using the Acrobat Reader program described later in this appendix.

- **Wnet95.pdf:** Bonus unit for this book that provides step-by-step instructions on installing AT&T WorldNet Service for Windows 95, an Internet sign-up kit described later in this appendix. Read this document using the Acrobat Reader program, which is also described later in this appendix.

- **Wnet31.pdf:** Bonus unit for this book that provides step-by-step instructions on installing AT&T WorldNet Service for Windows 3.1, an Internet sign-up kit described later in this appendix. Read this document using the Acrobat Reader program, which is also described later in this appendix.

- **WnetMac.pdf:** Bonus unit for this book that provides step-by-step instructions on installing AT&T WorldNet Service for the Macintosh, an Internet sign-up kit described later in this appendix. Read this document using the Acrobat Reader program, which is also described later in this appendix.

- **Bookmark.htm:** File crammed with 220 bookmarks pointing to the very best sites on the World Wide Web. To install this file, follow the instructions in Lesson 2-1. (**Note:** On the Macintosh, this file is named Bookmarks.html.)

- **Leonardo.jpg:** Self-portrait of Leonardo da Vinci that you use in Lessons 6-3 and 6-4 to learn how to send attached files by e-mail and receive attached files by e-mail.

- **Mounts.gif:** Picture of mountains that you use to help construct a personal Web page in Lesson 8-3.

- **Ferns.gif:** Picture of a fern that you use to help construct a personal Web page in Lesson 8-3.

◗ **Rainbow.gif:** Picture of a rainbow that you use to help construct a personal Web page in Lesson 8-3.

We hope you enjoy these files!

# System Requirements

The following are the minimum requirements needed to run most of the software on this book's CD-ROM:

◗ A PC that runs Windows 95, or a PC that runs some version of Windows 3.1 (such as Windows 3.11 or Windows 3.11 for Workgroups), or an Apple Macintosh or Macintosh-compatible (such as the Power Macintosh, Macintosh PowerBook, or PowerTower Pro) running System 7.5 or higher.

◗ At least 8MB of RAM (though 16MB or more is recommended).

◗ A 14,400 bps or faster modem (to connect to the Internet).

◗ A CD-ROM drive (for obvious reasons).

In addition, if you need some help with the basic operation of your computer, you might want to explore a book such as *Dummies 101: Windows 95* or *Dummies 101: Windows 3.1,* which are both by Andy Rathbone, or *Macs for Dummies* by David Pogue (published by IDG Books Worldwide, Inc.).

# Installing the Programs

What steps you should follow to install a program depend on the program, the computer you're using, and whether this is the first time you've used the *Dummies 101* CD-ROM:

◗ **If you want to install a plug-in:** Exit Netscape, use the instructions that follow to install a single plug-in, and then launch Netscape to test the plug-in before installing anything else. For more information, we strongly recommend that you read Unit CD-5, " Extending Netscape's Capabilities with Plug-Ins," which is a bonus unit that's stored in file Plugins.pdf on the CD-ROM. To learn how to view and print PDF documents, see the description of the Acrobat Reader program that appears later in this appendix.

◗ **If you've previously run the Windows SetIcons program:** Insert the *Dummies 101* CD-ROM into your CD-ROM drive. If you're using Windows 3.1, double-click the Dummies 101 - Netscape Communicator icon you created to run the Installer program. If you're using

*Notes:*

Windows 95, click the Start button and choose Programs⇨ Dummies 101⇨Dummies 101 - Netscape Communicator to run the Installer program.

▶ **If you're using a Macintosh:** Insert the *Dummies 101* CD-ROM into your CD-ROM drive and wait for the disc's window to open. When it does, locate and double-click a file named Read Me First to open a text document. Follow the instructions in this document to install the program you're interested in. (In many cases, this will involve nothing more than using your mouse to copy the program's folder to your hard disk.)

Finally, if you're using Windows and have *not* previously run the SetIcons program, follow these steps to run the CD-ROM's Installer program:

**1** **Insert the *Dummies 101* CD-ROM into your computer's CD-ROM drive.**

Be careful to touch only the edges of the CD-ROM and to insert the disc with its label side up.

- If you're using Windows 95, then within a minute the CD-ROM's Installer program should start running automatically and display an initial window. If you see a license agreement, skip to Step 6. If you see an Installer program window instead, skip to Step 7.

- If you're using Windows 3.1, or if you find that the Installer program doesn't run automatically on your Windows 95 computer, continue to Step 2.

**2** **If you're using Windows 3.1, click the File menu from the Program Manager and choose the Run option. If you're using Windows 95, click the Start button (located in the bottom-left corner of your screen) and choose the Run option.**

A Run dialog box appears that lets you type the name of a program you want to run. If a program name already appears highlighted in the box, ignore it; the text will be replaced as soon as you begin typing.

**3** **In the Run dialog box that appears, type d:\seticons — that is, the letter d, a colon (:), a backslash (\), and the program name seticons.**

If your CD-ROM isn't drive D, type the letter appropriate for your drive instead of D. (If you're not sure what letter to type, see the "If you don't know the letter of your computer's CD-ROM drive" paragraph that appears at the end of this exercise.)

**4** **Press Enter or click OK.**

The Run dialog box closes, and an icon is created to run the CD-ROM. Specifically:

- If you're using Windows 3.1, a Program Group and Dummies 101 - Netscape Communicator icon are created for the CD-ROM on your desktop. You can run the CD-ROM's Installer program in the future by double-clicking the icon.

- If you're using Windows 95, a folder and icon are added to your Start menu. You can run the CD-ROM's Installer program in the future by clicking the Start button and choosing Programs⇨Dummies101⇨ Dummies 101 - Netscape Communicator.

After the icon is created, you're asked whether you want to run the Installer program now.

**5** **Click the Yes button.**

The CD-ROM's Installer program launches and displays an IDG Books Worldwide, Inc. license agreement. This is the only time you'll see this document.

**6** **Read (or at least skim) the license agreement to make sure you're comfortable with its terms. When you're ready, click the Accept button.**

If you don't click Accept, you can't use the Installer program. After you click, an opening screen appears.

**7** **Follow the on-screen prompts until you see a menu with software categories.**

The menu displays four software categories: Getting Connected (for programs that get you connected to the Net), Communicating (for programs that let you interact on the Net), Using Plug-Ins (for plug-ins that enhance Netscape's capabilities), and Working Offline (for programs that help you deal with files you've downloaded from the Net). This is the Installer's *main menu,* which is so named because all your other selections stem from this initial menu.

**8** **Click a category you're interested in.**

A submenu displays the particular programs grouped under the category you selected.

**9** **Click a program you're interested in.**

A description of the program appears. Read the description carefully, because it may include steps you need to follow to install and run the program properly.

**10** **Click the Continue button near the bottom of the screen if you want the program installed on your hard disk.**

Alternatively, click the Cancel button in the lower-right corner to return to the previous screen and then skip to Step 12.

After you click the Continue button, installation for the program you selected begins.

**11** **Follow the prompts that appear on your screen to complete the installation of the program.**

When the installation is finished, you return to the submenu of programs in the last category you selected.

**12** **Return to Step 9 to explore another program on the submenu, or click the Go Back button repeatedly to return to previous screens (until you reach the main menu, which is as far back as you can go), or continue to Step 13 to exit.**

**13** **When you're done examining and installing all the programs you're interested in, click the Exit button or press Alt+F4.**

The Installer program closes. You can now start using the new software you've installed on your hard disk!

**If you don't know the letter of your computer's CD-ROM drive:** Most PCs assign the letter D to a CD-ROM drive. Here's how to find out which letter your CD-ROM drive uses:

- If you use Windows 95, double-click the My Computer icon on your Windows 95 desktop. A window appears that lists all your drives, including your CD-ROM drive (which is usually represented by a shiny disc icon), and shows you the letter of each drive. When you're done examining the My Computer display, exit by clicking the window's Close button in its upper-right corner.

- If you use Windows 3.1, double-click the File Manager icon in Program Manager. In the File Manager window, you see a row of disk icons. The CD-ROM drive is the one with the little CD-ROM sticking out of it.

- If you use a Macintosh, you don't have to worry about this. Shortly after you insert the CD-ROM, an icon for it appears on your desktop.

**To run the Installer program again:** If you've exited the Installer program and then want to run it again while the *Dummies 101* CD-ROM is still in your drive, simply double-click the Dummies 101 - Netscape Communicator icon (if you're using Windows 3.1) or click the Start button and choose Programs⇨ Dummies 101⇨Dummies 101 - Netscape Communicator (if you're using Windows 95 and have previously run the SetIcons program). Alternatively, if the Installer program runs automatically on your Windows 95 system, double-click the My Computer icon on your desktop and then double-click the icon that looks like a shiny CD, or just eject the CD-ROM and then reinsert it into your CD-ROM drive to make the Installer run automatically again.

**To examine the Dummies 101 CD-ROM's contents under Windows:** You can use the *Dummies 101* Installer program to install all the software on your CD-ROM. However, if you're simply curious about the CD-ROM, you can examine its contents after you exit the Installer. If you're using Windows 95, open a Windows Explorer window (as opposed to a My Computer window) and double-click the CD-ROM's icon. If you're using Windows 3.1, double-click the CD-ROM's icon in File Manager.

# CD-ROM Program Descriptions

Following are descriptions of the various programs you'll find on the CD-ROM.

## Acrobat Reader

Acrobat Reader 3.0 from Adobe Systems is a free program that lets you view and print Portable Document Format, or *PDF,* files. The PDF format is used by many programs that you'll find on the Internet for storing documentation, because it supports the use of such stylish elements as assorted fonts and colorful graphics, in contrast to the standard plain text format that doesn't allow for any special effects in a document.

For example, four documents on the CD-ROM are bonus units for this book that tell you how to participate in Internet mailing lists (Unit CD-1, "Joining Discussions by E-Mail"), how to use Netscape plug-ins (Unit CD-5, "Extending Netscape's Capabilities with Plug-Ins"), and how to install AT&T WorldNet software for Windows (see the "AT&T WorldNet" section directly following this one). All these documents are PDF files, and they require you to use the Acrobat Reader program to view or print them.

## Installing Acrobat Reader

To install Acrobat Reader, do this:

**1** **Follow Steps 1 through 7 of the "Installing the Programs" section.**

You see the main menu.

**2** **Click the Working Offline category, click the Acrobat Reader option, read the installation information that appears, and then click the Continue button.**

The Acrobat Reader installation program is launched.

**3** **Click the Yes button to confirm installation.**

After some initial data copying, the Adobe Acrobat 3.0 Setup screen appears.

**4** **Click the Next button.**

A license agreement appears.

**5** **Read or skim the agreement and then click the Yes button to accept it.**

You're told that the software will be installed in a folder named C:\Acrobat3\Reader. If you're comfortable with this folder name and location, skip to Step 7.

**6** **Click the Browse button, and use the Choose Directory dialog box that appears to select a different drive and/or folder name to store the software. When you're done, click the OK button.**

The name of the folder you selected is displayed in the dialog box.

**7** **Click the Next button.**

The software is copied to your hard disk. When the installation is completed, a dialog box appears.

**8** **Click the Finish button.**

A text file shows you last-minute technical notes about the program.

**9** **Skim the document for anything that might apply to your particular PC and then exit the Notepad file and click the OK button that appears.**

The installation is completed, and you're returned to the *Dummies 101* Installer program.

*Notes:*

*Notes:*

If you use Windows 95, you can now run Acrobat Reader at any time by clicking the Start button and choosing Programs⇨Adobe Acrobat⇨ Acrobat Reader 3.0. If you use Windows 3.1, you can now launch the program by opening the Adobe Acrobat Program Group and then double-clicking a program icon named Acrobat Reader 3.0.

## Reading documents with Acrobat Reader

After you run Acrobat Reader, follow these steps to use it:

**1  Click the File menu and choose the Open option.**

A dialog box prompts you to select the PDF file you want to view.

**2  Use the dialog box to select the drive and folder that contain the file you want.**

For example, if you want to view one of the bonus units for this book, switch to the top level of your CD-ROM drive, which contains four such PDF files.

**3  Scroll through the list of PDF files until the one you want is listed; then double-click the file's name.**

For example, if you want to view bonus unit CD-1, "Joining Discussions by E-Mail," double-click Maillist.pdf; or if you want to view bonus unit CD-5, "Extending Netscape's Capabilities with Plug-Ins," double-click Plugins.pdf.

Alternatively, if you want to view the installation instructions for AT&T WorldNet Service for Windows 95, double-click Wnet95.pdf; if you want to view the instructions for AT&T WorldNet Service for Windows 3.1, double-click Wnet31.pdf.

After you've double-clicked the name of the desired file, the document appears in the Acrobat Reader window. Use the VCR-like Forward and Backward buttons on the Toolbar near the top of the window to move to the next or previous page or to the end or beginning of the document.

**4  If you want to print the document you're viewing (which we recommend doing for long documents), make sure your printer is on and has paper in its paper tray, click the File menu, click the Print option, and click OK (or Print on the Mac).**

The document is printed, making it easier to read.

**5  If you want to open additional documents, repeat Steps 1 through 3.**

Each document opens in its own window. You can switch to any document by clicking the window it's in, or by clicking the Window menu and then clicking the name of the file you want (which is listed near the bottom of the menu).

**6  When you're done using Acrobat Reader, click the File menu and choose the Exit option (or the Quit option on the Mac).**

All your PDF documents close and then the Acrobat Reader program exits.

## Getting more information about Acrobat Reader

To learn more about using Acrobat Reader, click the Help menu and the Reader Online Guide option. You can also get more information by visiting the Adobe Systems Web site at www.adobe.com.

# Anarchie

Anarchie 2.0.1 from Stairways Shareware is a Macintosh shareware File Transfer Protocol, or *FTP,* program that you can employ to find files on the Net, and to copy files between your Mac and a computer on the Net. FTP programs were more useful before the World Wide Web took hold and made finding and downloading files a snap. However, FTP programs are still handy for activities not supported by the Web, such as uploading files for your own Web pages.

To install Anarchie, drag the Anarchie folder from the CD-ROM's Bonus Software folder and then drop it on your hard disk icon to copy the program. After you do so, you can run the program by double-clicking the Anarchie icon from its folder.

To use Anarchie to find a file on the Internet, first click the File menu, then click either the MacSearch option (for a Macintosh file) or the Archie option (for any file). Type part of the name of the file you want and click the Find It button. If a matching list of files is displayed, double-click the one you're after; the file will be downloaded to your hard disk. After the file is saved, if it turns out that it's compressed, use StuffIt Expander (which is also on the *Dummies 101* CD-ROM) to decompress the file and make it useable.

For more information on downloading and uploading files, see Lesson 3-2; for more information on publishing Web pages, see Unit 8; and for more information about Anarchie, see its Web site at `www.share.com/peterlewis/anarchie`.

# AT&T WorldNet℠ Service

AT&T WorldNet Service is a world-class Internet provider that, for a monthly charge, will supply you with an Internet e-mail account and full access to all Internet features. AT&T WorldNet Service also provides such fine services as free technical support via an 800 number that's available 24 hours a day, seven days a week.

The *Dummies 101* CD-ROM contains three AT&T WorldNet sign-up kits for Windows 95, Windows 3.1, and the Macintosh. Each software kit includes a free, fully registered copy of Netscape Navigator, which is the previous version of Netscape Communicator and can be used to download a copy of Netscape Communicator from the Web. (For more information about downloading a recent copy of Netscape, see Lessons 1-1 and 3-2.)

To launch an AT&T WorldNet sign-up kit, follow Steps 1 through 7 of the "Installing the Programs" section. When you see the main menu, click the Getting Connected category, click the AT&T WorldNet Service option appropriate for your PC, click the Continue button to start the installation, and follow the prompts that appear on your screen to complete the installation.

Detailed information about AT&T WorldNet Service hardware requirements and monthly charges, as well as step-by-step installation instructions for Windows, are stored on the CD-ROM in three Acrobat Reader documents:

*Notes:*

> ◗ Wnet95.pdf for the Windows 95 kit
>
> ◗ Wnet31.pdf for the Windows 3.1 kit
>
> ◗ WnetMac.pdf for the Macintosh kit

For information on how to view and print out these PDF documents, see the preceding section on Acrobat Reader.

## BBEdit Lite

BBEdit Lite 4.0 from Bare Bones Software, Inc. is a Macintosh shareware program that helps you to create Web pages. If you aren't entirely satisfied with the Netscape Composer program covered in Unit 8, or if you're simply interested in seeing another approach to creating Web pages, you can try out BBEdit Lite.

To install BBEdit Lite, drag the BBEdit Lite 4.0 folder from the CD-ROM's Bonus Software folder and then drop it on your hard disk icon to copy the program. After you do so, you can run the program by double-clicking the BBEdit Lite 4.0 icon from its folder on your hard disk.

For more information about BBEdit Lite, visit the program's Web site at `www.barebones.com/freeware.html`.

## Disinfectant

Disinfectant 3.6 from shareware author John Norstad is a Macintosh utility that detects a nasty type of program known as a *virus*. Defined broadly, a virus is a program — typically hidden inside another, benign program — that's created to deliberately wreak havoc with computers by destroying their data.

The odds of encountering a virus are relatively low, but it's a good idea to play it safe by scanning any program you're about to run for the first time using a tool such as Disinfectant. We also recommend that you at least occasionally scan your entire hard disk for viruses. If you detect a virus, you can also use Disinfectant to eliminate it.

To install Disinfectant, drag the Disinfectant icon from the CD-ROM's Bonus Software folder and then drop it on your hard disk icon. For more information about Disinfectant, visit the program's Web site at `charlotte.acns.nwu.edu/jln/jln`.

## DropStuff with Expander Enhancer

DropStuff with Expander Enhancer 4.0 from Aladdin Systems, Inc. is a shareware utility for the Macintosh that boosts the capabilities of StuffIt Expander (see the "StuffIt Expander" entry near the end of this appendix) in four ways:

- It allows StuffIt Expander to deal with a much wider ranger of compressed file formats. After you've installed both programs, you'll be set to handle virtually any compressed file you encounter.

- It makes StuffIt Expander decompress files up to five times faster on Power Macintoshes.

- It allows you to compress and decompress files directly from any program you're using that's written to support StuffIt Expander.

- It lets you compress files and folders easily. Specifically, if you use your mouse to drag and drop a file or folder onto the DropStuff with Expander Enhancer icon, the program will automatically create a compressed version of the file or folder in the same window that you dragged from.

To install DropStuff with Expander Enhancer, double-click the DropStuff w/ EE Installer icon in the Bonus Software folder and then follow the on-screen prompts. After you've installed the program, the features of DropStuff with Expander Enhancer will run automatically whenever StuffIt Expander is activated.

For more information about decompressing files, see Lesson 3-2. For more information about both StuffIt Expander and DropStuff with Expander Enhancer, visit the Web site of these two programs at www.aladdinsys.com.

## Eudora Light

Eudora Light 3.0.1 from Qualcomm, Inc. is a free but powerful electronic mail program. If you're not entirely satisfied with the Netscape Messenger program covered in Units 5 and 6, or if you'd simply like to see another approach to e-mail, Eudora Light is an excellent choice.

To install Eudora Light, follow Steps 1 through 7 of the "Installing the Programs" section. When you see the main menu, click the Communicating category, click the Eudora Light option, and follow the prompts that appear on your screen to complete the installation. To run the program, double-click the Eudora Light 3.0.1 icon from its folder.

For more information about e-mail, see Units 5 and 6. To learn more about Eudora Light, read the program's manual (which is stored in a PDF file in the Eudora Light folder of the CD-ROM) using the Acrobat Reader program described earlier in this appendix. You can also learn more by selecting options from Eudora Light's Help menu and by visiting the program's Web site at www.eudora.com.

## Formula One/NET plug-in

Formula One/NET from Visual Components is a free Netscape plug-in that lets you view and interact with spreadsheets on Web pages. To install Formula One/NET, follow the instructions in Lesson PI-2 of bonus unit CD-5 (see the Acrobat Reader section that appears earlier in this appendix to learn how

*Notes:*

to read this document). For more information about Formula One/NET, see Lesson PI-6 in Unit CD-5 and visit the program's Web site at `www.visualcomp.com`.

# Free Agent

Free Agent 1.11 from Forté, Inc. is a free Windows program that lets you read and participate in ongoing group discussions that take place over the Internet via Usenet newsgroups. There are tens of thousands of newsgroups devoted to virtually every topic under the sun, ranging from knitting to high finance and from decoding DNA to dating, and Free Agent is one of the best programs available for accessing them. If you aren't entirely satisfied with the Netscape Collabra program covered in Unit 7, or if you'd simply like to explore a different approach to reading newsgroups, Free Agent is an excellent choice.

To install Free Agent, follow Steps 1 through 7 of the "Installing the Programs" section. When you see the main menu, click the Communicating category, click the version of Free Agent appropriate for your version of Windows, and follow the prompts that appear on your screen to complete the installation.

To run Free Agent, double-click the Agent icon from its folder or Program Group. Alternatively, if you use Windows 95, click the Start button, click Programs, and click the Agent option that appears.

For more information about Usenet newsgroups, see Unit 7. To learn how to use Free Agent, click its Help menu and choose Contents to launch its online manual. You can also visit Free Agent's Web site at `www.forteinc.com`.

# FreePPP

FreePPP 2.5v3 from Rockstar Studios is a Macintosh shareware program that provides the foundation TCP/IP software your computer needs to get connected to the Internet. This type of software is usually provided automatically when you sign up with an Internet provider. (For example, FreePPP itself is bundled in with the AT&T WorldNet sign-up kit for the Macintosh included on the *Dummies 101* CD-ROM.) If you lack TCP/IP software, however, or if you're not satisfied with the software you currently have, you can try using the excellent FreePPP instead.

To install FreePPP, double-click the FreePPP folder from the CD-ROM's Bonus Software folder, double-click the Install FreePPP icon, and then follow the on-screen prompts to complete the installation. After you do so, run the program by double-clicking the FreePPP Setup icon.

To learn more about FreePPP, visit the program's Web site at `www.rockstar.com/ppp.shtml`.

# GraphicConverter

GraphicConverter 2.8 by shareware author Thorsten Lemke is a Macintosh program that allows you to view images in virtually any graphics format you're likely to encounter on the Internet. In addition, it lets you convert the most common Windows, DOS, Amiga, and Atari computer images to Macintosh formats, and vice versa; and it provides a rich set of image editing options. The latter two features are especially useful if you're interested in creating your own Web pages.

To install GraphicConverter, drag the GraphicConverter 2.8 folder from the CD-ROM's Bonus Software folder and then drop it on your hard disk icon to copy the program. To run the program, double-click the GraphicConverter icon from its folder.

To learn more about the utility of a graphics converter program in creating Web pages, see Unit 8. For more information about GraphicConverter, double-click the Documentation icon in the program's folder.

# ichat plug-in

ichat 2.22 from ichat, Inc. is a free Netscape plug-in that lets you participate in live chat sessions via Web page chat rooms or Internet Relay Chat. To install ichat, follow the instructions in Lesson PI-2 of bonus unit CD-5 (see the Acrobat Reader section that appears earlier in this appendix to learn how to read this document). For more information about ichat, see Lesson PI-7 of Unit CD-5, and visit the program's Web site at www.ichat.com.

# InterNews

InterNews 2.0.2 from Moonrise Software is a Macintosh shareware program that lets you read and participate in ongoing discussions that take place over the Internet via Usenet newsgroups. There are tens of thousands of newsgroups devoted to virtually every topic under the sun, ranging from knitting to high finance and from decoding DNA to dating, and InterNews is one of the best Mac programs available for accessing them. Among this program's charms is that it's trim and quick — that is, it doesn't require a lot of memory or a super-fast Mac to operate effectively. In addition, it's highly customizable, so you can tailor it to your tastes. If you aren't entirely satisfied with the Netscape Collabra program covered in Unit 7, or if you'd simply like to explore a different approach to reading newsgroups, InterNews is a good choice.

To install InterNews, double-click the InterNews installer icon from the CD-ROM's Bonus Software folder and then follow the on-screen prompts to complete the installation. After you do so, run InterNews by double-clicking the program's icon from its folder on your hard disk.

For more information about Usenet newsgroups, see Unit 7; and for more information about InterNews, visit the program's Web site at www.dartmouth.edu/~moonrise.

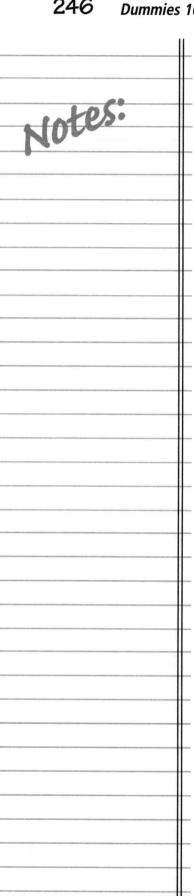

Notes:

## Ircle

Ircle 2.5 is a Macintosh shareware program from MacResponse that lets you participate in Internet Relay Chat (*IRC*), a worldwide system that enables you to receive messages over the Internet within seconds of when other people send them, and vice versa. Much more information about IRC appears in the "Chatting via IRC" sidebar in Lesson PI-7 of bonus unit CD-5 (see the Acrobat Reader section that appears earlier in this appendix to learn how to read this document).

To install Ircle, drag the Ircle folder from the CD-ROM's Bonus Software folder and then drop it on your hard disk icon to copy the program. To run Ircle, double-click its icon on your hard disk.

To learn more about Ircle, click the program's Apple menu and choose the Help option, and visit Ircle's Web site at `www.xs4all.nl/~ircle`.

## mIRC

mIRC 5.02 is an excellent Windows program from shareware author Khaled Mardam-Bey. It lets you participate in Internet Relay Chat (*IRC*), a worldwide system that enables you to receive messages over the Internet within seconds of when other people type them, and vice versa. Much more information about IRC appears in the "Chatting via IRC" sidebar in Lesson PI-7 of bonus unit CD-5 (see the Acrobat Reader section that appears earlier in this appendix to learn how to read this document).

To install mIRC, follow Steps 1 through 7 of the "Installing the Programs" section. When you see the main menu, click the Communicating category, click the mIRC option, and follow the prompts that appear on your screen to complete the installation.

To run mIRC, double-click the mIRC icon from its folder or Program Group. If you use Windows 95, alternatively click the Start button, click Programs, click mIRC, and click mIRC again.

To learn how to use mIRC, click the program's More Info button on the first window that appears. You can get further information after you're past the opening window by pressing F1, clicking a Help button that looks like a life preserver, or clicking the Help menu and choosing the Contents option.

For more facts about mIRC, visit its home page at `www.mirc.co.uk`.

## Netopia Virtual Office plug-in

Netopia Virtual Office 1.0 from Farallon Communications is a Netscape plug-in that lets you quickly create an electronic office on a Web page. This version is a demo that expires after 30 days if you don't register it by paying a fee to its publisher. To install Netopia, follow the instructions in Lesson PI-2 of bonus unit CD-5 (see the Acrobat Reader section that appears earlier in this appendix to learn how to read this document). For more information about Netopia, see Lesson PI-7 of Unit CD-5, and visit the program's Web site at `www.farallon.com`.

## Paint Shop Pro

Paint Shop Pro from JASC, Inc. is a multipurpose graphics tool for Windows. This superb shareware program lets you view images in virtually any graphics format you're likely to encounter on the Internet. In addition, it lets you edit and crop images, convert images from one file format to another, and even create pictures from scratch, which can all be useful in helping you create your own World Wide Web pages. The *Dummies 101* CD-ROM installs Paint Shop Pro Version 4.12 for Windows 95 and Version 3.11 for Windows 3.1.

To install Paint Shop Pro, follow Steps 1 through 7 of the "Installing the Programs" section. When you see the main menu, click the Working Offline category, click the version of Paint Shop Pro appropriate for your version of Windows, and follow the prompts that appear on your screen to complete the installation.

To run Paint Shop Pro, double-click the program's icon in its folder or Program Group. Alternatively, if you use Windows 95, click the Start button, click Programs, click Paint Shop Pro, and click Paint Shop Pro 4.

To learn about Paint Shop Pro's utility in creating Web pages, see Unit 8. For information on how to use Paint Shop Pro, click the floating question mark icon on the program's Toolbar, or click its Help menu and Help Topics option. Also, visit the program's Web site at `www.jasc.com/psp.html`.

## Quick View Plus plug-in

Quick View Plus 4.0 from Inso Corporation is a Netscape plug-in that lets you display and print virtually any file on your hard disk using the Netscape browser window. This version is a demo that expires after 30 days if you don't register it by paying a fee to its publisher. To install Quick View Plus, follow the instructions in Lesson PI-2 of bonus unit CD-5 (see the Acrobat Reader section that appears earlier in this appendix to learn how to read this document). For more information about Quick View Plus, see Lesson PI-6 of Unit CD-5 and visit the program's Web site at `www.inso.com`.

## Shockwave Director plug-in

Shockwave Director Version r4 from Macromedia is a free and essential Netscape plug-in that lets you play movies, animations, and sound on multimedia Web pages. To install Shockwave Director, follow the instructions in Lesson PI-2 of bonus unit CD-5 (see the Acrobat Reader section that appears earlier in this appendix to learn how to read this document). For more information about Shockwave Director, see Lesson PI-4 of Unit CD-5 and visit the program's Web site at `www.macromedia.com/shockwave`.

## Shockwave Flash plug-in

Shockwave Flash Version r4 from Macromedia is another free Netscape plug-in that lets you play movies, animations, and sound on multimedia Web pages. To install Shockwave Flash, follow the instructions in Lesson PI-2 of bonus unit CD-5 (see the Acrobat Reader section that appears earlier in this appendix to learn how to read this document). For more information about Shockwave Flash, see Lesson PI-4 of Unit CD-5 and visit the program's Web site at www.macromedia.com/shockwave.

## StuffIt Expander

StuffIt Expander 4.0.1 from Aladdin Systems, Inc. is an invaluable file decompression shareware utility for the Macintosh. Many files on the Internet are compressed — that is, shrunken in size via special programming tricks — both to save disk storage space and to cut down on the amount of time they require to be downloaded. You may also occasionally receive compressed files as e-mail attachments. After you have a compressed file on your hard disk, you should use StuffIt Expander to decompress it and make it useable again.

To install the program, double-click the DropStuff w/EE Installer icon from the CD-ROM's Bonus Software folder and then follow the on-screen prompts to complete the installation.

You'll typically run StuffIt Expander indirectly, because it activates automatically when you download a compressed file or double-click a compressed file. When StuffIt has finished its work, you can toss the compressed file in the trash can and use the normal files that have been generated.

StuffIt Expander can operate on its own, but we recommend that you improve both its abilities and performance by also installing the complementary program DropStuff with Expander Enhancer, which is described in the previous "DropStuff with Expander Enhancer" section.

For more information about decompressing files, see Lesson 3-2. For more information about both StuffIt Expander and DropStuff with Expander Enhancer, visit the Web site of these two programs at www.aladdinsys.com.

## ThunderBYTE Anti-Virus

ThunderBYTE Anti-Virus Version 7.07 (for Windows 3.1) and version 8.0 (for Windows 95) are Windows shareware utilities from Authentex Software Corporation that detect a nasty type of program known as a *virus*. Defined broadly, a virus is a program — typically hidden inside another, benign program — that's created to deliberately wreak havoc with computers by destroying their data.

The odds of encountering a virus are relatively low, but it's a good idea to play it safe by scanning any program you're about to run for the first time using a tool such as ThunderBYTE. We also recommend that you at least occasionally scan your entire hard disk for viruses. If you detect a virus, you can also use ThunderBYTE to eliminate it.

To install ThunderBYTE Anti-Virus, follow Steps 1 through 7 of the "Installing the Programs" section. When you see the main menu, click the Working Offline category, click the ThunderBYTE Anti-Virus option, and follow the prompts that appear on your screen to complete the installation.

For more information about ThunderBYTE Anti-Virus, visit the program's Web site at www.authentex.com.

## Trumpet WinSock

Trumpet WinSock 3.0 from Trumpet Software International is Windows shareware that provides the foundation TCP/IP software your PC needs to get connected to the Internet. Windows 95 comes with TCP/IP software built-in, and such software is usually provided automatically when you sign up with an Internet provider. If you're using Windows 3.1 and need to get a TCP/IP program on your own, though, or if you're not satisfied with the TCP/IP software you already have, you can use the excellent Trumpet WinSock.

To install Trumpet WinSock, follow Steps 1 through 7 of the "Installing the Programs" section. When you see the main menu, click the Getting Connected category, click the Trumpet WinSock option, and follow the prompts that appear on your screen to complete the installation.

For more information about Trumpet WinSock, visit the program's Web site at www.trumpet.com.au.

## VDOLive plug-in

VDOLive 2.1 from VDOnet Corporation is a free Netscape plug-in that lets you play video clips on Web pages without having to wait for the clip to fully download, using *streaming video* technology. To install VDOLive, follow the instructions in Lesson PI-2 of bonus unit CD-5 (see the Acrobat Reader section that appears earlier in this appendix to learn how to read this document). For more information about VDOLive, see Lesson PI-4 of Unit CD-5 and visit the program's Web site at www.vdo.com.

## WinZip

WinZip 6.2 from Nico Mak Computing is an invaluable file compression/decompression Windows shareware utility. Many files you'll find on the Internet are compressed — that is, shrunken in size via special programming tricks — both to save disk storage space and to cut down on the amount of time they require to be downloaded. You may also occasionally receive compressed files as e-mail attachments. After you have a compressed file on your hard disk, you should use WinZip to decompress it and make it useable again.

*Notes:*

To install WinZip, follow Steps 1 through 7 of the "Installing the Programs" section. When you see the main menu, click the Working Offline category, click the WinZip option, and follow the prompts that appear on your screen to complete the installation.

To run WinZip, double-click the WinZip icon from its folder or Program Group. If you use Windows 95, alternatively, click the Start button, click Programs, click WinZip, and click WinZip 6.2 32-bit.

The first time you launch WinZip, it will display a bunch of messages and configuration questions. When asked whether you want the program to operate in WinZip Wizard or WinZip Classic mode, we recommend you choose WinZip Classic, which we consider easier to use. After you've answered all the questions, WinZip is ready to go.

For additional information on WinZip, see Lesson 3-2. To find out more about how to use the program, click its Help menu and choose the Contents option or double-click the program's Online Manual icon from its folder. To learn yet more about WinZip, visit the program's Web site at www.winzip.com.

## WS_FTP LE

WS_FTP LE 4.12 from Ipswitch, Inc. is a free (for noncommercial use) Windows File Transfer Protocol, or *FTP,* program that you can employ to find files on the Net and to copy files between your PC and a computer on the Net. FTP programs were more useful before the World Wide Web took hold and made finding and downloading files a snap. However, FTP programs are still handy for activities not supported by the Web, such as uploading files and your own Web pages.

To install WS_FTP LE, follow Steps 1 through 7 of the "Installing the Programs" section. When you see the main menu, click the Communicating category, click the WS_FTP LE option, and follow the prompts that appear on your screen to complete the installation.

To run the program, double-click the WS_FTP icon from its folder or Program Group. If you use Windows 95, alternatively, click the Start button, click Programs, click Ws_ftp, and click WS_FTP95 LE.

For more information on downloading and uploading files, see Lesson 3-2, and for more information on publishing Web pages, see Unit 8.

To get details on using WS_FTP LE, click the Help button from the program's main window or Session Profile dialog box, or double-click the WS_FTP Help icon from the WS_FTP folder. You can also visit WS_FTP LE's Web site at www.ipswitch.com.

# Removing Icons and Programs

Just because you install an icon or program doesn't mean that you want to keep it forever. For example, after you're finished using the *Dummies 101* CD-ROM, you may want to delete any CD-ROM icon you've created for it. You may also decide that a program you've installed isn't very useful — or just isn't as good as another program you recently discovered that does the same thing. Even if you have no problems with the program, you may eventually want to remove, or *uninstall,* it so that you can install a new and improved version of it. The following exercises tell you how.

## Removing the CD-ROM's Windows icon

If you installed an icon under Windows for running the CD-ROM's Installer and you don't need the icon any longer, you can quickly delete it. Always think twice before deleting, however, to ensure that you don't mistakenly erase an item you want to keep.

If you're using Windows 3.1, follow these steps to delete the CD-ROM icon:

**1** **Locate and (if necessary) double-click the Dummies 101 Program Group to open it.**

**2** **From the Dummies 101 window, click the icon you want to delete to select it.**

**3** **Press Delete or choose File⇨Delete.**

If you're asked to confirm the deletion, do so. The icon is eliminated.

*Note:* If you delete the wrong icon by accident and realize it immediately, press Ctrl+Z or choose Edit⇨Undo; the icon you deleted is restored.

**4** **Optionally, repeat Steps 2 and 3 to eliminate any other icons in the Program Group.**

**5** **After the Program Group is empty, optionally repeat Step 3 to eliminate the Program Group itself.**

If you're using Windows 95, follow these steps to delete the CD-ROM icon:

**1** **Click the Start button and choose Settings⇨Taskbar.**

A Taskbar Properties dialog box appears.

**2** **Click the Start Menu Programs tab at the top of the dialog box.**

**3** **Click the Remove button.**

A list of all the items on your Start menu appears.

**4** **Click the tiny plus sign to the left of the Dummies 101 folder.**

If this is the only *Dummies 101* CD-ROM you've used, you'll see only the Dummies 101 - Netscape Communicator CD-ROM icon. If you've used other *Dummies 101* CD-ROMs, you'll see icons for those discs as well.

*Notes:*

**5** **Click the icon you want to delete.**

The icon is highlighted to show that it's selected.

**6** **Click the <u>R</u>emove button.**

The icon is eliminated.

**7** **Optionally, repeat Steps 5 and 6 to eliminate any other icons in the folder.**

**8** **After the folder is empty, optionally repeat Step 6 to eliminate the folder itself.**

**9** **After you're done deleting, click the Close button and then the OK button to exit the dialog box.**

## Removing Windows programs

Many Windows programs include some sort of uninstall feature. Therefore, first try the following:

- Open the program's folder or Program Group, and look for a program named something like Uninstall or Remove. If you see such a file, double-click it to run it and then follow the on-screen prompts to remove the software.

- If you're using Windows 95, click the Start button, choose <u>S</u>ettings⇨<u>C</u>ontrol Panel, and double-click the icon named Add/Remove Programs to display a list of software you can uninstall. Scroll through the alphabetical list. If you see the name of the program you want to delete, click it to select it, click the Add/<u>R</u>emove button, and then follow the on-screen prompts to remove the software.

If those two suggestions don't work, and if you're certain the program's files don't affect anything on your PC other than the program itself, simply locate and manually delete the program's folder or Program Group. For example, if you're using Windows 95, open a My Computer or Windows Explorer window to locate the folder, right-click the folder (that is, click it with your *right* mouse button), click the <u>D</u>elete option from the menu that appears, and (if necessary) click a <u>Y</u>es button to confirm the deletion.

**heads up**

*Note:* Always think twice before deleting to ensure that you don't mistakenly erase an item you want to keep. Also, never delete a file, folder, or Program Group unless you know exactly what you're doing. If you have any doubts, create a temporary folder named Trash or Junk, and *move* the items you want to eliminate into this folder; if no problems occur over the next month as a result of the move, delete the folder's contents.

## Removing Macintosh programs

How you remove software from your Mac depends on how you installed it. If you dragged the program folder from the CD-ROM to your hard disk, just drag the folder from your hard disk window to the Trash and then choose Special⇨Empty Trash.

If the software came with an installer program, run the installer again and select its Remove option. Alternatively, locate and run an uninstaller program from the program's folder. This hunts down and eliminates all files related to the program that were copied anywhere on your hard disk.

If the installer program doesn't have a Remove option and you can't find an uninstaller program, simply drag the program's folder from your hard disk to the Trash and choose Special⇨Empty Trash.

# If You've Got Problems (Of the CD-ROM Kind)

If a program you've installed from the CD-ROM doesn't work, the two likeliest reasons are that your computer doesn't have enough memory (RAM) for that particular program or that you have other programs running that are affecting the installation or running of the program. If you see error messages such as Not enough memory or Setup cannot continue, try one or more of these suggestions, and then try installing or launching the program again:

- **Turn off any anti-virus software you have running.** Installers sometimes mimic virus activity and may make your computer incorrectly believe that it is being infected by a virus.

- **Close all other programs you have running.** The more programs you're running, the less memory is available to other programs. Other programs may also confuse the installation program.

- **If you're on a Mac, turn Virtual Memory on from the Memory control panel.** This will make your Mac use your hard disk for extra memory. If you're on a PowerPC computer (such as the Power Macintosh), we recommend always leaving Virtual Memory on. Otherwise, though, this setting may cause your Mac to operate slower.

- **Add more RAM to your computer.** You can have this done by your local computer store. More memory can both significantly boost the speed of your computer and allow you to run more programs at the same time.

If you still have trouble with installing the items from the CD-ROM, please call the IDG Books Worldwide Customer Service phone number: 800-762-2974 (outside the U.S.: 317-596-5261).

# A Final Reminder about Shareware

Some programs on the *Dummies 101* CD-ROM are free, but most of them are shareware. As we mentioned near the beginning of this appendix, shareware programs are available to you for an evaluation period, after which you're expected to either stop using them or pay for them. Sending a registration fee to a shareware publisher typically entitles you to technical support and notifications about new versions . . . and it also makes you feel good. Most shareware operates on an honor system, but it's just plain sensible to support the shareware concept and encourage the continued production of quality low-cost software by sending in your payment for the programs you use. You can typically get information about where to send your payment for a shareware program by checking its online help and/or by visiting its Web site. When you do, tell them that Hy and Margy sent you!

# Index

## ◆ C ◆

## ◆ D ◆

# AT&T WorldNet℠ Service

## A World of Possibilities...

Thank you for selecting AT&T WorldNet Service — it's the Internet as only AT&T can bring it to you. With AT&T WorldNet Service, a world of infinite possibilities is now within your reach. Research virtually any subject. Stay abreast of current events. Participate in online newsgroups. Purchase merchandise from leading retailers. Send and receive electronic mail.

AT&T WorldNet Service is rapidly becoming the preferred way of accessing the Internet. It was recently awarded one of the most highly coveted awards in the computer industry, *PC Computing*'s 1996 MVP Award for Best Internet Service Provider. Now, more than ever, it's the best way to stay in touch with the people, ideas, and information that are important to you.

You need a computer with a mouse, a modem, a phone line, and the enclosed software. That's all. We've taken care of the rest.

## If You Can Point and Click, You're There

With AT&T WorldNet Service, finding the information you want on the Internet is easier than you ever imagined it could be. You can surf the Net within minutes. And find almost anything you want to know — from the weather in Paris, Texas — to the cost of a ticket to Paris, France. You're just a point and click away. It's that easy.

AT&T WorldNet Service features specially customized industry-leading browsers integrated with advanced Internet directories and search engines. The result is an Internet service that sets a new standard for ease of use — virtually everywhere you want to go is a point and click away, making it a snap to navigate the Internet.

When you go online with AT&T WorldNet Service, you'll benefit from being connected to the Internet by the world leader in networking. We offer you fast access of up to 28.8 Kbps in more than 215 cities throughout the U.S. that will make going online as easy as picking up your phone.

## Online Help and Advice
## 24 Hours a Day, 7 Days a Week

Before you begin exploring the Internet, you may want to take a moment to check two useful sources of information.

If you're new to the Internet, from the AT&T WorldNet Service home page at www.worldnet.att.net, click on the Net Tutorial hyperlink for a quick explanation of unfamiliar terms and useful advice about exploring the Internet.

Another useful source of information is the HELP icon. The area contains pertinent, time saving information-intensive reference tips, and topics such as Accounts & Billing, Trouble Reporting, Downloads & Upgrades, Security Tips, Network Hot Spots, Newsgroups, Special Announcements, etc.

Whether online or off-line, 24 hours a day, seven days a week, we will provide World Class technical expertise and fast, reliable responses to your questions.  To reach AT&T WorldNet Customer Care, call **1-800-400-1447**.

Nothing is more important to us than making sure that your Internet experience is a truly enriching and satisfying one.

## Safeguard Your Online Purchases

AT&T WorldNet Service is committed to making the Internet a safe and convenient way to transact business. By registering and continuing to charge your AT&T WorldNet Service to your AT&T Universal Card, you'll enjoy peace of mind whenever you shop the Internet. Should your account number be compromised on the Net, you won't be liable for any online transactions charged to your AT&T Universal Card by a person who is not an authorized user.\*

\*Today, cardmembers may be liable for the first $50 of charges made by a person who is not an authorized user, which will not be imposed under this program as long as the cardmember notifies AT&T Universal Card of the loss within 24 hours and otherwise complies with the Cardmember Agreement. Refer to Cardmember Agreement for definition of authorized user.

## Minimum System Requirements

IBM-compatible Personal Computer Users:
- IBM-compatible personal computer with 486SX or higher processor
- 8MB of RAM (or more for better performance)
- 15–36MB of available hard disk space to install software, depending on platform
  (14–21MB to use service after installation, depending on platform)
- Graphics system capable of displaying 256 colors
- 14,400 bps modem connected to an outside phone line and not a LAN or ISDN line
- Microsoft Windows 3.1*x* or Windows 95

Macintosh Users:
- Macintosh 68030 or higher (including 68LC0X0 models and all Power Macintosh models)
- System 7.5.3 Revision 2 or higher for PCI Power Macintosh models: System 7.1 or higher for all 680X0 and non-PCI Power Macintosh models
- Mac TCP 2.0.6 or Open Transport 1.1 or higher
- 8MB of RAM (minimum) with Virtual Memory turned on or RAM Doubler; 16MB recommended for Power Macintosh users
- 12MB of available hard disk space (15MB recommended)
- 14,400 bps modem connected to an outside phone line and not a LAN or ISDN line
- Color or 256 gray-scale monitor
- Apple Guide 1.2 or higher (if you want to view online help)
  *If you are uncertain of the configuration of your Macintosh computer, consult your Macintosh User's guide or call Apple at 1-800-767-2775.*

## Installation Tips and Instructions

- If you have other Web browsers or online software, please consider uninstalling them according to the vendor's instructions.
- If you are installing AT&T WorldNet Service on a computer with Local Area Networking, please contact your LAN administrator for setup instructions.
- At the end of installation, you may be asked to restart your computer. Don't attempt the registration process until you have done so.

IBM-compatible PC users:
- Insert the CD-ROM into the CD-ROM drive on your computer.
- Select *File/Run* (for Windows 3.1*x*) or *Start/Run* (for Windows 95 if setup did not start automatically).
- Type *D:\setup.exe* (or change the "D" if your CD-ROM is another drive).
- Click *OK*.
- Follow the onscreen instructions to install and register.

Macintosh users:
- Disable all extensions except Apple CD-ROM and Foreign Files Access extensions.
- Restart Computer.
- Insert the CD-ROM into the CD-ROM drive on your computer.
- Double-click the *Install AT&T WorldNet Service* icon.
- Follow the onscreen instructions to install. (Upon restarting your Macintosh, AT&T WorldNet Service Account Setup automatically starts.)
- Follow the onscreen instructions to register.

## Registering with AT&T WorldNet Service

After you have connected with AT&T WorldNet online registration service, you will be presented with a series of screens that confirm billing information and prompt you for additional account set-up data.

The following is a list of registration tips and comments that will help you during the registration process.

I. Use one of the following registration codes, which can also be found in Appendix B of *Dummies 101: Netscape Communicator 4*. Use L5SQIM631 if you are an AT&T long-distance residential customer or L5SQIM632 if you use another long-distance phone company.
II. During registration, you will need to supply your name, address, and valid credit card number, and choose an account information security word, e-mail name, and e-mail password. You will also be requested to select your preferred price plan at this time. (We advise that you use all lowercase letters when assigning an e-mail ID and security code, since they are easier to remember.)
III. If you make a mistake and exit or get disconnected during the registration process prematurely, simply click on "Create New Account." Do not click on "Edit Existing Account."
IV. When choosing your local access telephone number, you will be given several options. Please choose the one nearest to you. Please note that calling a number within your area does not guarantee that the call is free.

## Connecting to AT&T WorldNet Service

When you have finished installing and registering with AT&T WorldNet Service, you are ready to access the Internet. Make sure your modem and phone line are available before attempting to connect to the service.

For Windows 95 users:
- Double-click on the *Connect to AT&T WorldNet Service* icon on your desktop.
  OR
- Select *Start, Programs, AT&T WorldNet Software, Connect to AT&T WorldNet Service.*

For Windows 3.1*x* users:
- Double-click on the *Connect to AT&T WorldNet Service* icon located in the AT&T WorldNet Service group.

For Macintosh users:
- Double-click on the *AT&T WorldNet Service* icon in the AT&T WorldNet Service folder.

## Choose the Plan That's Right for You

The Internet is for everyone, whether at home or at work. In addition to making the time you spend online productive and fun, we're also committed to making it affordable. Choose one of two price plans: unlimited usage access or hourly usage access. The latest pricing information can be obtained during online registration. No matter which plan you use, we're confident that after you take advantage of everything AT&T WorldNet Service has to offer, you'll wonder how you got along without it.

AT&T

Explore our AT&T WorldNet Service site at http://www.att.com/worldnet.

# IDG Books Worldwide, Inc., End-User License Agreement

**READ THIS.** You should carefully read these terms and conditions before opening the software packet(s) included with this book ("Book"). This is a license agreement ("Agreement") between you and IDG Books Worldwide, Inc. ("IDGB"). By opening the accompanying software packet(s), you acknowledge that you have read and accept the following terms and conditions. If you do not agree and do not want to be bound by such terms and conditions, promptly return the Book and the unopened software packet(s) to the place you obtained them for a full refund.

1. **License Grant.** IDGB grants to you (either an individual or entity) a nonexclusive license to use one copy of the enclosed software program(s) (collectively, the "Software") solely for your own personal or business purposes on a single computer (whether a standard computer or a workstation component of a multiuser network). The Software is in use on a computer when it is loaded into temporary memory (RAM) or installed into permanent memory (hard disk, CD-ROM, or other storage device). IDGB reserves all rights not expressly granted herein.

2. **Ownership.** IDGB is the owner of all right, title, and interest, including copyright, in and to the compilation of the Software recorded on the disk(s) or CD-ROM ("Software Media"). Copyright to the individual programs recorded on the Software Media is owned by the author or other authorized copyright owner of each program. Ownership of the Software and all proprietary rights relating thereto remain with IDGB and its licensers.

3. **Restrictions on Use and Transfer.**

   (a) You may only (i) make one copy of the Software for backup or archival purposes, or (ii) transfer the Software to a single hard disk, provided that you keep the original for backup or archival purposes. You may not (i) rent or lease the Software, (ii) copy or reproduce the Software through a LAN or other network system or through any computer subscriber system or bulletin-board system, or (iii) modify, adapt, or create derivative works based on the Software.

   (b) You may not reverse engineer, decompile, or disassemble the Software. You may transfer the Software and user documentation on a permanent basis, provided that the transferee agrees to accept the terms and conditions of this Agreement and you retain no copies. If the Software is an update or has been updated, any transfer must include the most recent update and all prior versions.

4. **Restrictions on Use of Individual Programs.** You must follow the individual requirements and restrictions detailed for each individual program in Appendix B of this Book. These limitations are also contained in the individual license agreements recorded on the Software Media. These limitations may include a requirement that after using the program for a specified period of time, the user must pay a registration fee or discontinue use. By opening the Software packet(s), you will be agreeing to abide by the licenses and restrictions for these individual programs that are detailed in Appendix B and on the Software Media. None of the material on this Software Media or listed in this Book may ever be redistributed, in original or modified form, for commercial purposes.

5. **Limited Warranty.**

   (a) IDGB warrants that the Software and Software Media are free from defects in materials and workmanship under normal use for a period of sixty (60) days from the date of purchase of this Book. If IDGB receives notification within the warranty period of defects in materials or workmanship, IDGB will replace the defective Software Media.

   (b) **IDGB AND THE AUTHORS OF THE BOOK DISCLAIM ALL OTHER WARRANTIES, EXPRESS OR IMPLIED, INCLUDING WITHOUT LIMITATION IMPLIED WARRANTIES OF MERCHANTABILITY AND FITNESS FOR A PARTICULAR PURPOSE, WITH RESPECT TO THE SOFTWARE, THE PROGRAMS, THE SOURCE CODE CONTAINED THEREIN, AND/OR THE TECHNIQUES DESCRIBED IN THIS BOOK. IDGB DOES NOT WARRANT THAT THE FUNCTIONS CONTAINED IN THE SOFTWARE WILL MEET YOUR REQUIREMENTS OR THAT THE OPERATION OF THE SOFTWARE WILL BE ERROR FREE.**

   (c) This limited warranty gives you specific legal rights, and you may have other rights that vary from jurisdiction to jurisdiction.

6. **Remedies.**

   (a) IDGB's entire liability and your exclusive remedy for defects in materials and workmanship shall be limited to replacement of the Software Media, which may be returned to IDGB with a copy of your receipt at the following address: Software Media Fulfillment Department, Attn.: *Dummies 101: Netscape Communicator 4*, IDG Books Worldwide, Inc., 7260 Shadeland Station, Ste. 100, Indianapolis, IN 46256, or call 800-762-2974. Please allow three to four weeks for delivery. This Limited Warranty is void if failure of the Software Media has resulted from accident, abuse, or misapplication. Any replacement Software Media will be warranted for the remainder of the original warranty period or thirty (30) days, whichever is longer.

   (b) In no event shall IDGB or the authors be liable for any damages whatsoever (including without limitation damages for loss of business profits, business interruption, loss of business information, or any other pecuniary loss) arising from the use of or inability to use the Book or the Software, even if IDGB has been advised of the possibility of such damages.

   (c) Because some jurisdictions do not allow the exclusion or limitation of liability for consequential or incidental damages, the above limitation or exclusion may not apply to you.

7. **U.S. Government Restricted Rights.** Use, duplication, or disclosure of the Software by the U.S. Government is subject to restrictions stated in paragraph (c)(1)(ii) of the Rights in Technical Data and Computer Software clause of DFARS 252.227-7013, and in subparagraphs (a) through (d) of the Commercial Computer–Restricted Rights clause at FAR 52.227-19, and in similar clauses in the NASA FAR supplement, when applicable.

8. **General.** This Agreement constitutes the entire understanding of the parties and revokes and supersedes all prior agreements, oral or written, between them and may not be modified or amended except in a writing signed by both parties hereto that specifically refers to this Agreement. This Agreement shall take precedence over any other documents that may be in conflict herewith. If any one or more provisions contained in this Agreement are held by any court or tribunal to be invalid, illegal, or otherwise unenforceable, each and every other provision shall remain in full force and effect.

# Dummies 101 CD-ROM Installation Instructions

The CD-ROM at the back of this book contains the exercise files that you'll use while you work through the lessons in this book. It also contains a handy installation program that copies this bonus software to your hard drive in a very simple process. See Appendix B for complete details about the CD (especially system requirements for using the CD).

**heads up**

If you're installing a plug-in, follow the instructions in Lesson 9-2.

If you're using a Macintosh and want to install a standalone program from the *Dummies 101* CD-ROM, insert the disc into your CD-ROM drive and wait for a folder to open. When it does, locate and double-click a file named Read Me First to open a text document. Follow the instructions in this document to install the program you're interested in. (In many cases, this will involve nothing more than using your mouse to copy the program's folder to your hard disk.)

If you're using Windows and have previously run the SetIcons program, insert the *Dummies 101* CD-ROM into your CD-ROM drive and use the icon you created to run the Installer program.

Otherwise, follow these steps:

**1** **Insert the *Dummies 101* CD-ROM that came with this book into your CD-ROM drive.**

Be careful to touch only the sides of the CD-ROM and to insert the CD-ROM with its printed side up.

If you're using Windows 95, then within a minute of your inserting the CD-ROM into the drive the CD-ROM's Installer program should start running automatically and display a license agreement. If this occurs, skip to Step 7.

**2** **If you're using Windows 3.1, click the File menu from the Program Manager and choose the Run option. Similarly, if you're using Windows 95 but the Installer program didn't run automatically, click the Start button (located in the bottom-left corner of your screen) and choose the Run option.**

**3** **In the Run dialog box that appears, type** d:\seticons — **that is, the letter** *d,* **a colon (:), a backslash (\), and the program name** *seticons.*

If your CD-ROM isn't drive D, type the letter appropriate for your drive instead of D.

**4** **Press Enter or click OK.**

The Run dialog box closes, and a message tells you that icons for running the CD-ROM's Installer program are about to be created.

**5** **Click OK.**

- If you're using Windows 3.1, a Program Group and icons are created for the CD-ROM on your desktop. You can start the CD-ROM's Installer program in the future by double-clicking its icon.

- If you're using Windows 95, a folder and icons are created on your Start menu. You can start the CD-ROM's Installer program in the future by clicking the Start menu and choosing Programs⇨Dummies 101⇨Dummies 101 - Netscape Communicator.

After the icons are created, you're asked whether you want to run the Installer program.

**6** **Click the Yes button.**

The CD-ROM's Installer program launches and displays an IDG Books Worldwide, Inc. license agreement.

**7** **Read (or at least skim) the license agreement to make sure you're comfortable with its terms. When you're ready, click the Accept button.**

If you don't click Accept, you can't use the Installer program. After you click, an opening screen appears.

**8** **Follow the on-screen prompts until you see a menu with software categories.**

The menu displays four software categories: Getting Connected (for programs that get you connected to the Net), Communicating (for programs that let you interact on the Net), Using Plug-Ins (for plug-ins that enhance Netscape's capabilities), and Working Offline (for programs that help you deal with files you've downloaded from the Net). This is the Installer's *main menu,* which is so named because all your other selections stem from this initial menu.

**9** **Click a category you're interested in.**

A submenu displays the particular programs grouped under the category you selected.

**10** **Click a program you're interested in.**

A description of the program appears.

**11** **If you want the program copied to your hard disk, click the Continue button at the bottom of the screen. (Otherwise, click the Cancel button and skip to Step 13.)**

After you click Continue, installation for the program you selected begins.

**12** **Follow the prompts that appear on your screen to complete the installation of the program.**

When the installation is finished, you return to the last category screen you visited.

**13** **Click the Go Back button to return to previous menus and explore the other contents of the CD-ROM.**

The Go Back button is available on each category screen, so you can always use it to retrace your steps back to the main menu.

**14** **When you're done examining all the options you're interested in and installing all the programs you want, click the Exit button.**

The Installer program closes. You can now start using the new software you've installed on your hard disk!

**To run the Installer program again:** If you've exited the Installer program and then want to run it again while the *Dummies 101* CD-ROM is still in your drive, double-click the icon you've created for the Installer program (if you're using Windows 3.1) or click the Start button and choose Programs⇨Dummies 101⇨Dummies 101 - Netscape Communicator (if you're using Windows 95 and have previously run the SetIcons program). Alternatively, if you're using Windows 95, double-click the My Computer icon on your desktop and then double-click the icon that looks like a shiny CD, or just eject the CD-ROM and then reinsert it into your CD-ROM drive to make the Installer run automatically again.

**To examine the *Dummies 101* CD-ROM's contents under Windows:** You can use the *Dummies 101* Installer program to install all the software on your CD-ROM. However, if you're simply curious about the CD-ROM, you can examine its contents after you exit the Installer. If you're using Windows 95, open a Windows Explorer window (as opposed to a My Computer window) and double-click the CD-ROM's icon. If you're using Windows 3.1, double-click the CD-ROM's icon in File Manager.

If you have problems with the installation process, you can call the IDG Books Worldwide, Inc., Customer Support number: 800-762-2974 (outside the U.S.: 317-596-5261).

*Note:* The files are meant to accompany the book's lessons. If you open a file prematurely, you may accidentally make changes to the file, which may prevent you from following along with the steps in the lessons.

# IDG BOOKS WORLDWIDE REGISTRATION CARD

**RETURN THIS REGISTRATION CARD FOR FREE CATALOG**

**Title of this book:** Dummies 101®: Netscape Communicator™

**My overall rating of this book:** ❑ Very good [1] ❑ Good [2] ❑ Satisfactory [3] ❑ Fair [4] ❑ Poor [5]

**How I first heard about this book:**

❑ Found in bookstore; name: [6] _____     ❑ Book review: [7] _____

❑ Advertisement: [8] _____     ❑ Catalog: [9] _____

❑ Word of mouth; heard about book from friend, co-worker, etc.: [10] _____     ❑ Other: [11] _____

**What I liked most about this book:**

_____

_____

**What I would change, add, delete, etc., in future editions of this book:**

_____

_____

**Other comments:** _____

**Number of computer books I purchase in a year:** ❑ 1 [12] ❑ 2-5 [13] ❑ 6-10 [14] ❑ More than 10 [15]

**I would characterize my computer skills as:** ❑ Beginner [16] ❑ Intermediate [17] ❑ Advanced [18] ❑ Professional [19]

**I use** ❑ DOS [20] ❑ Windows [21] ❑ OS/2 [22] ❑ Unix [23] ❑ Macintosh [24] ❑ Other: [25]_____
(please specify)

**I would be interested in new books on the following subjects:**
(please check all that apply, and use the spaces provided to identify specific software)

❑ Word processing: [26] _____     ❑ Spreadsheets: [27] _____

❑ Data bases: [28] _____     ❑ Desktop publishing: [29] _____

❑ File Utilities: [30] _____     ❑ Money management: [31] _____

❑ Networking: [32] _____     ❑ Programming languages: [33] _____

❑ Other: [34] _____

**I use a PC at** (please check all that apply): ❑ home [35] ❑ work [36] ❑ school [37] ❑ other: [38] _____

**The disks I prefer to use are** ❑ 5.25 [39] ❑ 3.5 [40] ❑ other: [41]_____

**I have a CD ROM:** ❑ yes [42] ❑ no [43]

**I plan to buy or upgrade computer hardware this year:** ❑ yes [44] ❑ no [45]

**I plan to buy or upgrade computer software this year:** ❑ yes [46] ❑ no [47]

Name: _____     Business title: [48] _____     Type of Business: [49] _____

Address (❑ home [50] ❑ work [51]/Company name: _____     )

Street/Suite# _____

City [52]/State [53]/Zipcode [54]: _____     Country [55] _____

❑ **I liked this book!** You may quote me by name in future IDG Books Worldwide promotional materials.

My daytime phone number is _____

**IDG BOOKS**®

THE WORLD OF COMPUTER KNOWLEDGE

 **YES!**
Please keep me informed about IDG's World of Computer Knowledge.
Send me the latest IDG Books catalog.

COMPUTER
BOOK SERIES
FROM IDG